# AN

# ENGLISH INDEX

# TO

# THE PLANTS OF INDIA

# AN
# ENGLISH INDEX
# TO
# THE PLANTS OF INDIA.

GYAN

*Published by*

GYAN

Gyan Publishing House
5, Ansari Road
Daryaganj, New Delhi-110002
Phone: 011-47034999, 9811692060
E-mail: books@gyanbooks.com

*Distribution Network*
gyanbooks.com
India, USA, Canada, UK, Australia



ISBN: 978-81-212-5579-0 (HB)
First Published, 1832

2nd Impression 2024

*Printed at:* Gyan Press, Delhi.



**AN ENGLISH INDEX TO THE PLANTS OF INDIA**
Compiler: H. PIDDINGTON

AN

# ENGLISH INDEX

TO

# THE PLANTS OF INDIA.

AN

# ENGLISH INDEX

TO

# THE PLANTS OF INDIA.

---

COMPILED BY

## H. PIDDINGTON,

*Foreign Secretary, Agricultural and Horticultural Society.*

---

"And in this founde wee oftimes muche trouble and vexation, with moreover losses, bothe of precious tyme and lucre. *Fyrste*, thatt wee coulde never aske in ye *Indian* tongues for suche herbes, or fruites, woodes, barkes, or gummes, as wee knewe full well, by expeerience in sundrye other partes, to bee wholesomme, (many of our crewe lyinge sicke at this tyme,) or savorye, or usefulle to trafficke withall. *Nexte*, thatt when anye were shewne us, we coulde in noewise tell, from ye names given toe them by ye *Gentooes*, whether or noe ye like were alreadye knowne in *Europpean* countryes: And yett these partes doe myghtylie abounde with herbes and woodes of sovraigne virtew."—*Master Richarde Kynge, his travells, and voyages, and traffickes, in foraygne countryes, in the Shippe Tamburlan. Lond. MSS. fol.* 1634.

---

**Calcutta:**

PRINTED AT THE BAPTIST MISSION PRESS, CIRCULAR; ROAD AND SOLD BY MESSRS. THACKER AND CO. ST. ANDREW'S LIBRARY.

1832.

# PREFACE.

A WORK enabling the European on his first landing to inquire for every Indian plant yet known to European botanists by its native name, if it has one; or to trace from the native name its scientific appellation, must be a desideratum to all; for there are none who, more or less, have not an interest in plants, either as studious pursuits, as amusements, as objects of commercial enterprise, or of domestic economy; and but too many of us in India find, that before we are sufficiently linguists to trace out a name, or botanists to ascertain a plant, years and climate, the pressure of business, or the deadening canker of disappointment, have taken from our pursuits the freshness, which alone can compensate that want of energy through which every thing in India so soon becomes stale and wearying, even to the most active minds.

A work then, which spares labour to all, to the Native as well as to the European, may claim the attention of every man who, either from motives of interest or of philanthropy, desires to see the science of Europe brought nearer to the resources of India; and such a work the Compiler has intended. It has been completed from every known source, principally the two volumes of Dr. Wallich's edition of

Roxburgh's Flora Indica, Ainslie's Materia Indica, Fleming, the Hortus Bengalensis, a valuable catalogue of Hindu names in the Gleanings of Science, &c. &c.

It is one of the many peculiarities of our situation in India, that those who have the most ability have generally the least disposable time ; no where too, do we so much find that, from the uncertainty of health, of situation, and even of life, things must be done as they best can, for the morrow is not ours : and this may plead as a motive that one, a tyro in Botany, should have undertaken such a work ; for, of the many so much better qualified than himself, not one probably could have had time to execute a plan requiring so much and such tedious detail. It is hoped then, that where imperfections are met with, it will be remembered, that its object is *to save time in research, and perhaps expence in books of reference;* and that thus it is one of those works which are better ill done than not done at all.

# INTRODUCTION.

In the following Vocabulary no attempt has been made to reduce the orthography of the native names to any fixed standard; for to do so would have required, both in the Compiler and the original collector of the plants, not only a correct knowledge of the different languages, but moreover one of the provincial dialects and of the pronunciation of the spoken language. How much these vary is well known to those who have paid attention to the subject; and, after all the attempts of those who have endeavoured to fix a standard, very much must be left which is almost of necessity arbitrary; for it is only a practised ear, and one aided by a knowledge of native orthography, which can distinguish between an *a*, an *u*, or an *o*, as in Mădar, Mudar; an Italian *i* for a *ee*, as Jitee, Jeetee: and then again, scarcely any two orientalists will use the same English letters to express the same sounds caught by the ear, even where they agree as to the system to be followed, unless they have first written the word in the native character.

From this difficulty the search for names in Part II. must always be to a certain degree vague and indefinite; but the smallest knowledge of Botany will correct any error which may take place; and to aid research as much as possible, repetition has been always preferred to omission, so that the same name, with but a trifling difference, will be often found repeated.

The innumerable Sanscrit synonymes which are found to some of the common plants in the Flora Indica, (there are 23 to Vangueria and 21 to Solanum *Jacquini,)* are however omitted, and the principal or first only preserved; because it is not intended to furnish a book of reference for the scholar, (for whom far better sources of information exist,) but a manual for common and every-day use.

Some names of plants will be found which are perhaps not indigenous or cultivated in India, and of which only the products are to be found in the bazar; as Ladan (Cistus *Creticus,)* Gum Labdanum; and Hing, (Ferula *asafœtida,)* asafœtida: but it was thought useful to leave these as a guide; to medical men more particularly.

The same names are often marked in both parts, or in the sections of Part II. as only belonging to one language, while they are, in fact, common to two or more; thus Dillenia *Indica* or *Speciosa*, is marked in Part I. as B. Chalta, while it is equally called by this name in Hindi.

To facilitate research, Part II. has been divided into two sections; but when any difficulty occurs, both should be examined in search of the name: for the different dialects often adopt the name used in the native country of the plant, with but at most a slight variation. The Karia-pilli of the Tamool, which is the Karia-phullee ofthe Bengalese (Bergera Kœnigii), (originally perhaps from Southern India, though now a common plant about the gardens of Calcutta, its leaf giving a peculiar flavour to curries,) is an example of this sort of corruption.

Blank spaces have been designedly left after each letter in both parts, that names which may be found may be noted in them by the possessor of the work.

The note of interrogation has been added when any uncertainty exists.

---

## ABBREVIATIONS.

S. Sanscrit.
B. Bengalee.
H. Hindee.
N. Nawar or the Napalese dialect.
Tam. Tamul.
T. Telinga.

Cyng. Cingalese.
Can. Canarese.
Mah. Mahratta.
G. Guzrattee.
M. Malabar.

# PART I.

## INDEX

FROM

## THE LINNÆAN GENERA AND SPECIES

TO

## The Native Names of Plants.

| *Gen. and Spec.* | *Native Names.* |
|---|---|
| ABROMA | |
| *augusta.* | B. Oolut-kumbul. |
| ABRUS | |
| *precatorius, (red.)* | S. Gunja; Goonja; Kaka-chinchi. B. Koonch. H. Guncha. TAM. Condumunnie. T. Goorie-ghenza. CYNG. Olinda. |
| *(white.)* | B. Sweta-koonch. |
| ACACIA, see MIMOSA. | |
| ACALYPHA | |
| *Indica.* | S. Arittamunjayrie. B. Shwet-busunta; Kunda-amadoo. H. Kooppie. TAM. Koopamaynie. CYNG. Koopamenya; Wæl-Koopamenya. |
| *betulina.* | H. Chinnie. TAM. Sinnie. T. Tsinniakoo. |
| ACANTHUS *Ilicifolius.* | S. Hari-Kussa. B. Hakooch; Harkuchkanta. M. Phaina-schelli; Painaschulli. |
| ACHRYANTHES | |
| *aspera.* | S. Upamarga. B. Upanga; Apanga; Hoorhooriya; Chichiria. H. Agareh; Lalchirchiri. CYNG. Gas-karal-sæbo. |
| *centrostachys.* | B. Hooeet. |
| *lappacea.* | B. Kuya-duya; Duya-kuya. |
| *alternifolia.* | B. Luta-muhooia. H. Gangatiah. T. Chancheli-kura. |
| *ferruginea.* | B. Rukta-sirinchee. H. Lal-sirinchee. |
| *scandens.* | H. Nooriya. |

| Gen. and Spec. | Native Names. |
|---|---|
| *triandra.* | S. H. Shalanchi. B. Shanchi; Shalooncha; Shelenga. T. Ponagunta-kura. |
| *lanata.* | S. Astma-bayda. B. H. Chaya; H. Khul. T. Pindie-conda. CYNG. Polkuda-pala. M. Scherubala. |
| ACONITUM | |
| *ferox.* | B. Butsnab-bish. |
| ACORUS | |
| *Calamus.* | S. Vucha; Golomi. B. Buch; Shwet buch. H. Bach; Kusseb-bewa; Igir. TAM. Vassamboo. T. Vudza. CYNG. Wadda-kaha-vaesamboo. M. Vaymboo. CAN. Bagy. |
| *(white var.)* | S. Haimavati. |
| ADELIA | |
| *Nereifolia.* | H. Heeaboka. |
| *Castanicarpa.* | B. Bool-kukra. |
| ADENANTHERA | |
| *pavonina.* | S. H. Koochunduna. B. Ructa-chunduna; Ranjuna. T. Manseni-kotta, CAN. Mandateea. CYNG. Mansiadi. |
| *aculeata.* | T. Shumi. |
| ADIANTUM | |
| *melanocaulon.* | S. Mayura-shikanda. TAM. Myle-conday. T. Nemilie-shega. |
| ÆGICERAS | |
| *majus.* | B. Hulsi. |
| ÆGLE | |
| *Marmelos.* | S. Vilva. H. and B. Bel. T. Maredoo. |
| *(small var.)* | S. H. B. Shreephula. CYNG. Beli. M. Covalum. |
| ÆSCHYNOMENE | |
| *grandiflora, (white and red.)* | B. Buka; Buk-pooshpa; Bok-phool. |
| *Sesban, (yellow and purple.)* | S. H. B. Juyuntee. H. B. Jainti. T. Siminta. |
| *spinulosa.* | T. Yerra-jeeloga. |
| *aspera.* | S. Damana. B. Fool-sola. H. Sothali. CYNG. Mahadiya-siyambala. |
| *arborea.* | S. Damana. H. Bhend; Shoola. TAM. Nettych-eddie. T. Bendoo-chittoo. |
| *paludosa.* | B. Shola; Sola; Kath-shola. |
| *cannabina.* | B. Dhuncha. |

| *Gen. and Spec.* | *Native Names.* |
|---|---|
| *procumbens.* | T. Manchi-jeeloga. |
| AGAVE | |
| *Cantala.* | S. Kuntala. |
| AGERATUM | |
| *cordifolium.* | B. Okunchi. |
| *aquaticum.* | B. Bura-keshuta. |
| AGLAIA | |
| *polystachya.* | B. Bandoor-pala. |
| AGROSTIS | |
| *tenacissima.* | B. Panee-doorba. T. Sema-gherka; Toema-gherika. |
| *diandra.* | B. Bena-joni. |
| *linearis.* | TAM. Arugam. |
| *Coromandelliana.* | T. Yelloo-tungoo-gaddi. |
| AILANTHUS | |
| *excelsa.* | S. Aralu. TAM. Perumaruttoo. T. Peddamanieputta. |
| AIRA | |
| *filiforme.* | B. Choota-pini-nuti. |
| AJUGA | |
| *disticha.* | B. H. Gobura. T. Mabera. |
| *fruticosa.* | TAM. Retti-pemeretti. |
| ALDROVANDA | |
| *verticillata.* | B. Malacca-jhanji. |
| ALEURITES | |
| *triloba.* | B. Akhoroot. CYNG. Kokuna. |
| ALLANGIUM | |
| *hexapetalum.* | S. Unkotha; Nekochuka. B. Baghankra. H. Akarkanta. |
| *tomentosum.* | B. Chela. |
| ALLIUM | |
| *Porrum.* | B. Puroo. |
| *sativum.* | S. Mahooshooda. B. Loshoon; Lushoona; Rushoon. TAM. Vullay-poondoo. T. Velligudda. CYNG. Soodooloonoo. CAN. Belluly. |
| *Cepa.* | S. Palandu; Latarka. B. Pulantoo. H. B. Peeaj. TAM. Venggayum. T. Woolligudda. CYNG. Loono. CAN. Kembally. |
| *Ascalonium.* | S. Pulandoo. B. Gundhuna; Rushoona. |
| ALNUS | |
| *dioica.* | H. Kokra. |

| *Gen. and Spec.* | *Native Names.* |
|---|---|
| **Aloe** | |
| *perfoliata v. littoralis.* | S. Kamari. S. B. Taruni. B. Ghrita-koomaree. H. Ghi-cumar ; Chota-kunwar. Tam. Kuttalay ; Sirrooghoo-kuttalay. T. Chini-kala-bunda. |
| **Alpinia** | |
| *Galanga.* | S. Koolanjuna ; Sogunda-yoga ; Dhu-moola. H. Kulingan. Tam. Pere-aretei. T. Dombrastacum. Cyng. Maha-kalooa. |
| *nutans.* | S. Poonnaga. B. Poonnag-champa. |
| *Cardamomum.* | B. Elachi ; Elaich. T. Sana-yallaci. M. Ailumchedy. |
| *Cardamom : medium.* | B. Doo-keswa. |
| **Althæa** | |
| *rosea.* | H. Gool-khirree. |
| *Alhugas.* | S. Taruka. B. Tara. |
| **Amaranthus** | |
| *polygonoides.* | S. Tundooleeya. B. Cheeloo-nuteeya. T. Chirra-kura. |
| *polygamus.* | B. Champa-nuteeya ; Poorika. H. Chundi-sag. T. Dayla-kura. |
| *tristis.* | Tam. Kuppei-kirei. T. Quoi-tota-kura. |
| *lividus.* | B. Gobura-nuteeya ; Gobura-dengooa. |
| *oleraceus.* | B. Shada-nuteeya. T. Tota-kura. |
| *Gangeticus.* | B. Lal-sag ; Dengooa. H. Rukta-shaka. |
| *lanceofolius.* | B. Bans-pata-nuteeya. |
| *atropurpureus.* | B. H. Lal-nuteeya. B. Ranganthеya. H. Bans-putta. |
| *fasciatus.* | B. Toontoonee-nuteeya ; Bun-nuteeya. T. Chilaka-tola-kura. |
| *tenuifolius.* | B. Geel-chumli. |
| *campestris.* | S. Maykanada. Tam. Sirroo-keeray. T. Tseerikoora. |
| *frumentaceus.* | Tam. Kiery. |
| *spinosus.* | H. B. Kanta-nuteeya. |
| **Amaryllis** | |
| *Zeylanica.* | Cyng. Goda-manel. |
| **Ambrosinia** | |
| *ciliata.* | B. Keralee. |
| *unilocularis.* | T. Pecheka-boora-gaddi. |
| **Ammania** | |
| *vesicatoria.* | B. Bun-murich. B. H. Dad-mari. T. Cyng. Agundra-pacoo. |

| *Gen. and Spec.* | *Native Names.* |
|---|---|
| AMOMUM | |
| *subulatum.* | B. Bungali-elachee. |
| *aromaticum v. Cardamomum.* | S. Ela. B. Morung-elachee. H. Ilachi. |
| *sericeum.* | B. Dooi-kesha. |
| *Zingiber, see Zingiber.* | |
| AMYRIS | |
| *Agallocha.* | S. B. Googoola ; Ogooroo. CYNG. Gugul. |
| *Protium.* | CYNG. Weeta-hik. |
| *heptaphylla.* | H. Karun-phul. |
| ANACARDIUM | |
| *occidentale.* | B. Hijilee-budam. |
| ANDERSONIA | |
| *cucullata.* | B. Amoora, |
| *Rohitoka.* | S. Rohitoka. B. Tikta-raj. H. Hurinhura. |
| ANDRACHNE | |
| *Cadishaw.* | S. Vishavriksha. TAM. Woodoowunghai. T. Nulloopoo-moostikaia. |
| ANDROPOGON | |
| *serratum.* | S. Deva-tara; Venee; Jeemota. B. Detara; Detto. |
| *contortum.* | T. Yedda; Yeddi. |
| *fascicularis.* | T. Kunda-jerri. |
| *montanum.* | T. Aurooch-hunguli; Auroots-hangali. |
| *Iwarancusa.* | B. H. Iwarancusha; Iberancusha; Kurankusha. |
| *aciculatum.* | S. Chora-pushpa; Shunkinee; Keshinee. B. H. Chor-kanta. |
| *punctatus.* | B. Goaliya. T. Kundi-jeri. |
| *muricatus.* | S. Veeruna; Viratara. B. Khor; Kuskus. H. B. Bena. H. Useer; Bala. TAM. Vakil; Woettiwear. T. Kassavoo; Cooroo-vayroo. |
| *glabrum.* | B. Gundha-goorana. |
| *bicolor.* | B. Kala-debdhanya. H. Dedhan; Kala-jooar. T. Muka-janoo. |
| *Sorghum.* | B. Deb-dhanya. B. H. Joar. T. Tella-janoo. |
| *saccharatum.* | H. Dedhan. |
| *laxum.* | H. Kula-moocha. T. Gadi-janoo. |

| *Gen. and Spec.* | *Native Names.* |
|---|---|
| *Schœnanthus.* | S. Bhoostrina; Malatrinukung. B. Gundha-bena. H. Ghundha-bela; Gund-bel. TAM. Camachie-pilloo; Wassina-pilloo; Cavatum-pilloo. T. Kamachie-kussoo. M. Sirek. |
| *Nardus.* | B. Koorunkosha. H. Iwarankosa. TAM. Sukkunaroo-pilloo. CYNG. Watussæwendara. |
| *Bladhii.* | B. Loari. |
| *scandens.* | H. Loari. |
| ANDROSACE | |
| *sarmentosa.* | N. Nita, Nitaha. |
| *cordifolia.* | N. Boollee-sowa. |
| ANETHUM | |
| *Sowa, v. graveolens.* | S. Shaleya; Misreya; Sitasiva. B. Suloopha. H. Sowa; Soie; Shuta-pooshpa. TAM. Saddacooppie. T. Suddapa. CYNG. Sattacooppa. GUZ. Suva. |
| *Panmorium, v. fœniculum.* | S. Mudoorika. B. Goowamooree; Mooree. H. Panmuhoree; Mayuri; Sonf. T. Perun-siragum. T. Pedda-gillakara. CYNG. Dewadooroo. |
| ANNESLEA | |
| *spinosa.* | B. Mukhana. |
| ANNONA | |
| *squamosa.* | S. Gunda-gatra. B. Loona; Meba. B. H. Ata. |
| *reticulata.* | B. H. Nona; Luvunee. |
| ANTHERICUM | |
| *tuberosum.* | S. Chitra. T. Cushelli. |
| ANTHISTIRIA | |
| *Cymbaria.* | T. Pedda-ghella. |
| ANTIDESMA | |
| *pubescens.* | T. Polaree. |
| *paniculata.* | B. H. Khoodi-jam. |
| ANTIRRHINUM | |
| *Cymbalarium.* | S. Karambha. H. Uttimarini. |
| APIUM | |
| *involucratum.* | B. Rhadonee; Rhadunee. H. Ujmood; Ajmood. |

| Gen. and Spec. | Native Names. |
|---|---|
| APLUDA | |
| *aristata.* | B. Choon-kuriki. H. Goruma. T. Pootstrangali. |
| APONOGETON | |
| *monostachyon.* | S. Kekanjee. H. Ghetchoo. T. Namma. |
| AQUILARIA | |
| *Agallocha.* | B. Agooroo ? |
| ARABIS | |
| *Chinensis.* | S. Rohita-sarushapa. H. Haleem. TAM. Aliverie. T. Addalavittiloo. |
| ARALIA | |
| *digitata.* | H. Dain. |
| ARACHIS | |
| *fruticosa.* | T. Sakilli-kampa. |
| *hypogea.* | H. Moong-phullee. |
| ARDISIA | |
| *Solanacea.* | B. Bun-jam. T. Conda-mayoor. |
| *glandulosa.* | H. Bun-nurukalee. |
| *anceps.* | B. Lal-jam. |
| *colorata.* | B. Umur-kalee. |
| ARECA | |
| *Catechu.* | S. Goovaka ; Kramuka. B. Gowa ; Oodbeg. H. B. Sooparee; Supearie. TAM. Paak. T. Poka. CYNG. Puwak. |
| *triandra.* | B. Ran-goowa. |
| *gracilis.* | B. Ran-goowa-sooparee. |
| ARGEMONE | |
| *Mexicana.* | S. Brumhadundie ; Bramhie. B. H. Bura-shial-kanta. B. Shial-kanta. H. Bherband; Faringie-datura. TAM. Brumhadundoo ; Brumarakash. T. Brumhadundie. CAN. Dotury. |
| ARISTIDIA | |
| *setacea.* | T. Shippuroo-gaddi ; Shippur-gaddi. |
| *hystrix.* | T. Shippuroo-kali. |
| *depressa.* | T. Nali-pootika. |
| ARISTOLOCHIA | |
| *Indica.* | S. Urka-moola ; Ishwara ; Hari. B. H. Isarmel ; Ishurmool. H. Isrievayl. TAM. Perumarundoo. T. Doolagovila; Eesaravayroo. CYNG. Sat-sanda ; Sacasander. M. Catelæ-vegon. |

| *Gen. and Spec.* | *Native Names.* |
|---|---|
| *bracteata.* | S. Cattrabungha. Tam. Addatinapalay. T. Gardi-garapa ; Gadidaygudda-purra. |
| Artemisia | |
| *Maderaspatana.* | H. Mustaroo. Tam. Mashipattiri. Cyng. Wæl-kolundoo. M. Nelampala. Can. Dorana. |
| *Indica.* | S. Duna-dana. H. Duna; Mustaroo; Ghundumar. Tam. Mashiputrie. Cyng. Wol-kolundo. |
| *Austriaca.* | S. Dawanakaha. H. Downah; Gundmar. Tam. Marikolindoo. T. Dawanum. |
| *elegans.* | H. Abuttna. |
| *sternutatoria.* | B. Hachittee ; Nukchiknee. |
| Artocarpus | |
| *integrifolia.* | B. Kantal; Kental. |
| *Lacucha.* | S. Lukoocha. B. Dephul. |
| *Chaplasha.* | B. Chapalasha. |
| *hirsuta.* | Mah. Anjeli. |
| Arum | |
| *Colocasia.* | S. Kuchoo; Kuchwee. |
| 1*st var.* | B. Goori-kuchoo. T. Shama-kura. |
| 2*d var.* | B. Ashoo-kuchoo. |
| 1*st var.* | B. Kala-kuchoo. |
| 2*d var.* | B. Char-kuchoo. |
| 3*d var.* | B. Bun-kuchoo. |
| *macrorhizon.* | S. Hasti-carni. Tam. Verrughung. Cyng. Abara-balloorakashie; Habarala. |
| *Nymphæafolia.* | B. Sar-kuchoo. T. Ishama. |
| *montanum.* | T. Konda-rakis. |
| *Indicum.* | B. H. Man; Man-kuchoo; Man-giri. |
| *cucullatum.* | B. Bish-man. |
| *fornicatum.* | B. Kuchiree. T. Balrakis. |
| *Orixense.* | B. Ghetkool; Ghet-kuchoo. |
| *gracile.* | H. Harpung. |
| *curvatum.* | H. Beer-buka. |
| *sessiliflorum.* | H. Binda-gooea. |
| *campanulatum.* | S. Kunda. B. H. Ol. T. Munchakunda. |
| *bulbiferum.* | B. Umbla-bela. |
| *lyratum.* | T. Adivi-kunda. |
| *sylvaticum.* | T. Adivi-chama. |

| *Gen. and Spec.* | *Native Names.* |
|---|---|
| ARUNDO | |
| *bifaria.* | B. Anol. T. Potoo-ederoo. |
| *Karka.* | S. Nula; Dhumuna; Potugala. B. H. Nul. T. Naga-sara-ma-dantoo; Maitantos. |
| *Bengalensis.* | B. Durma; Gaba-nul. |
| ASCLEPIAS | |
| *gigantea. (red var.)* | S. Axka. S. H. Urka. B. Akund. H. Ark; Mudar. TAM. Yercum. T. Nella-jeeleeroo. CAN. Yecada. |
| *(white.)* | S. Alarka; Ulurca. B. Shwet-akund; Shwet-urka. T. Tella-jelladoo. |
| *acida.* | S. B. Soma-luta. T. Tiga-chumoodoo. |
| *asthmatica.* | H. Unta-mool. T. Kaka-palla. |
| *tunicata.* | B. Chagul-patee. H. Callia-lata. |
| *volubilis.* | S. Madhu-malati. H. Teet-conga; Nukchiknie. TAM. Kodie-palay. T. Palay; Doodi-palla. |
| *annularia.* | T. Palla-gurgi; Poola-gurgi. |
| *prolifera.* | TAM. Nangarapanjam. M. Nanjeramoorchuni. |
| *pseudosarsa. (narrow leaved.)* | H. Sada-booree. T. Palla-soucundi. |
| *(broad leaved.)* | S. Ununta. B. H. Ununta (or Anonto) mool. T. Ghadi-Soucundi. |
| *rosea.* | S. Doogdhika. B. Dood-luta; Doodeyabeera. T. Doodi-palla. |
| *lactifera.* | TAM. Vilpalei. |
| *echinata.* | H. Sagwanee. T. Jatuga. |
| *geminata.* | H. Chota-dood-luta. |
| *odoratissima.* | H. Kunja-lata. |
| *tenacissima.* | H. Jitee. |
| *vomitoria.* | H. Automel; Untamool. TAM. Coorinja. T. Coorinja. CYNG. Kuringyan. |
| *microphylla.* | T. Poola-palla. |
| ASPALATHUS | |
| *Indica.* | S. Shivanimba. TAM. Shevenar-vaymboo. M. Manelli. |
| ASPARAGUS | |
| *sarmentosus.* | H. Suffaid-mooslie. TAM. Tanneervittang. T. Tsulla-ghedaloo. M. Schædaveli-kelungu. |
| *officinalis.* | H. Nakdoun. |

| *Gen. and Spec.* | *Native Names.* |
|---|---|
| *racemosus.* | S. Wari. S. B. Shuta-moolee. T. Challa. |
| *Curillus.* | N. Kurella. |
| ASTER | |
| *Chinensis.* | N. Gaynatuka. |
| ATHANASIA | |
| *Indica.* | T. Bugati-bunda. |
| ATRAGENE | |
| *Zeylanica.* | H. Chagool-batee. |
| ATROPA | |
| *Mandragora.* | B. Yeb-rooj. H. Luckmuna-luckmunnie. TAM. Caat-jootie. |
| *Belladonna.* | H. Sug-unggoor; Ungoor-shefa. |
| AVERRHOA | |
| *Carambola, (acid.)* | S. Kurmu-runga. B. H. Kamarunga. |
| *(sweet.)* | B. H. Meetha-kamarunga. |
| AVICENNIA | |
| *tomentosa.* | B. H. Bina. |

| *Gen. and Spec.* | *Native Names.* |
|---|---|
| # B. | |
| BŒOBOTRYS | |
| *ramentacea.* | B. Mulmooriya. |
| *nemoralis.* | B. Mul. |
| BALLOTA | |
| *disticha.* | S. Buta-ghni. TAM. Vuttei-pemayruttie; Vaydoo-booriki; Eerumottie. T. Andaberakoo. CYNG. Heen-yakwanassa. |
| BAMBUSA | |
| *arundinacea.* | S. Vungsha. B. Bansh. T. Vedroo. |
| *stricta.* | T. Sadanapa-vedroo. |
| *baccifera.* | B. Bish-bansh. H. Paya-tullu. |
| *Tuldu.* | B. Tulda-bashini; Pea bansh, Tulda-bansh. |
| *spinosa.* | B. Behoor-bansh. |
| *Balcua.* | B. Dhooli-bansh. T. Puloo; Bhalkoo. |
| BARLERIA | |
| *Prionitis.* | S. Kuruntuka. B. Kanta-jatee; Puroosha. TAM. Shemmoolie; Varamoolie. T. Moolloogorinteh. CYNG. Katukarundu. M. Coletta-veetla. |
| *longifolia.* | S. Ikshugandha. H. Gokshura. TAM. Neer-moollie. T. Neer-gobbie. CYNG. Katu-iriki. |
| *cristata, (purple.)* | S. B. Jhintee. |
| *(rosy.)* | H. Pia-bausa. |
| *ciliata.* | S. Kuruvuka. B. Oojootee. |
| *dichotoma.* | B. Sada-jatee. |
| *cærulea.* | S. Dasee; Vana. |
| BARRINGTONIA | |
| *acutangula.* | S. Jul. B. Hijjul. T. Kadami. |
| BASELLA | |
| *rubra.* | S. Pootika. B. Racta-bun-pooi; Pooi; Pooi-shak. T. Yerra-batsalla. |
| *alba.* | B. H. Suffet-pooi. T. Alla-batsalla. |
| *lucida v. cordifolia.* | B. H. Pooi. T. Pedda-batsalla. |
| BASSIA | |
| *latifolia.* | S. Mudhooka; Madooka. B. H. Moula. T. Ipie. |

| Gen. and Spec. | Native Names. |
|---|---|
| *longifolia.* | S. Madooka. B. Mooa. H. Mohe. Tam. Eloopei; Illipee. T. Ippa. Cyng. Tel-mee. |
| *butyracea.* | H. Phul-wara. |
| Batis | |
| *spinosa.* | S. Sakotuka. H. Suhoora. Tam. Barinka. T. Koriti. |
| Bauhinia | |
| *variegata.* | S. B. Kovidara; Yooga-putra. B. Rukta-kanchun; Beedul. |
| *candida.* | B. Kana-raj. |
| *purpurea.* | B. Deb-kanchun. H. Sona. |
| *parviflora.* | S. Vana-raja. Tam. Areka-marum. T. Arræ. |
| *tomentosa.* | S. Usmadugha. Tam. Ati; Caat-ati. M. Chanschena. |
| *racemosa.* | H. Mawal. T. Ada. |
| *anguina.* | B. Nag-poot. |
| *scandens.* | B. Gundha-gila. |
| *acuminata.* | B. Kanchun; Chutka. |
| Begonia | |
| *laciniata.* | B. Hoowurjo. |
| Bentinckia | |
| *Condapana.* | Tam. Kunda-pana. |
| Berberis | |
| *pinnata.* | B. Huding-nioong-mari. |
| Bergera | |
| *Kœnigii.* | S. Kristna-nimboo. B. Karia-phullee. H. Bursunga. Tam. Kari-pilli; Karaway-pillay. T. Kari-vepa; Karrivaympakoo. |
| *integerrima.* | H. Bun-kooncha. |
| Bergia | |
| *verticillata.* | B. H. Lal-keshura. T. Neeroo-pavala. |
| *Ammanioides.* | H. Doolacheri. |
| Berria | |
| *Ammonilla.* | Cyng. Amonilla. |
| Beta | |
| *Bengalensis.* | B. H. Palung; Palunka. |
| Betula | |
| *Bhoorja.* | B. Bhoorj. |
| Bignonia | |
| *spatheacea.* | T. Woodi. |
| *suaveolens.* | S. Patuli. B. Parool; Ghunta; Moog. H. Purula. |

| Gen. and Spec. | Native Names. |
|---|---|
| *Chelonoides.* | TAM. Poupadyræ ; Padrie-vayr. T. Tagada ; Kalighotroo. CYNG. Ela-palol. |
| *Indica.* | S. Shyonaka. B. H. Shona. TAM. Vaag-marum. |
| BIXA | |
| *Orellana.* | B. H. Lut-kun. CAN. Kuppa-manhala. |
| BŒOBOTRYS | |
| *ramentacea.* | B. Mulmooriya. |
| BOERHAVIA | |
| *diffusa.* | S. Sinadika ; Punarnava. B. Shoo-thugnee. H. Tikrie. TAM. Mooka-rutty. T. Attika-mamedie. |
| *procumbens, (red.)* | S. Shoothugnee ; Poonarnava. B. Ga-dha-poorna. |
| BOLETUS | |
| *igniarius.* | H. Agarikoon. TAM. Garikoon. |
| BOMBAX | |
| *pentandrum.* | S. Mullie. B. H. Shwet-shimool. H. Huttian. TAM. Elavum. T. Kadami; Booraga. CYNG. Pulun-imbul. M. Pania-paniala. |
| *heptaphyllum.* | S. B. Shalmuli. B. Rukta-shimool ; Shimool. |
| BORAGO | |
| *Indica.* | B. Chota-kulpa. |
| *officinalis.* | TAM. Karpoorawullie. |
| BORASSUS | |
| *flabelliformis.* | S. Tala. B. H. Tal. H. Tarie. TAM. Pan-nang-kulloo. T. Putoo-toadi ; Peati-toadi ; Tati-kulloo ; Penty. M. Am-pana ; Carimpana. CYNG. Tal-gaha. |
| BOSWELLIA | |
| *thurifera v. serrata.* | S. Sallaci ; Shullokee. B. Luban. H. Salaee. TAM. Moræda. T. Tsaroo-mamadi. |
| *glaber.* | T. Googoolapoo-chittoo. |
| BRADLEIA | |
| *nitida.* | B. Ungootee. |
| *lanceolaria.* | B. Ungootee. |
| BRASSICA | |
| *Rapa.* | B. Shalgram. |
| *oleracea.* | B. H. Kopee. |

| *Gen. and Spec.* | *Native Names.* |
|---|---|
| *Erucoides.* | S. Siddartha. B. Shwet-surisha. |
| BRIEDELIA | |
| *spinosa.* | T. Kora-maun. |
| *montana.* | T. Patunga. |
| *scandens.* | T. Dooki-boora. |
| BROMELIA | |
| *Ananas.* | S. Anarush. B. H. T. Ananus. TAM. CYNG. Anasie. M. Koida-cheeka. |
| BRYONIA | |
| *scabrella.* | H. Agumukee. T. Putri-budinga. |
| *Garcini.* | T. Gheedi-moraloo. |
| *glabra.* | T. Naga-dunda. |
| *grandis.* | S. Jivaka; Vimba; Patuparni. H. Tselkacha; Telkacha; Koondoorie. TAM. Covay. T. Donda. CYNG. Ken-kekiri. |
| *epigœa.* | H. Rawkus-gudda. TAM. Kolung-kovay-kalung. T. Akasagherooda-gudda. |
| *scabra.* | S. Ahilaykum. H. Musmusa. TAM. Mosumooski. T. Noodhosa. |
| *callosa.* | TAM. Tomettikai. T. Boddama-kaia. |
| *pilosa.* | T. Kukuma-dunda. |
| *rostrata.* | TAM. Appekovay. |
| *laciniosa.* | H. Gurga-naroo. |
| BUCHANNIA | |
| *latifolia.* | S. B. Piyala. TAM. Moræda. T. Tsaroo-mamadi. |
| BUCHNERIA | |
| *Asiatica.* | T. Woolisi. |
| BUDDLEIA | |
| *Neemda.* | B. Nimda. |
| BURMANNIA | |
| *disticha.* | H. Tala-kattee. |
| BUTEA | |
| *frondosa.* | S. Pulasha; Kingshooka; Kinouka. B. H. Pulas. H. Dhak. T. Porasum-cottay. T. Maduga; Moduga. CYNG. Gas-kæla. M. Plaso. |
| *superba.* | T. Tiga-maduga. |
| BÜTTNERA | |
| *aspera.* | B. Dhootura-luta. |

| Gen. and Spec. | Native Names. |
|---|---|
| **C.** | |
| CACALIA | |
| *Kleinia.* | TAM. Erminakullie. T. Yennapotoo-na-likeh-jemmoodoo. |
| *sonchifolia.* | S. Udiram-panum. B. Shudi-mudi. CYNG. Bookadu-para. M. Muel-schevy. |
| CACTUS | |
| *Indicus.* | B. Moonsa-kanta. B. H. Nag-phunee. H. Juppal-saynd; Phoonee-monsa. TAM. Nagatallee-kullie. CYNG. Judu-kata-patuk. |
| CÆSALPINIA | |
| *Sappan.* | S. Patanga; Potunga. B. Bukum. H. Bukum-kulija. TAM. Vatungha-cut-tay; Patinga-cuttay. CYNG. Patan-gee. M. Tsiapangum. |
| *Bonducella.* | S. Pootikarunja. B. Nata-kanta; Kut-karanja. H. Kat-kuleja. CAN. Kom-boorel. |
| *lacerans.* | T. Wallikadooda. |
| *Mimosoides.* | CYNG. Coda-wawul-ætiya. |

| Gen. and Spec. | Native Names. |
|---|---|
| CALAMUS | |
| *erectus.* | H. Sun-gootta. |
| *Rotang.* | S. Vetra ; Vetusa. B. H. Bet ; Beta. |
| *fasciculatus.* | S. Umba-vetusa. B. H. Bura-beta. |
| *gracilis.* | B. Mapoori-bet. |
| *latifoluis.* | B. Karak-bet. |
| *polygamus.* | B. Koodoom-bet. |
| *tenuis.* | B. Bandhari-bet. |
| *extensus.* | H. Dew-gullar. |
| *quinquenervius.* | H. Hurmur-gullar. |
| CALLA | |
| *virosa.* | H. Bish-kuchoo. |
| *aromatica.* | H. Kuchoo-gundhubee. |
| CALLICARPA | |
| *lanata.* | S. Mashandari. B. Massandari. H. Bastra. CYNG. Ella. |
| *incana.* | S. Mashandari. B. Mattura. |
| *lancæolaria.* | H. Koamoora. |
| CALLOPHYLLUM | |
| *Calaba.* | CYNG. Gæta-keena. M. Tsierou-ponna. |
| *Inophyllum.* | H. Sultan-champa ; H. Surpunka. TAM. Pinnay. T. Poona. CYNG. Tel-domba. M. Ponna-maram. |
| *angustifolium.* | M. Poon. |
| CALOTROPIS | |
| *gigantea.* | B. Adeetya ; Akon ; Urko ; Arko ; Asphoot. |
| CALYPTRANTHES | |
| *caryophyllifolia.* | S. Kaka-jamba. H. Jamoon. TAM. Nawel. T. Nereddie. CYNG. Bata-domba. |
| *jambolana.* | S. Turkolum. H. Jamoun. TAM. Turkolum ; Takkelam. CYNG. Alu-bodan. |
| CAMPANULA | |
| *fulgens.* | N. Usery-soah. |
| CANARIUM | |
| *commune.* | CYNG. Rata-kækuna. |
| *balsamiferum.* | CYNG. Mala-kækuna. |
| CANNA | |
| *Indica, (red.)* | S. Vana-keli. S. B. Surba-juya. H. Lalsurbjuya. T. Kristmatamara. |
| *(yellow.)* | B. Surba-juya. H. Subjuya. |

| *Gen. and Spec.* | *Native Names.* |
|---|---|
| CANNABIS | |
| *sativa.* | S. Bhanga; Gunjika. B. TAM. T. Ganja. H. Bhang. |
| CANTHIUM. | |
| *parviflorum.* | S. Naga-vala. TAM. Caray-cheddy. T. Ballusoo-kura; Ballusoo-chetto. M. Tsjerou-kara. |
| *angustifolium.* | B. Katha-mooli; Kota-mulli. |
| *didymum.* | T. Naum-papala. |
| CAPPARIS | |
| *acuminata.* | H. Kalu-kera. T. Palliky. |
| *Zeylanica.* | T. Adonda. |
| *sepiaria.* | B. Kanta-goor-kamaee. T. Nella-upi. |
| *aphylla.* | H. Keril. |
| *heteroclita.* | T. Putta-tiga. |
| *trifoliata.* | S. Vuroona; Tikta-shaka. B. Buroon. T. Tella-woolymera. |
| *bisperma.* | T. Gooli. |
| *corymbosa.* | T. Aguba. |
| CAPRARIA | |
| *gratissima.* | H. Kala-kurpoor. |
| CAPSICUM | |
| *frutescens.* | S. Bran-maricha. B. Lunka-murich. TAM. Mollaghai. T. Merapakaia. CYNG. Gas-miris. MAH. Tambhudda-meerchingay. CAN. Meneshena. |
| ——— *red.* | B. Lall-lunka-murich. |
| ———*yellow.* | B. Huldi-lunka-murich. |
| *minimum.* | B. Dhan-lunka-murich. H. Dhan-murich. |
| *annuum.* | B. Gach-murich. |
| CARDIOSPERMUM | |
| *Halicacabum.* | S. Karavi; Jyotishmutee. B. Shibjool; Noaphutuki. TAM. Mooda-cottan. T. Boodda-kanka-rakoo; Nallagolivinda. |
| CAREYA | |
| *herbacea.* | S. Bhoomi-darimba. B. Bhooi-dalim. |
| *arborea.* | TAM. Kumbi. T. Pootta-tanni-marum. |
| CARICA | |
| *Papaya.* | B. H. M. Papeya; Papaya. TAM. Puppali. |
| CARISSA | |
| *Carandas, (black.)* | S. Krishnapak-phula; Avigna. B. Karumcha. H. Kurunda. T. Waka. |

| *Gen. and Spec.* | *Native Names.* |
|---|---|
| *diffusa.* | S. Kurumurdika. B. San-kurumcha. T. Wakloo ; Wakoyloo. |
| CARPOPOGON | |
| *monospermum.* | T. Enuga. |
| *pruriens.* | S. Atma-goopta ; Murkutee. B. Alkooshi. B. H. Kiwach. |
| *atropurpurea.* | T. Tilla-kodi. |
| *niveum.* | H. Kamach. |
| *capitatum.* | T. Surootoo. |
| CARTHAMUS | |
| *tinctorius.* | S. Cusumbha ; Kamalottara. S. B. H. T. Koosumbha. B. Kajeerah. H. Koosum. TAM. Seendoorkum. T. Koosumba. CAN. Cossumba. |
| CARYOTA | |
| *urens.* | T. Teerooga. |
| CASEARIA | |
| *tomentosa.* | T. Garugoodoo. |
| *vareca.* | B. Sitta-cheera. |
| *esculenta.* | T. Kunda-jungira. |
| *glomerata.* | B. Loorjoor. |
| CASSIA | |
| *Tora.* | S. Chukra-murda ; Brabhunatha. B. Chakoonda ; Kalkashunda. TAM. Tagaray ; Tagashay. T. Chakunda ; Tagarish-akoo. CYNG. Petitora. |
| *purpurea.* | B. Kala-kulkashinda. T. Kunda-kashinda. |
| *Fistula.* | S. B. Soovurnuka. B. Sonali ; Soodali. H. Amultus ; Pykassie. TAM. Konnekai ; Sarakon-nekai. T. Rela ; Rayla-kaia. CYNG. Ahilla. CAN. Cakay. |
| *Senna.* | S. Amshunatty-divandiva ; Botallapotaka. B. Sona-pat. H. Soona-mookhee. TAM. Nilaverei ; Nilavaghei. T. Nela-ponna ; Nayla-tunghadoo. CYNG. Nilaverie. |
| *esculenta.* | B. Kas-murdun. T. Nitty-kashinda-kura. |
| *prostrata.* | T. Nalla-Teelooga. |
| *Sophora.* | S. Talpota. Mayharie ; Swarnamayharie. B. Kulkashinda. TAM. Po- |

| Gen. and Spec. | Native Names. |
|---|---|
| | naverie. T. Pydu-tenghadoo. CYNG. Oorootora; Ranawara. M. Ponnamtaghera. |
| *auriculata.* | S. Mayharie; Talpota. H. Turwer. TAM. Avery. T. Tangheeroo; Tangheedoo. CYNG. Ranawara. CAN. Tangayree. |
| *alata.* | S. Dudrooghna. B. Dadoo-murdun. H. Velatie-aghatie; Dadmerdun. TAM. Wandukolli; Seemi-aghatee. T. Seema-avisee; Metta-tamara. CYNG. Ætora. |
| CASSYATA | |
| *filiformis.* | S. Akasha-vullee. B. Akash-bulee. T. Pauncha-tiga. |
| CASTANEA | |
| *Indica.* | H. Badam-gota. |
| CASUARINA | |
| *equisitifolia.* | CYNG. Kasagaha. |
| *muricata.* | H. Huri. B. Jow. |
| CEDRELA | |
| *Toona.* | S. Tunna: Toona; Kooveruka; Cuveraca. B. H. TAM. Toon; Tood. CAN. Tunda. |
| CELASTRUS | |
| *montanus.* | T. Pedda-chintu. |
| *emarginatus.* | T. Chinny-chintu. |
| *verticillatus.* | N. Tibiliti. |
| *monospermus.* | B. Tiara. |
| *robustus.* | B. Sheelkoil. |
| CELOSIA | |
| *argentea.* | B. Shwet-moorga; Chooa. H. Debkhotee. |
| *cristata, (red.)* | B. Deepuk. B. H. Lall-moorga. |
| *(yellow.)* | S. Vurhichoora. B. Huldi-moorga. |
| *corymbosa.* | T. Rajuma. |
| CELSIA | |
| *Coromandeliana.* | B. Kookshima. |
| CELTIS | |
| *Orientalis.* | S. Jeevunee. B. Jubuna. CYNG. Gaedumba. M. Mallam-toddali. |
| CENTAUREA | |
| *moschata.* | H. Shah-pusund. |
| CERATOPHYLLUM | |
| *verticillatum.* | H. Jhanji. |

| Gen. and Spec. | Native Names. |
|---|---|
| **Ceratostema** | |
| *variegata.* | B. Tala-moot. |
| *vaccinacea.* | B. Kesa-proom. |
| **Cerbera** | |
| *Manghas.* | T. Caat-aralie. Cyng. Gonkaduru? M. Odallam. |
| **Ceropegia** | |
| *tuberosa.* | T. Batsala-mandu. |
| *juncea.* | T. Bella-mandu. |
| *bulbosa.* | T. Munchi-goodi-munda. |
| *acuminata.* | T. Kumoo-mundoo. |
| **Chara** | |
| *involucrata.* | B. Jhanjī. |
| *furcata.* | B. Jhanji. |
| **Chaulmoogra** | |
| *odorata.* | B. Chaulmoogra; Piturkurra. |
| **Cheiranthus** | |
| *Cheiri.* | H. Lahoori-shuboo. |
| **Chenopodium** | |
| *album.* | B. Beto-sag; Betoya. |
| **Chionanthus** | |
| *Smilacifolia.* | B. Chunalata. |
| **Chironia** | |
| *centauroides.* | B. Geema; Girmi. |
| **Chironjia** | |
| *sapida.* | H. Cheeroojee. |
| **Chloroxylon** | |
| *Dupada.* | Tam. Chadacula. M. Payana. |
| **Chrysanthemum** | |
| *Indicum.* | B. Chundra-mullika. H. Gool-daoodi. T. Chamunti. |
| **Chrysophyllum** | |
| *acuminata.* | B. H. Peetakara. |
| **Cicer** | |
| *Lens.* | B. Mussoor. |
| *arietinum.* | S. Chennuka. B. Chala; Boot; Chŭna-batoola; Boot-kalai. H. Hurbhury; Chenna. Tam. Cadalei. T. Sanigheloo: Guz. Chana. |
| **Cichorium** | |
| *Endivia.* | T. Koshee. |
| **Cinchona** | |
| *excelsa.* | H. Kala-buchnak. T. Bundaroo; Bundoorob; Pundaroo. |

| Gen. and Spec. | Native Names. |
|---|---|
| *gratissima.* | B. Usookooli. |
| CISSAMPELOS | |
| *hexandra.* | S. Patha-umbusta. H. Nimookka; Beedrookoron. |
| *Pareira.* | TAM. Pooi-mooshtie; Poon-mooshtie; Vata-tirupie. |
| *convolvulacea.* | T. Pata. |
| *glabra.* | H. Peer-grooj. |
| CISSUS | |
| *vitiginea.* | B. Gwali-lata. CAN. Marata-tiga. |
| *glauca.* | B. Goor-gwaliya. |
| *quadrangularis.* | S. Vajra-valli. B. Har; Harchara. H. Harjora; Nillur. TAM. Perundie-codie. T. Nullerootingeh. CYNG. Wael-heerasa. |
| *latifolia.* | CYNG. Galberaya. M. Schunambu-valli. |
| *acida.* | TAM. Pooliarileh. T. Woorsipala. |
| *carnosa.* | T. Canapa-tiga. |
| *setosa.* | T. Barubutsali. |
| *elongata.* | B. Dhena; Dhemna. |
| *pedata.* | S. Godha-pudu. B. Gwaliya. |
| CITRUS | |
| *acida v. medica.* | S. Jumbeera; Nimbooka. B. Neboo. H. Leemo; Lemboo. |
| 1*st var.* | B. H. Patee-neboo. |
| 2*d var.* | —— Kagujee-neboo. |
| 3*d var.* | —— Gora-neboo. |
| 4*th var.* | —— China-gora-neboo. |
| 5*th var.* | —— Kamaral-neboo. |
| 7*th var.* | —— Taba-neboo. |
| 9*th var.* | —— Meetha-neboo. |
| *medica.* | —— Korna-neboo. |
| 1*st var.* | S. Beeja-poora. B. H. Beg-poora. |
| *aurantium.* | S. Nagrunga. B. Kumla; Komla-neboo. H. Nerunga. |
| *decumanus.* | B. H. Batavi-neboo. |
| CLEOME | |
| *pentaphylla.* | S. Kara-vela; Varvar. B. H. Karela. B. Hurhuriya. H. Hoolhool. TAM. Vaylee; Nellei-vaylie. T. Vaivinta; Wawinti. CYNG. Awusada-wœla-kola. M. Karaveela. CYNG. Wominta. |
| *Chelidonii.* | T. Kar-wominta. |

| Gen. and Spec. | Native Names. |
|---|---|
| *felina.* | S. H. Swarnakshira. |
| *viscosa.* | S. Kooka-vaivinta ; Kooka-vumitie ; Shunaca-barbara. B. H. Hoor-hooriya. TAM. Nayavaylei. CYNG. Walaba. M. Aria-veela. |
| CLERODENDRUM *Phlomoides.* | S. Vata-ghni. TAM. Taloodalei. T. Teloki ; Nellie. |
| CLITORIA *ternata, (blue.)* | S. Neela-gherie ; Asphota ; Upurajita. B. Upurajita ; Aporajita. H. Kalizer. TAM. Karkakartan. T. Neeladintona; Nella-ghentana. CYNG. Nilkatarodu. M. Shlonga-kuspi. |
| *(white.)* | B. Shwet-Upurajita. |
| CLUYTIA *collina.* | TAM. Wodachie. T. Kodisha. |
| *oblongifolia.* | B. Dookesswa. |
| CNESTIS *monadelpha.* | B. Spokur-thooti. |
| COCOS *nucifera.* | S. Narikela. B. Narikel. H. Naril; Naryel. TAM. Taynga. T. Tenkaia. Narikadam. M. Tangha ; Tengha. |
| *Maldivica.* | S. Ubdie-narikaylum. H. Dirya-kanaril. TAM. Kaddil-taynghai. T. Samatrapoo-tainkaya. |
| COFFEA *tetrandra.* | B. Chilmuri ; Chilmaree. |
| *Bengalensis.* | B. Bun-kawa. |
| *Arabica.* | B. Kawa. |
| COIX *lacryma.* | S. Guberoo. B. H. Jul-gurgur ; Jeelgurgur ; Kanch. |
| *barbata.* | H. Gurgur. T. Ghella-gaddy. |
| *gigantea.* | B. Danga-gurgur. |
| COLDENIA *procumbens.* | S. Tripakshi. H. Tripungkhi. |
| COLUMNEA *balsamica.* | B. Kursoor. |
| *tomentosa.* | B. Chota-bhooi-kamadi. |
| COMBRETUM *decandrum.* | T. Arry-kota. |
| *pilosum.* | B. Jooni-ugur. |

| Gen. and Spec. | Native Names. |
|---|---|
| *acuminatum.* | B. Pat-jooniya. |
| *costatum.* | B. Tali-jooniya. |
| *rotundifolium.* | B. Kowa-luta. |
| *laxum.* | T. Bandi-koota. |
| COMMELINA | |
| *communis.* | B. Juta-kanchura. |
| *Bengalensis.* | B. Kanchura. B. H. Kanuraca. |
| *salicifolia.* | S. Langulee. B. Languli; Panee-kanchura. |
| *nudiflora.* | B. Kanduli; Kendru. |
| *scapiflora.* | H. Kurelli. |
| CONNARUS | |
| *nitidus.* | H. Toog. |
| CONOCARPUS | |
| *latifolia.* | T. Sirimaun. |
| *acuminata.* | T. Panch-maun. |
| CONVOLVOLUS | |
| *bicolor.* | H. Jurud-kulmee. |
| *speciosus.* | S. Samudra-patra. TAM. Samutra-cheddie. T. Samutrapatsa. CYNG. Mahadumuda. |
| *Turpethum.* | S. Priputa. B. H. Doodh-kulmee; Teorie. H. Niswut; Tikura. TAM. Shevadie. T. Tegadu; Tella-tagada. CYNG. Trasta-walu. |
| *grandiflorus.* | S. Puthmapoo-todemie. TAM. Vul-ademboo; Naga-mooghatei-kai. T. Nagara-mookutty-kai. CYNG. Alanga. M. Munda-valli. |
| *Malabaricus.* | TAM. Paymoostey. M. Kattu-kelangie. |
| *Batatas.* | S. Ruktaloo. B. Lal (or Suffet) sukur-kunda. H. Pendaloo. TAM. Sukkaray-vullie. T. Sukkara-vela. CAN. Ghenasa. |
| *paniculatus.* | S. Vidaree. B. H. Bhooi-komra. M. Phal-modeca. |
| *reptans.* | S. Kulumbee. B. Kulmee-shak. |
| *dentatus.* | T. Tella-antoo-tiga. |
| *pes-capra.* | B. Chagul-khoori. H. Dobutee-luta. |
| CONYZA | |
| *lacera.* | B. Bura-kooksima; Kookura-shonga. |
| *cinerea.* | S. Sahadevi. TAM. Seera-shengalameer. T. Gherutti-kamma. CYNG. Heen-monara-kudimbiya. |

| *Gen. and Spec.* | *Native Names.* |
|---|---|
| *balsamifera.* | Cyng. Lewærælla. |
| *bifoliata.* | H. Jurud-banghra. |
| *lanceolaria.* | B. Tejmool. |
| Corallia | |
| *lucida.* | T. Koralli. |
| Corchorus | |
| *olitorius, (green v.)* | B. Pat; Koshta; Bhungee. H. Singginganascha. |
| *(red var.)* | B. H. Bun-pat. |
| *capsularis, (red v.)* | H. Ghinalita; Pat; Koshta. |
| *(green.)* | B. Koshta; Tittha-pat. |
| *fascicularius.* | H. Junglee-pat. |
| Cordia | |
| *Myxa.* | S. Buhoovaruka; Bukampadaruka. B. Buhooari. H. Lesora; Lusoora. Tam. Vidi-maram. T. Nekra. Cyng. Lolu. |
| *Sebestena.* | T. Shaeshtmantaka; Tenka. |
| *latifolia.* | S. Sheloo. B. Buhooari. H. Buralesoora. |
| *monoica.* | H. Pida. T. Panagheri. |
| *acuminata.* | B. Ramutti. |
| Coriandrum | |
| *sativum.* | S. B. H. Dhunya; Dhanyaca. Tam. T. Cottamillie. Cyng. Cotumbaroo. M. Danga. Can. Cottimbirry. |
| Cornus | |
| *capitata.* | H. Bhumowra. N. Chungwa. |
| Coronilla | |
| *picta.* | S. Krishna-rajam. Tam. Carim-chembai. T. Nulla-somuttie. |
| Corypha | |
| *umbraculifera.* | T. Conda-pani. Cyng. Tala. |
| *Taliera.* | S. Talee. B. Tariyat. H. Taliera. |
| *elata.* | B. H. Bujra; Bujra-batool. |
| Costus | |
| *speciosus.* | S. Kemboo; Kemooka. B. H. Keoo. |
| Cotyledon | |
| *laciniata.* | S. Hema-sagura. B. H. Hemsagur. |
| Cratæva | |
| *Tapia.* | S. Varuna; Varana. H. Tapia; Birmi. Tam. Mavilinghum. T. Maredoo. |
| *religiosa.* | S. Vilwa. B. H. Bel. Tam. Veelvie. T. Bilva. Cyng. Lunee-warna. M. Niivala. |

| *Gen. and Spec.* | *Native Names.* |
|---|---|
| *Marmelos.* | TAM. M. Covalam. CYNG. Beli. |
| CRINUM | |
| *Asiaticum.* | S. Vishamandala. H. Sookh-durshun. TAM. Veshei-moonghei. T. Vesha-mangaloo. CYNG. Heentolabo. M. Belutta-pola-taly. |
| *toxicarum.* | B. H. Burra-kanoor. CYNG. Maha-tolabo. |
| *Zeylanicum.* | B. H. Kanoor. |
| *defixum.* | B. Soodurshun. |
| CROCUS | |
| *sativa.* | S. Kasmirajamma ; Kunkuma. H. Zafran ; Keysur. TAM. Khoongoo-mapoo. T. Khoon-koomapoo. CYNG. Kohoon. |
| CROTALARIA | |
| *juncea.* | S. Shuna. B. H. Sun. T. Shanamoo. |
| *stricta.* | T. Moonga. |
| *prostrata.* | B. Bhooi-sun. T. Seri-galla-gheetsa. |
| *retusa.* | H. Beel-jhunjhun. |
| *sericea.* | S. Peeyooksha. B. Peeyoli ; Jhun-jhun. |
| *verrucosa.* | B. H. Bun-sun. TAM. Vuttei-khilloo-khilloopie. T. Alla-galli-gheetsa ; Ghelegherinta. CYNG. Kiligilippe ; Nil-adana-hiriya. |
| *Laburnifolia.* | B. Muna. T. Pedda-galli-gheetea. |
| *trifoliastrum.* | T. Naga-galli-gheetsa. |
| *quinquefolia.* | T. Neeru-galli-gheetsa. |
| *cespitosa.* | T. Nella-guri-galli-gheetsa. |
| *uniflora.* | T. Nella-benda. |
| *nummularia.* | T. Pili-wata-tiga. |
| *Orixcensis.* | T. Koona-galli-gheetsa. |
| CROTON | |
| *Tiglium.* | S. Nepala ; Jipala ; Dunti. B. Re-chuk. B. H. Jumalgota. TAM. Ner-valum-cottay. T. Naypalum-vittiloo. CYNG. Nepalam. CAN. Jayapala. |
| *sebiferum.* | S. Tayapippali. H. Pippalyang. |
| *oblongifolium.* | H. Bura-gach. |
| *plicatum.* | S. Suryavarti. B. H. Khoodi-okra. H. Sonballi. |
| *Jouffiah.* | B. Joffai. |

| Gen. and Spec. | Native Names. |
|---|---|
| CUCUMIS | |
| *Colocynthis.* | S. Indra-varoonee; Vishala. B. Makhal. H. Indraini. TAM. Peycoomutikai; Varriecoomutiekai. T. Pootsakaia; Sheti-putsa. CYNG. Tittacommodoo. |
| *Melo.* | B. H. Khurbooja. TAM. Molam. |
| *sativus.* | S. Sookasa. B. Susha. H. Keera. |
| *Momordica.* | B. Sphootee. B. H. Footi. T. Pedda-dos-kay. |
| *utilissimus.* | B. Kankoor; Kurktee. H. Kakni. T. Dos-kay. |
| *trigonus.* | T. Pam-budinga. |
| *turbinatus.* | T. Nella-budinga. |
| *Maderaspatanus.* | H. Bun-gumuk. T. Kodi-budinga. |
| CUCURBITA | |
| *lagenaria.* | S. Ulavoo. B. Laoo; Kudoo; Toombo. |
| *Pepo.* | S. Kurkaroo. B. Koshnanto. B. H. Koomra. T. Boorda-gomodoo. |
| *Melopepo.* | B. H. Suphuree-koomra. |
| *citrullus.* | S. Chaya-pula. B. H. Turbooz; Turmooz. TAM. Pitcha; Shakara-koomatei. T. Darboojee. CYNG. Pitchaghedie; Komadu-diya. |
| *bitter var.* | S. Kutoo-toombie. B. Titu-laoo. |
| CUMINUM | |
| *Cyminum.* | S. Jeeruka; Ajaji. B. H. Jeera; Zira. TAM. Siragum. T. Gilakara. CYNG. Dooroo. CAN. Jeeraga. |
| CUPRESSUS | |
| *sempervirens.* | B. Suruss. H. Sarass. |
| CUCURLIGO | |
| *Orchioides.* | S. Warahi. B. Tal-moolee; Tal-noor; Moohol. H. Siah-mooslie. TAM. Nelepannay. T. Nella-tady. |
| CURCUMA | |
| *Zedoaria.* | S. Nirbisha; Vuna-huridra; Sholee; Shoolika. B. H. Bun-huldi. H. Nirbisi. |
| *Zerumbet.* | S. Karkhura. B. Shoothee. H. Kakhur; Kuchoora. TAM. Pulang-kilunggu; Capoor-kichlie. T. Keech- |

| *Gen. and Spec.* | *Native Names.* |
|---|---|
| | lie; Kuchoora. CYNG. Hinhoroo-peealliculla. |
| *Cæsia.* | B. Neel-kantha; Kala-huldi. |
| *angustifolia.* | H. Teecor; Ticor; Tikur. TAM. Kooamaoo. H. M. Kooa-koghei. |
| *longa.* | S. Peeta. S. B. Huridra. S. B. H. Huldi; Pit-ras. TAM. Munjil. T. Passapoo; Pampi. CYNG. Haradul. M. Mangellacua. MAH. Hulud. CAN. Arsina. |
| *Amada.* | B. Amada. |
| *Amhuldi.* | B. Shuthee; Amba-huldi. |
| *reclinata.* | B. Kurboor. B. H. Amba-huldi. |
| *xanthorhiza.* | B. Kasta-purjnee. |
| CUSCUTA | |
| *reflexa.* | B. Huldi-algosa; Huldi-algusi-luta. T. Sitama-poorgoonooloo. |
| *capitata.* | B. H. Algosa. |
| CYMBIDIUM | |
| *tessalloides.* | S. Vrisha-roha. B. Alugnuta. H. Bunda; Algooch. |
| CYNANCHUM | |
| *extensum.* | S. Yugaphala. H. Utrun. TAM. Vaylie-partee-ootamunnie. T. Zootupakoo. |
| CYNARA | |
| *Scolymus.* | H. Kunjir. |
| CYNOMETRA | |
| *polyandra.* | B. Peng. |
| CYNOSURUS | |
| *(see Eleusine)* | |
| CYPERUS | |
| *nudus, v. seminudus* | H. Goola-methi. T. Ghadoo-tunga. |
| *dubius.* | B. Choota-gothoobi. T. Tagada-tunga. |
| *juncifolius.* | S. Musta. H. Nagur-motha. TAM. Koray-kalung. T. Toonga-gudda. |
| *monocephalus.* | B. Gothoobi. |
| *compressus.* | B. H. Choonchi. T. Salli-tunga. |
| *diformis.* | B. Behooa. |
| *rotundus.* | S. Moosta. B. H. Mootha; Ghun. |
| *pertenuis.* | B. Naga; Nagur-mootha. |
| *odoratus.* | TAM. Camachie-pilloo. |
| *tenuiflorus.* | T. Ghelaba-tunga. |
| *Iria.* | B. H. Bura-choocha. |

| Gen. and Spec. | Native Names. |
|---|---|
| *inundatus.* | B. H. Patee. |
| *Pangorii.* | B. H. Chumali-patee. |
| *elatus.* | B. Gol-mulunga. T. Rakesha. |
| *verticillatus.* | B. Burethi. |
| *distans.* | B. Panee-mulunga. |
| *tegetus.* | B. Majoor-kati. B. H. Madoor-kati. |
| *Jemenicus.* | T. Poora-gaddi. |
| *Haspan.* | T. Poo-cushalie. |
| *umbellatus.* | T. Pedda-shoka. |
| *spinulosus.* | T. Kurra-tunga. |
| CYRILLA | |
| *aquatica.* | T. Baggapatti. |
| CYTISUS | |
| *Cajan.* | S. Arhuku. B. H. Urur. B. Orol. TAM. Towaray. T. Kandy; Carpoo-woolandoo. MAH. Toor. |

| Gen. and Spec. | Native Names. |
|---|---|
| **D.** | |
| DALBERGIA | |
| *arborea.* | S. Karanja; Naktamala. H. Kurunje; Caranj. TAM. Poonga-marum. T. Kanoogamanoo. CYNG. Mogulkaranda. CAN. Canaga. |
| *Ougeinensis.* | S. Tinisha; Sejanduna. |
| *latifolia.* | B. Sweta-shala. T. Veru-gudu-chawa. |
| *Sissoo.* | S. Singshupa. B. H. Sissoo. |
| *paniculata.* | T. Patseroo. CAN. Hasur-gunni. |
| *Zeylanica.* | CYNG. Belloo-labba. |
| *robusta.* | H. Krowee. |
| *marginata.* | B. Mahara-gila. |
| *scandens.* | B. Noa-luta. T. Scheratalli-bador. |
| *tamarindifolia.* | B. Tentolee. |
| *rimosa.* | B. Koogroom. |
| *reniformis.* | B. Kurissa. |
| *Crowey.* | B. Krooee. |
| *rubiginosa.* | T. Tella-tiga. |
| *volubilis.* | T. Bandi-girgin. |
| DALRYMPELIA | |
| *pomifera.* | B. Junki-jam. |
| DAMASONIUM | |
| *Indicum.* | B. Panee-kula. T. Neer-veneki. |
| DATURA | S. B. H. Dhotura. TAM. Oomatay. |
| *fatuosa.* | S. Doostoora. Khrishna-dhattura. B. H. Kala-dhootura. H. Lal-datura. TAM. Karoo-oomatay. T. Nulla-oomatie. CYNG. Kaloo-attana, or Antenna. M. Umana. |
| *Metel.* | B. Dhootura. B. H. Sada-dhootura; Sada-dhustura. |
| *ferox.* | TAM. Munjil-oomatay. |
| DAUCUS | |
| *carota.* | S. Grinjuna. B. H. Gajer. T. Gazeragedda. |
| DEERINGIA | |
| *Celosoides.* | B. Gola-muhunee. H. Lutmun. |
| DENDROBIUM | |
| *veratrifolium.* | B. Kathaeea-bun-jhoopee. |

| *Gen. and Spec.* | *Native Names.* |
|---|---|
| *clavatum.* | B. Titur-keoo. |
| DENTELLA | |
| *repens.* | B. Bhoomi-pat. |
| DILLENIA | |
| *Indica, v. speciosa.* | S. B. Ruvya. B. Chalta. T. Uva. |
| *pentagyna.* | T. Rawadam. |
| *scabrella.* | B. Agosthyo. |
| DIPSACUS | |
| *inermis.* | N. Barberi-gooja. |
| DIOSCOREA | |
| *globosa.* | B. H. Choopri-aloo. |
| *alata.* | B. H. Kam-aloo. TAM. Yamskalung. CYNG. Rosakenda. M. Perinvullie-kalungha. |
| *rubella.* | B. H. Guranya-aloo. |
| *purpurea.* | B. H. Lal-guranya-aloo. |
| *aculeata.* | B. H. Mou-aloo. |
| *fasciculata.* | B. H. Soosni-aloo. |
| *anguina.* | B. H. Kookoor-aloo. |
| *nummularia.* | B. H. Shora-aloo. |
| *pentaphylla.* | B. H. Kanta-aloo. |
| *oppositifolia.* | T. Ava-tenga-tiga. |
| DIOSPYROS | |
| *melanoxylon.* | S. Kakindoo. B. Kiew ; Kendoo. TAM. Tumbali. T. Trimeda. |
| *tomentosa.* | S. B. Tumala. |
| *glutinosa.* | S. Sindica ; Tembiri. B. Gab. H. Gaub. TAM. Panichekai ; Toombikai. T. Tumika. CYNG. Mahatimbiri. M. Panitsjika-marum. |
| *racemosa, v. lancæfolia.* | B. Goolal. |
| *montana.* | T. Yerra-gada. |
| *chloroxylon.* | T. Nella-wooly-mera. |
| *cordifolia.* | B. Bun-gab. T. Kawoolimera. |
| *ramiflora.* | B. Oori-gab. |
| DIPTEROCARPUS | |
| *turbinatus.* | B. Shweta-gurjun. |
| *costatus.* | B. Telia-gurjun. |
| *incanus.* | B. Gurjun. |
| DOLICHOS | |
| *gladiatus.* | S. Shimbee. B. Makhun-shim. |
| *gladiatus, (red.)* | B. Ranga-makhun-shim. |

| *Gen. and Spec.* | *Native Names.* |
|---|---|
| *(large white.)* | Burra-makhun-shim. |
| *(small white.)* | Makhun-shim. |
| *virosus.* | B. H. Kala-shim. |
| *Sinensis.* | H. Lobia. |
| *Catjang.* | H. Burbutee. |
| *Lablab.* | S. Shimbee. |
| 1*st var.* | B. Bun-shim. |
| 3*d var.* | T. Annapa. |
| 4*th var.* | T. Annapa-chicureay. |
| 5*th var.* | B. Jeea-shim. |
| 6*th var.* | B. Goordal-shim. |
| *hexandrus.* | B. Kussa-gila. |
| *pruriens.* | S. Capicachu ; Atmagupta ; Kapacachlie. H. Kiwach ; Kaunch-koorie. TAM. Poonaykalie. T. Peeliadugookaila. CYNG. Kosambiliwail ; Dewipagura. M. Nai-corana. |
| *lignosus,* 1*st var.* | B. Panch-shim. |
| 2*d var.* | B. Bagh-nukhooa-shim. |
| 3*d var.* | B. Sada-jamai-pooli-shim. |
| 4*th var.* | B. Pitulee-jamai-pooli-shim. |
| 5*th var.* | B. Doodha-pitulee-shim. |
| 6*th var.* | B. Kanchi-shim. |
| *Gangeticus.* | H. Bun-burbutee. |
| *falcatus.* | T. Itoo-moonghy-tiga. |
| *glutinosus.* | H. Shimi-batrajee. T. Kar-kandi. |
| *pilosus.* | B. Masha-kulai. |
| *biflorus.* | S. Kooluttha. H. Kooltee. T. Woolawooloo. |
| *medicagineus.* | T. Gadi-chikurea. |
| *scarabæoides.* | B. Banur-kulai. H. Bela-chooi. |
| *fabæformis.* | T. Goor-chikurkai. |
| *prostratus.* | T. Kanchi-chikurkai. |
| DORONIUM | |
| *calcaratum.* | T. Paleroopoo. |
| DRACÆNA | |
| *ferrea.* | B. Byolee-chutuk. |
| *terniflora.* | H. Bhoonamtol. |
| DRACONTIUM | |
| *polyphyllum.* | S. Kanana-cunda. H. Junglai-kandi. TAM. Caat-karnay. T. Adivie-cunda. CYNG. Kana-kideran. |

| Gen. and Spec. | Native Names. |
|---|---|
| **E.** | |
| ECHITES | |
| *acuminata.* | H. Pinguree. |
| *antidysenterica.* | S. Kootuja. H. Koorchi; Curayja. TAM. Veppalei. T. Palla-codija; Manoopala. M. Codaga-palla. |
| *scholaris.* | S. Supta-purna. B. Chatin. |
| *venenata.* | T. Ganda-ganeroo. |
| *frutescens.* | S. Syama; B. H. Shyama-luta. T. Nalla-tiga. |
| *dichotoma.* | S. Vishulya-krit. H. Hapur-malee. |
| *caryophyllata.* | S. B. Malutee. |
| *macrophylla.* | B. Harkee. |
| *marginata.* | B. Dood-luta. |
| *cymosa.* | B. Ootaso-braba. |
| ECLIPTA | |
| *prostrata.* | S. Brinraja. B. H. Keshooriya. H. Bungrah; Brinraj. TAM: Kaiantagarie; Kursalankunnie. T. Goontagelinjeroo. CYNG. Sadu-kirindi. |

| Gen. and Spec. | Native Names. |
|---|---|
| EHRETIA | |
| *serrata.* | B. Kala-oja. |
| *aspera.* | T. Tella-juvi. |
| *lævis.* | T. Serigada. |
| *buxifolia.* | H. Palé. TAM. Cooruvingie. T. Bapanaboorie. CYNG. Heen-tambala. |
| *umbellulata.* | B. Kunuka. |
| EKEBERGIA | |
| *Indica.* | T. Pooroodonda. CAN. Bettuda-bewoo. |
| ELEAGNUS | |
| *dulcis.* | B. Shooshuna. |
| *conferta.* | B. Gwara. |
| ELETTARIA | |
| *Cardamomum.* | S. Ela. TAM. Yadersie. T. Yaylakooloo. CYNG. Ensal. M. Elettari; Ailum-cheddy. |
| ELEOCARPUS | |
| *aristatus.* | B. Ramduliya. |
| *serratus.* | B. H. Julpai. |
| *Ganitrus.* | S. Roodraksha. B. Roodrakya. |
| *rugosus.* | B. Bun-julpai. |
| *robustus.* | B. Dulpai. |
| *lancæofolius.* | B. Shweta-pai. |
| ELEPHANTOPHUS | |
| *scaber.* | S. Gojihwa. B. Sham-dulun. H. Samdulun. CYNG. Artadiya. M. Anashovadi. |
| ELEUSINE | |
| *Coracana.* | S. Rajika. B. H. Marooa; Murooa. H. Maud. TAM. Kelwaragoo. T. Sodi; Tamidaloo; Ponassa. M. Mootamy; Tsjettipulli. CAN. Raggi. |
| *stricta.* | H. Raggie. T. Pedda-sooloo; Pedasodi; Muddiruba. |
| *Ægyptica.* | B. Makur-jali. |
| *Indica.* | H. Mal-ankuri. T. Kar-sodi; Kuroosoloo. |
| *calycina.* | T. Wodata-toka-guddie. |
| ELSHOLTZIA | |
| *villosa.* | B. Riyunta. |
| EMBELIA | |
| *ribes.* | B. Baberung. |
| *vestita.* | B. Oaour-baberung. |

| Gen. and Spec. | Native Names. |
|---|---|
| EPIDENDRUM | |
| *tenuiflorum.* | M. Tsjerou-mou-maravara. |
| *Vanilla.* | CYNG. Hin-nil-wœlla. |
| EPIPACTIS | |
| *Babianifolia.* | H Chetiya-shooker. |
| *plicata.* | B. H. Lall-ghurree. |
| ERANTHEMUM | |
| *pulchellum.* | B. Kala-jatee. H. Gool-sham. |
| *strictum.* | B. Neel-vasooka. |
| ERVUM | |
| *hirsutum.* | S. Mussoora. B. Mussoor. |
| ERYCIBE | |
| *paniculata.* | B. Luta-bichuttee. |
| ERYTHRINA | |
| *Indica.* | S. Mundara. B. H. Palta-mandar ; Furrud. T. Badata. |
| *stricta.* | CAN. En-mouricon. |
| *ovalifolia.* | S. Paribhudra. H. Huri-kekra. |
| *suberosa.* | T. Mooni-matuga. |
| *sublobata.* | T. Badadoomoo. |
| *fulgens.* | B. Pareejat ; Madar ; Mundaruka. |
| ERYTHROXYLON | |
| *areolatum.* | S. Amava-buruhi. H. Dewudar. TAM. Semanatty ; Tevadarum ; Devadarum. T. Dewadari. |
| *monogynum.* | T. Udivi-gorinta. |
| ERYTHRONIUM | |
| *Indicum.* | H. Junglie-piaz ; Kanda. T. Nurrivungyum. T. Addivitella-guddaloo. CYNG. Nurriala. |
| EUGENIA | |
| *Malaccensis.* | B. Malacca-jamrool. |
| *racemosa.* | S. Neepa. TAM. Cadapum. T. Kanitee. |
| *caryophyllifolia.* | B. Chota-jamb. |
| *fruticosa.* | B. Bun-jamb. |
| *claviflora.* | B. Lumba-nuli-jamb. |
| *bracteata.* | H. Hijulee-mindee. T. Garoog-moodi. |
| *ternifolia.* | H. Phull-jamb ; Lall-phull-jamb. |
| *cymosa.* | H. Buti-jamb. |
| *alba.* | B. Jamrool. |
| *aquea, (white.)* | B. Jamb. |
| *(rose colour.)* | B. Ayer-jamb. |
| *oblata.* | H. Goolum. |

| *Gen. and Spec.* | *Native Names.* |
|---|---|
| *lancæofolia.* | H. Poora-jamb. |
| *lancæolaria.* | H. Panee-jamb. |
| *Jamboo.* | S. Jambu. B. H. Gulab-jamb. |
| *caryophyllata.* | S. Luvunga. H. B. Lung. |
| *Panialla.* | B. Panialla-jamba. |
| *Zeylanica.* | B. Nagkeshura-jamba. |
| EUONYMUS | |
| *tingens.* | N. Kasoori. |
| *garcinifolia.* | N. Mooee. |
| EUPATORIUM | |
| *Ayapana.* | B. Ayapana. T. Ayapanie. |
| EUPHORBIA | |
| *antiquorum.* | S. Sihoonda ; Vajra ; Vajrakantaka. B. Nagree. B. H. Nara-shij. H. Sayord. TAM. Shadray-kullie. T. Boontajemmoodoo. CYNG. Dalook-gaheh. M. Shadraij-kullie. |
| *nereifolia.* | S. Puttakarie ; Seej. B. H. Shij. H. Putteoon. TAM. Elekullie. T. Akoojemmoodoo. CYNG. Paluk. |
| *ligularia.* | B. H. Munsa-shij. |
| *thymifolia.* | S. Rukta-vindu-chada. B. Shwet-kheerooee. TAM. Chin-amam-patchyarisee ; Sattrapaladi. T. Biddarienana-beam. CYNG. Bindada-keeriya. |
| *Tirucalli.* | B. Lunka-shij ; Gool. TAM. Kalli. T. Tirucalli. |
| *terecaulis.* | CYNG. Gas-nawa-handi. |
| *hirta.* | B. Bura-kheerooee; Kyeeree. |
| *Chamæsyce.* | H. Chota-kheerooee. |
| *dracunculoides.* | H. Chagul-putputee. |
| *pilulifera.* | TAM. Amaum-patcheh-arisa. |
| EVOLVULUS | |
| *alsinoides.* | S. Vaishnava. TAM. Vistnoo-krandie. T. Vistnoo-krandum. CYNG. Wistnu-kranti. |
| EXACUM | |
| *tetragonum.* | B. Koochuri. |
| *hyssopifolium.* | T. Voellarekoo. |
| EXCOECARIA | |
| *Agallocha.* | S. Ugooroo. H. Gewa. CYNG. Telakeeriya. |
| *Cochinchinensis.* | TAM. Tsillay-cheddie; Tillay-chedday. |

| *Gen. and Spec.* | *Native Names.* |
|---|---|
| **F.** | |
| FAGARA | |
| *Rhetsa.* | T. Rhetsa-maun. |
| *Budrunga.* | B. Budrunga. |
| FAGRÆA | |
| *obovata.* | B. Saom. |
| FERONIA | |
| *elephantum.* | S. Kupittha ; Bhu-kapittham. B. H Kuth-bel. H. Booien-kavite. TAM Cootivella ; Nilavoola ; Vullam-ma rum ; Vellangay. T. Nelavelaga CYNG. Dewul. |

| *Gen. and Spec.* | *Native Names.* |
|---|---|
| Ferriola *buxifolia.* | Tam. Irumbilli-marum. T. Pishanna. |
| Ferula *Assafœtida.* | S. Cyng. Hingoo. S. B. H. Hing. Tam. Perungyum. T. Ingoova. |
| Ficus *Carica.* | S. Udumvara. B. Doomoor. Tam. Simicattie. T. Maydipoondoo. Cyng. Rata-attika. |
| *hirsuta.* | B. Dungura. |
| *hirta.* | B. Bun-doomoor. |
| *heterophylla.* | B. Gooti-sheora. T. Burong. |
| *repens.* | B. Bhooi-doomoor. |
| *Goolooreea.* | H. Kuth-golurea. |
| *Wassa.* | M. Wassa. |
| *elastica.* | B. Kusmeer. |
| *Indica.* | S. Vuta; Nijugrodha. B. Bur; But. Tam. Alaverei. T. Murri; Marri. |
| *religiosa.* | S. Pippula. B. Ashwuttha. H. Pipul. Tam. Arasum. T. Ray; Raghi. Cyng. Bogaha. |
| *cordifolia.* | B. Guya-ashwuttha. |
| *infectoria.* | S. Plucsha. B. Pakur. |
| *laccifera.* | B. Kutul-but. |
| *vagans.* | B. Luta-doomoor. |
| *glomerata.* | S. Oodumbura. B. Jugya-doomoor. H. Doombur. T. Bruma-madi. |
| *oppositifolia.* | S. Kaka-doomborica. B. Kaka-doomoor. H. Koriya-doombar. T. Boda-mamadi. |
| *laminosa.* | M. Chun-cheri. |
| *scabrella.* | B. Bullum-doomoor. |
| *fruticosa.* | B. Purkutta-doomoor. |
| *Luducca.* | H. Looduka; Debra. |
| *Chincha.* | H. Chincha. |
| *hederacca.* | B. Luta-purkutti-doomoor. |
| *Benjamina.* | T. Yerra-yerra. |
| *tomentosa.* | T. Peta-mari. |
| *comosa.* | T. Pootra-jivee. |
| *racemosa.* | Tam. Attie. T. Maydi. |
| *Ampelos.* | T. Tella-barinha. |
| *asperrima.* | T. Karakar-booda. |
| *tuberculata.* | T. Kooda-juvee. |

| Gen. and Spec. | Native Names. |
|---|---|
| FLACOURTIA | |
| *cataphracta.* | S. Videra; Talisha. B. H. Paniyala. H. Talisputrie. TAM. T. Talisha-putrie. |
| *sepiaria.* | T. Kanrew. |
| *sapida.* | S. Swadoo-kuntuka. B. Bincha. T. Pudda-kanrew. |
| FLAGELLARIA | |
| *Indica.* | B. H. Bun-chundur. T. Poindi-pooti. H. Harchara. |
| FLEMINGIA | |
| *nana.* | H. Lipta-busunt. |
| *congesta.* | B. Bura-salpan. |
| *stricta.* | T. Guida. |
| FLUGGEA | |
| *leucopyrus.* | S. Sweta-camboji. H. Suffaid-mahommad. T. Tella-pooliyoodu. |
| FUIRENA | |
| *ciliaris.* | T. Elaga-boro-gaddi. |
| FUMARIA | |
| *parviflora.* | B. Sholoopha. H. Bun-shulpha. |
| *officinalis.* | H. Shahtra; Pitpapra. |

| Gen. and Spec. | Native Names. |
|---|---|
| **G.** | |
| GADELUPA | |
| *arborea.* | S. Kurunjuka. B. H. Kurunja. |
| *religiosa.* | B. Panee-luta. |
| *piscidia.* | B. Chunkee. |
| *marginata.* | H. Ooknee. |
| GALEGA | |
| *purpurea.* | S. Shura-punkha; Poonkie. B. Sur-punka. T. Vayampalie. CYNG. Gampila. |
| *spinosa.* | TAM. Mookavullie. T. Mulla-yampala. |
| GARCINIA | |
| *lancæofolia.* | H. Kurendra. |
| *Boobicowa.* | B. Bhoomi-kuwa. |
| *Zeylanica.* | CYNG. Goorka. |
| GARDENIA | |
| *florida.* | S. B. H. Gundha-raj. |
| *latifolia.* | H. Papura. T. Karinga. |
| *arborea.* | T. Karinga-marum. T. Garga. |
| GARDNERIA | |
| *ovata.* | B. Huldi. N. Oocha-soa. |
| GARUGA | |
| *pinnata.* | B. H. Toom. T. Garugo. |
| GELONIUM | |
| *fasciculatum.* | H. Bun-naringa. T. Soora-gada. |
| GENTIAN | |
| *verticillata.* | T. Nella-gulli. |
| *Cherayti.* | S. Chirataka; Chirata-tikta; Kirata-ticta. B. H. Cherayti; Cheretta; Keerat. TAM. Shayraat-coochie. T. Sheelasuttoo-coielloo. |
| GETONIA | |
| *floribunda.* | T. Bandi-mooroodoodoo. |
| GLECHOMA | |
| *erecta.* | H. Nagbo. |
| GLOBBA | |
| *bulbifera.* | T. Conda-pooshpoo. |
| GLORIOSA | |
| *superba.* | B. Langool; Eesha-nungula; Kookora-neja. |

| Gen. and Spec. | Native Names. |
|---|---|
| GLYCINE | |
| *debilis.* | S. Masha-purnee. B. Panta. B. H. Mashanee. |
| *labialis.* | B. H. Bun-kulai. |
| GLYCIRRHIZA | |
| *glabra.* | S. Yastimaduca. B. H. Jyosthi-madhoo. |
| GMELINA | |
| *arborea.* | S. Gumbharee. B. H. Gumhar. |
| *Asiatica.* | S. Biddari. TAM. Neelacomul. T. Goomoodoo. CYNG. Gæta-demata. |
| *parviflora.* | TAM. Goomadi. T. Shieri-goomoodoo. CAN. Koomatha. |
| GNETUM | |
| *scandens.* | B. Nana-wita. |
| GÆRTNERA | |
| *racemosa.* | S. Utimookta; Madhuveeluta. B. Malutee. B. H. Madhubeeluta. |
| GOMPHRENA | |
| *globosa, (red.)* | S. Umlana. B. Lall-gool-mukhmul. H. Gool-mukhmul. |
| *(white.)* | H. Suffet-gool-mukhmul. |
| GORDONIA | |
| *integrifolia.* | B. Bun-mukh. H. Makurjal. |
| *oblata.* | B. Makri-shala. |
| GOSSYPIUM | |
| *herbaceum.* | S. Karpasee. B. Kapase; Tula. H. Rooi; Kapas. TAM. Paratie; Vunparatie. T. Puttie. |
| GRATIOLA | |
| *Monniera,* | S. Jala-brimni. B. Ada-beerna. H. Shwet-chamni. TAM. Neerpirimie. T. Sambrani-chittoo. CYNG. Lunuwila. |
| *amara.* | B. Khai-nim. |
| *serrata.* | B. Bhoomi- nim. |
| GREWIA | |
| *orientalis.* | T. Peyar. |
| *Asiatica.* | B. H. Phulsha. |
| *carpinifolia.* | T. Nullie. |
| *sepiaria.* | B. H. Panee-syora; Panshiooli. |
| *salvifolia.* | T. Pastiki. |
| *hirsuta.* | T. Javelliki. |
| *didyma.* | T. Alpear. |

| Gen. and Spec. | Native Names. |
|---|---|
| GRISLEA | |
| *tomentosa.* | S. Ugni-jwala; Dhatri-pooshpika. B. Dhub; Dhangaphul. |
| GUAREA | |
| *paniculata.* | B. Kalee-koura. |
| GUILANDINA | |
| *Moringa.* | *See* HYPERANTHERA. |
| *Bonducella.* | S. Koobayratchie; Prakirya; Calimarca. B. Nata-kanta. H. Gudgega; Cat-caleji; Nata-caranja. CYNG. Wiel-kumburu. *See* CÆSALPINIA. |
| *Benduc.* | H. Lota. CYNG. Kalu-wawul-œtiya. |
| GYROCARPUS | |
| *Jacquini.* | T. Tanacoo; Tanukoo. |

| Gen. and Spec. | Native Names. |
|---|---|
| **H.** | |
| HARDWICKIA | |
| *binata.* | TAM. Acha; Atti. CAN. Caratchu. |
| HARPULLIA | |
| *cuponioides.* | B. Harpolli. |
| HASTINGIA | |
| *coccinea.* | B. Ungootee; Doodmari. |
| *scandens.* | B. Doodmari. |
| HEDYCHIUM | |
| *coronarium.* | B. Doolala-champa; Goruk-natha. |
| *flavum.* | B. Kattea-tilook-seer; Kattia-rit-yam. |
| *speciosum.* | B. Kattia-lung-mutti. |
| *angustifolium.* | B. Bhoovada; Bhoo-ada. |
| *gracile.* | B. Kattea-laffear; Laphya. |
| *villosum.* | B. Kattea-ram-rait. |
| HEDYOTIS | |
| *scandens.* | B. Guji. |
| *gracilis.* | N. Goshega-soa. |
| *auricularia.* | B. Muttia-lata. |
| HEDYSARUM | |
| *Sennoides.* | S. Kanana. H. Junglaie-moonghie. TAM. Caat-moorunghie. T. Adivie-monaga. |
| *diphyllum.* | CYNG. Maha-kakawœna; Nelam-mari. |
| *Alhagi.* | S. Yasa; Yavusa. H. Juwasa. |
| *gramineum.* | B. Pan-luta. H. Bunka-jooli. |
| *bupleurifolium.* | H. Allorie. |
| *alatum.* | H. Kusrunt. |
| *Gangeticum.* | S. Shala-purnee. B. H. Shalpani. |
| *gyrans.* | H. Gora-chand. |
| *vespertilionis.* | B. Chilia-tangi. |
| *triflorum.* | H. Kodaliya. |
| *Lagopodioides.* | H. Gorukhya-chakoolya. |
| *orbiculatum.* | B. Moonjiwra. |
| *pulchellum.* | B. Juta-shalpanee. |
| *tuberosum.* | B. Shimeeya-batrajee. |
| *gyroides.* | B. Biniyar. |
| *pictum.* | B. Shunkur-juta. H. Dabra. |
| *lagenaria.* | B. H. Phool-shola. |
| *Neli-tali.* | T. Tiga-jeelooga. |
| *sororium.* | T. Nala-sara-kada. |

| *Gen. and Spec.* | *Native Names.* |
|---|---|
| *biarticulatum.* | T. Nalla-kavani. |
| *umbellatum.* | T. Chitkinta. |
| *styracifolium,* *v. glumaceum.* | T. Nella-mandu. |
| HELIANTHUS *annuus.* | B. Soorjya-mookhee; Bhramoka. |
| HELICTERES *Isora.* | S. Avurtunnie. B. Antomoora. H. Merowrie. TAM. Valumbirikai. T. Valumbrikaca. CYNG. Liniya-gaha. M. Isora-murri. CAN. Ky-walla. |
| HELIOTROPIUM *Indicum.* | S. Shree-hustinee; Bhooroondee. B. Hatee-shoora. H. Siriari. TAM. Tayl-kodugoo. T. Tayl-munnie. CYNG. Ek-sætiya. M. Bena-patsja. |
| *Coromandelium.* | B. Naga-phoollee. |
| HEMEROCALLIS *fulva.* | H. Gool-nurgis. |
| HEMIONITIS *cordifolia.* | B. Chakoolya. |
| HEMISDEMUS *Indicus.* | B. Kural. |
| HERITIERA *minor.* | B. Sonduree. |
| HIBISCUS *populneus.* | S. Sooparshavaka. B. H. Porush. H. Parspipal; Paris. TAM. Poursun-ghai. T. Gangari; Ghengheravie. CYNG. Sooriya-gaha. |
| *populneoides.* | S. Gurdhubhanda. B. H. Purush-pipool. |
| *obtusifolia.* | TAM. Kaat-toottie. T. Mooni-gangari. |
| *tortuosus.* | S. B. Bala. H. Bola. |
| *pistus.* | B. Khojlee. |
| *macrophyllus.* | H. Kasya-pal. |
| *Rosa-sinensis.* | S. Juva. B. Juba; Jupa; Patkili. H. Jasoon. TAM. Sapatoo-cheddie. T. Dasanie. M. Scheru-pariti. |
| *(yellow.)* | B. Patkili. |
| *phœniceus.* | S. Soorya-muni; Soora-yamuni. |
| *(white.)* | B. H. Sufet-Sooryamuni. T. Tella-salla-burta. |

| *Gen. and Spec.* | *Native Names.* |
|---|---|
| *(red.)* | B. H. Lall-soorya-muni. T. Yerra-salla-burta. |
| *Syriacus.* | B. Juba. |
| *(sing. white.)* | H. Sada-juba. |
| *(purple.)* | H. Neel-juba. |
| *rigidus.* | T. Salla-burta. |
| *collineus.* | T. Konda-gong. |
| *vitifolius.* | S. Bharudwajee. B. Bun-kapasi. |
| *mutabilis.* | S. Pudma-charinee; Sthula-pudma. B. Thol-pudma. |
| *Abelmoschus.* | H. Kala-kustooree. CYNG. Kapu-kinaissa. M. Cattu-gasturi. |
| *strictus.* | H. Buri-harul; Bun-harul. |
| *cannabinus.* | B. H. Mesta-pat; Nalkee; Pulooa. T. Gong-kura. |
| *esculentus.* | B. Dhenroos. |
| *longifolius.* | B. Dhenroos. H. Ram-turi. T. Binda. |
| *fragrans.* | B. Kurunder. |
| *tetralocularis.* | T. Kunda-putta. |
| HINGCHA | |
| *repens.* | S. Hilumochika. B. Hingcha. H. B. Heluncha. |
| HIPPOCRATIA | |
| *arborea.* | H. Kotta-paharia. |
| HIRÆA | |
| *Indica.* | T. Rigrak-tiga. |
| HORDEUM | |
| *hexastichon.* | S. Yuva. B. Jub. H. Jow. N. Tosa. |
| HOUTTUYNIA | |
| *cordata.* | N. Kalla; Kullum-soa. |
| HOVENIA | |
| *dulcis.* | N. Mun-kokoshi. |
| HUMEA | |
| *alata.* | H. Mous-jat. |
| HYDROCOTYLE | |
| *Asiatica.* | S. Bheka-purni; Manduka-parni. B. Thall-kuri. TAM. Vullarei. TAM. T. Babassa. CYNG. Heen-gotu-kola. M. Codagam. |
| HYPERANTHERA | |
| *Morunga.* | S. B. Sigroo; Sobhanjuna. B. Shajina. H. Moongay; Sujna. TAM. Morunghy. T. Moorunga; Moonaga. CYNG. Merikoolu. CAN. Nugga. |

| *Gen. and Spec.* | *Native Names.* |
|---|---|
| **I.** | |
| Ichnocarpus | |
| *frutescens.* | B. Salsa. |
| Illecebrum | |
| *v. Achyranthes.* | |
| Illicium | |
| *anisatum.* | H. Anaspool. Tam. Anaseepoo. |
| Impatiens | |
| *Balsamina.* | S. Dwiputru. B. Doopatee. H. Goolmendi. |
| *natans.* | T. Neer-ganeroo. |

| Gen. and Spec. | Native Names. |
|---|---|
| INDIGOFERA | |
| *linifolia.* | B. Bhanga. |
| *glandulosa.* | T. Bura-gadam. |
| *enneaphylla.* | T. Cheppoo-neringie. T. Cherra-gaddam. CYNG. Bin-awari. |
| *hirsuta.* | T. Penni-vempali. |
| *cærulea.* | T. Kar-neelee. |
| *tinctoria.* | S. Neelee. B. H. Neel. TAM. Neelum: Averie. T. Neelee. CYNG. Nil. |
| *echinata.* | T. Nalla-paleroo. |
| *cinerea.* | T. Veri-nalli. |
| *Anil.* | TAM. Averie; Neelie. |
| IPOMOEA | |
| *grandiflora.* | S. Munda-vulee. H. Dhol-kulmee. |
| *sepiaria.* | CAN. Metta-tooti. |
| *cærulea.* | H. Neel-kulmee. |
| *pes-tigrides.* | B. Langulee-luta. |
| *Quamoclit.* | S. B. H. Lall or Shwet-turoo-luta; Kamaluta. |
| IRIS | |
| *florentina.* | H. Irsa. |
| ISCHŒMUM | |
| *aristatum.* | B. Meluncha. B. H. Munta. |
| ITEA | |
| *macrophylla.* | B. Uchuleeyaja. |
| IXORA | |
| *Pavetta.* | S. Pappana. B. Kookoora-choora. TAM. Pavuttay. T. Pavatti; Nooni-papoota; Paputta. CYNG. Pawatta. M. Malleamothe; Carnicara. |
| *undulata.* | B. H. Paluk-jooi. |
| *Bandhuca.* | S. Bandhuka; Ruktuka. B. Rungun; Bandoonee. H. Ranjun. |
| *parviflora.* | B. Gundhul-rungun. T. Tadda-pullu. |
| *tomentosa.* | B. H. Jooi. T. Nuni-papata; Nampapoota. |
| *villosa.* | H. Choonaree. |
| *rosea.* | B. Mattia-chanda. |

| *Gen. and Spec.* | *Native Names.* |
| --- | --- |
| **J.** | |
| JASMINUM | |
| *angustifolium.* | S. Kannana-mallica; Vana-mallé. TAM. Caat-mallica. T. Adwie-mallé. CYNG. Walsaman-pichha. |
| *Zambac.* | S. Asphota. B. Moorga; Mullika; Kanth-mullika; Belphool. H. Bun or Deshi-mullika. |
| *(double.)* | S. B. Mullika. |
| *(rose.)* | S Suptula. B. Moota-bela; Patna-mullika. |

| *Gen. and Spec.* | *Native Names.* |
|---|---|
| *pubescens.* | S. Maghya. B. Kath-bel; Mukurundo-hyun. S. B. Koonda. H. Chumbeli. |
| *latifolium.* | T. Udivi or Adivi-mulli. |
| *arborescens.* | S. Suptula. S. B. Niwa-mullika. B. Bura-koonda. |
| *elongatum.* | B. Pantub. |
| *attenuatum.* | B. Bun-nowaree. |
| *auriculatum.* | S. Yoothika. B. H. Joothi-pooshpika; Jooi. |
| *chrysanthemum.* | S. B. H. Hema-pooshpika. B. Swu-run-yoothee. |
| *grandiflorum.* | S. Malutee. S. B. H. Jatee. |
| JATROPHA | |
| *Curcas.* | S. Kanana-kerundum; Nepala. B. H. Bag-bherenda. TAM. Caat-amunah; Caar-noochie. T. Næpalam; Adi-vie-amida. CYNG. Rata-endaru. CAN. Mara-harulee. |
| *Manihot.* | TAM. Maravullie. CYNG. Mangyokka. |
| *glauca.* | S. Nikumba. TAM. Addaleyunnay. T. Nela-amida. |
| JOHNIA | |
| *salacioides.* | B. Goluck-laroo. |
| JONESIA | |
| *Asoca.* | S. B. Ushoka. H. Ussu. |
| JUGLANS | |
| *regia.* | S. Unkotha. H. Akrot. |
| JUSSIEUA | |
| *repens.* | S. Langulee. B. Kachura-dam. H. Canchara. T. Neer-batsala. |
| *suffruticosa.* | S. Bhalava-anga. CYNG. Hæmarago. M. Carambu. |
| *exaltata.* | S. Bhoo-luvunga. B. Bun-lung. T. Neeroo-aghiondraparoo. |
| JUSTICIA | |
| *bivalvis.* | S. Adulasso. TAM. Adatodey. CYNG. Ayiyapana. |
| *Ecbolium.* | H. Oodoo-jatee. |
| *paniculata.* | S. Cairath. B. Kala-megh. H. B. Calapnath; Maha-tita; Crëat. T. Nella-vemoo. CYNG. Attadie. M. Cara-caniram. |
| *repens.* | TAM. Kodaga-saleh. CYNG. Sulunayi. |

| *Gen. and Spec.* | *Native Names.* |
|---|---|
| *polysperma.* | B. Choota-mecheta. |
| *acaulis.* | T. Nella-meera. |
| *nasuta.* | S. Yoothika-purnie. B. Jooi-pana. H. Palek-joohie; Kabuter-ka-jar. TAM. T. Naga-mulli. CYNG. Anitia. M. Pulcolli; Peelcollie. |
| *lanceolaria.* | H. Toogee. |
| *tinctoria.* | B. Beta-rung; Batia-rung. |
| *Adhatoda.* | S. Utoorusha. B. Basoka. B. H. Bakus. H. Arus; Asganda; Anis. TAM. Adatodey. T. Adasara. CYNG. Adhatoda. |
| *Tranquebarensis.* | S. Pindi. TAM. Tavashoo-morunghie. Poonaka-poondoo. T. Pindi-koonda. |
| *Gendarussa.* | S. Nila-nirgandi. B. Jugut-mudun. H. Kali-shumbali. TAM. Caroonoochie. T. Nulla-vaviloo. CYNG. Kalu-wæraniya. M. Vada-kodi. |
| *verticillata.* | H. Koostoola. |
| *procumbens.* | TAM. Nereipoottie. T. Nakapoottachittoo. CYNG. Manayi. |
| JUNIPERUS *Cedrus.* | H. Lalchandan. |

| *Gen. and Spec.* | *Native Names.* |
|---|---|
| **K.** | |
| KÆMPFERIA | |
| *galanga.* | S. Chundra-moolika ; Kumula. B. Kumula ; Chundra-moola. TAM. Katsjula-kelengu. |
| *rotunda.* | S. Bhoomi-chumpuka. B. H. Bhooi-chumpa. H. Bhuneampa ; Chambak. CYNG. Kaha. |
| *secunda.* | B. Kattia-jorung. |
| *linearis.* | H. Kanjam-boora. |
| *angustifolia.* | B. H. Madun-nirbish. |
| KYDIA | |
| *calycina.* | H. Chouputeeya. T. Pandika. |
| *paterna.* | T. Potri. |
| KYLLINGIA | |
| *monocephala.* | B. Shwet-gothoobi ; Nirbisee. |
| *umbellata.* | B. Bura-gothoobi. |

| *Gen. and Spec.* | *Native Names.* |
|---|---|
| **L.** | |
| LACTUCA | |
| *sativa.* | H. Cahu. |
| LAGERSTRŒMIA | |
| *Indica.* | H. Telinga-china. |
| *regina.* | S. Urjoona. B. H. Jarool. |
| *grandiflora.* | S. Indradroog. |
| *parviflora.* | T. Chinamanghie. |
| LATHYRUS | |
| *Aphaca.* | B. Chuna; Bura-chuna. |
| *sativus.* | B. Khesaree; Teora. |
| LAURUS | |
| *Cinnamomum.* | S. Darasita. B. H. Dar-cheeni. TAM. Karruwa. T. Sanalinga. CYNG. Kurunda; Rassu-coronde. M. Katukarua. |
| *Cassia.* | S. Tamala-putra. B. Tej; Tej-pat. H. Taj. |
| *obtusifolia.* | B. Kintun. |
| *glaucescens.* | B. Oorook. |
| *lanceolaria.* | B. Sundighool. |
| *involucrata.* | T. Narrha. |
| *camphorifera.* | S. Kurpoora. |
| LAVENDULA | |
| *carnosa.* | S. Waluka. H. Sitakepungerie. TAM. T. Kapoorwullie. T. Kuruwehla. CYNG. Gol-kapra-walli. M. Katukurka. |
| LAWSONIA | |
| *inermis.* | S. Sakachera. B. H. Shudee. H. Hina. TAM. Moroo-danie. T. Goruntagorinta. CYNG. Maritondi. M. Pontaletsce. |
| LIGUSTICUM | |
| *Ajouan.* | S. Brumhadurbha; Juvanika. B. H. Ajouan; Juvanee. |
| *diffusum.* | B. Bun-ajouan; Moduyuntee. |
| LIMODORUM | |
| *virens.* | B. Goruk-phuna. H. Goorooma. |
| *nutans.* | H. Pankula. |
| *bicolor.* | B. Budbuhuri. |
| *Tankervillia.* | B. Louralee. |
| *spatulatum.* | S. Swarna-pushpa; Vanda. M. Ponnampou-maravara. |

| Gen. and Spec. | Native Names. |
|---|---|
| *candidum.* | B. Miarmee. |
| *longifolium.* | B. Telungshoora. |
| LIMONIA | |
| *monophylla.* | T. Udivi-nima. |
| *scandens.* | S. Luvunga-luta. B. Lubung-lota. |
| *pentaphylla.* | S. Ushwa-shakota. B. Ash-shoura. T. Gollunga. |
| *crenulata.* | T. Torellega. |
| *pentagyna.* | T. Chitruka. |
| *arborea.* | T. Kunda-gulloonga. |
| LEEA | |
| *staphylea.* | B. Kookoor-jeehwa; Cheetkee. T. Ancados. |
| *hirta.* | S. Kakangee. B. Kaka-jungha. |
| *crispa.* | B. H. Bun-chalta. |
| *macrophylla.* | S. Samoodruka. B. Dholsumoodra. |
| *integrifolia.* | T. Boora-deepaki. |
| LEERSIA | |
| *aristata.* | B. Kolshia. |
| LEPIDIUM | |
| *sativum.* | B. H. Halim. H. Chansur; Tara; Tezac. |
| LETTSOMIA | |
| *aggregata.* | T. Yerra-katha. |
| *nervosa.* | B. H. Bish-taruk. T. Koakaiti. |
| *speciosa.* | B. H. Chota-bish-taruk; Sumoodra-shoka. |
| *uniflora.* | T. Boordi-tiga. |
| *bona-nox.* | B. Kulmi-luta. |
| LEUCACEPHALA | |
| *graminifolia.* | B. Gooree. |
| LICHEN | |
| *rotundatus.* | H. Puttir-ka-phool. TAM. Kull-pashie. T. Ratipanchie. |
| LILIUM | |
| *(sp?)* | H. Sosan; Gul-i-sosun. |
| LINDSEA | |
| *odorata.* | H. Pullee. |
| LINUM | |
| *usitatissimum.* | S. Ooma; Matusee; Atasi. B. Musina. Moosnee. B. H. Tisi. H. Alsi. TAM. Allé-seroo-sanul. |
| *trigynum.* | H. Gool-ashroopi; Gooldadee; Jafari; Basant. |

| Gen. and Spec. | Native Names. |
|---|---|
| LIRIODENDRUM | |
| *grandiflorum.* | B. Doodiya-chumpa. H. Dhaulichampa. |
| *liliifera.* | B. Auoa-champa. |
| LODOICEA | |
| *Sechellarum.* | S. Ubdie-narikaylum. H. Dirya-kanaril. TAM. Kaddil-tayngai. T. Sumatrapoo-tainkaya. |
| LONICERA | |
| *quinquelocularis.* | H. Loung-phool. |
| *Japonica.* | B. Tea-parooa. N. Socha. |
| *Leschenaultia.* | T. Moullee-quedi. |
| LORANTHUS | |
| *bicolor.* | S. Vunda; Vrikshadunee. B. H. Bura-munda; Pat-reem. T. Yellinga-waddinika. |
| *globosus.* | B. Chota-munda. |
| *scurrula.* | T. Wadimki. |
| *ampullaceus.* | B. Am-puraroha. |
| LUDWIGIA | |
| *parviflora.* | B. H. Bun-lubunga. |
| LUFFA | |
| *pentandra.* | B. Dhoondool; Ghoosa. H. Purula. T. Nuni-beera. N. Pulo. |
| *acutangula.* | B. Jinga. H. Turi; Jhinga. |
| *amara.* | H. Kerula. T. Shelti-beera. |
| *fœtida.* | H. Bantarai. |
| LUPINUS | |
| *(sp ?)* | H. Turmas. |
| LYCOPODIUM | |
| *imbricatum.* | B. H. Hati-jori. |
| *phlegmaria.* | B. Sheetahar. |

| Gen. and Spec. | Native Names. |
|---|---|
| **M.** | |
| MANGIFERA | |
| *Indica.* | S. Amra. B. H. Am. T. Mamadichitoo. |
| *sylvatica.* | S. Koshamra; Ruktamra. B. Lukshmee-am. |
| MANISURUS | |
| *myurus.* | T. Nali-poonookoo. |
| *granularis.* | S. Palanggini. H. Trinpali. |
| MARANTA | |
| *paniculata.* | CYNG. Get-olua. |
| MARICA | |
| *paludosa.* | H. Chuka-tipatti. |
| MARLEA | |
| *Begonifolia.* | B. Marliya. |
| MARSILEA | |
| *quadrifolia.* | S. Sooni-shunnuka. B. Shoshuni-shak. T. Chick-linta-kura. |
| MELASTOMA | |
| *aspera.* | S. Citnaqueri. B. Chota-phootika. T. Katou-kadali. CYNG. Heen-bowitiya. |
| *Malabathrica.* | B. Bura-phootika. CYNG. Maha-bowitiya. |
| *spec. nov.* | B. Juya-phootika. |
| MELIA | |
| *Azadirachta.* | S. Nimba. B. H. Nim; Arishto. TAM. Vepam; Vaypum. T. Vepa; Vaympa. CYNG. Tel-kohomba; Nimba. M. Aria-bepou. CAN. Bewa. |
| *sempervirens.* | S. Maha-nimb. H. Bukain. T. Turkavepa. |
| MELILOTUS | |
| *Baumetta.* | H. Chini. |
| *nigellosa.* | H. Metha. |
| MELISSA | |
| *(sp ?)* | H. Badranjboyu. |
| MELOCHIA | |
| *corchorifolia.* | B. Tiki-opra. H. Beel-pat. TAM. Chiruparam. CYNG. Hingul-kura; Keen-gal-kura. M. Asjerroo-uren. |

| *Gen. and Spec.* | *Native Names.* |
|---|---|
| MELODINUS | |
| *monogynus.* | H. Sadul-kuwa. |
| MENISPERMUM | |
| *cordifolium.* | S. Goruksha; Guduchi; Amrita. B. Golunchee; Beeshulyo-kurunee. B. H. Gorkha; Gool; Goluncha. H. Goolbayl; Gurcha. TAM. Sheendie-codie. T. Tippa-tiga; Tippa-tingay. M. Cit-amerdoo. |
| *glabrum.* | B. Goluncha. H. Gilau; Gurch. |
| *tomentosa.* | B. Pudma-goluncha. |
| *Columba.* | B. Kolumbo. |
| *hirsutum.* | H. Di-er; Hi-er; Faridbuti. T. Doosera-tiga. |
| *polycarpum.* | H. Bagha-luta. T. Tiga-mushadi. |
| *laurifolium.* | B. Pudma-goluncha. |
| *fenestratum.* | CYNG. Wuriwal; Veni-vell-getta. |
| *cocculus.* | S. Kakamari. H. Kakmari. TAM. Kakacollie. T. Kakichempoo. |
| MENTHA | |
| *verticillata.* | B. H. Panee-kula. |
| *secunda.* | H. Beel-luta. |
| *sativa.* | B. H. Podeena. TAM. Widdatilam. |
| *quadrifolia.* | T. Konda-jajari. |
| MENYANTHES | |
| *Indica.* | S. Koomooda. B. H. Bura-chooli. T. Tamara-antara. |
| *aristata.* | S. Koomoodwutee; Koomoodinee. H. Chooli. T. Antara-tamara. |
| MESPILUS | |
| *Japonica.* | H. Lokat. |
| MESUA | |
| *ferrea.* | S. Naga-keshura. B. H. Nagkeshur. |
| MICHELIA | |
| *Champaca.* | S. B. H. Champuka. B. Kotoo. |
| MILIUM | |
| *filiforme.* | H. Kan-koojooriya; Kanka-juriya. |
| *sanguinale.* | H. Chiri-chira. |
| MILLINGTONIA | |
| *simplicifolia.* | B. Dunta-rungee. |
| *pinnata.* | B. Batiwa. |
| MILNEA | |
| *edulis.* | B. Gumee. |

| Gen. and Spec. | Native Names. |
|---|---|
| MIMOSA | |
| *xylocarpa.* | T. Konda-tangheroo. |
| *Sirissa.* | S. B. H. Shireesh. |
| *adhenanthera.* | H. Lajwanta. |
| *heterophylla.* | B. Kawa-purunee. |
| *odoratissima.* | TAM. Sælæ-marum. T. Shinduga. |
| *amara.* | TAM. Shikræn. T. Nella-renga. |
| *Smithiana.* | B. Suris. |
| *stipulata.* | B. Amlukee. |
| *microphylla.* | B. Teetooleeya. |
| *natans.* | B. Lajoolshya. H. Pan-lajuk; Lajalu; Lajwanti; Ruthni. T. Neerootavalapoo. |
| *scandens.* | H. Gela. T. Gila-tiga. CYNG. Mahapus-wæla. |
| *Farnesiana.* | S. Urimeda. B. Gooya-babula. T. Kustoori; Peetoma. |
| *Arabica.* | S. Barbura. B. Gursoonder; Babla. B. H. Babula. TAM. Karoovelum. H. Kalikeper. T. Nella-toomi; Nulla-tooma. |
| *leucophlea.* | T. Veel-velum. T. Tella-tooma. |
| *tomentosa.* | B. Shalshaeei-babula. TAM. Kodi-velæ. |
| *latronum.* | T. Peeki-tooma. |
| *cinerea.* | S. Yeltoor; Viravriksha. H. Vurtuli. TAM. Wara-tara; Vedditarung. T. Yettroo-vellitooroo. |
| *ferruginea.* | S. Khadira. TAM. Vulvaylum. T. Tella-tooma; Woni. |
| *Catechu.* | S. Khadira. B. H. Khuera. H. K'hayar. T. Podeelmaun. CYNG. Khehiree. |
| *Sundra.* | T. Sundra. |
| *Suma.* | S. Shumee. B. Shaee. H. Saee-kanta. |
| *abstergens.* | H. Seekekai. TAM. Sheeakai. T. Sheeikaia. |
| *pudica.* | S. B. Lujjaloo. S. Samangga. B. Lajuk. TAM. Total-vadie. T. Moonooghoo-tamara. |
| *octandra.* | B. Koochee-kanta. T. Wallag-doora; Poota-korinta. |
| *Intsia.* | T. Korinta. |
| *concina.* | B. Reetha. T. Chikai. |

| *Gen. and Spec.* | *Native Names.* |
|---|---|
| *cæsia.* | T. Konda-koriuta. |
| *pinnata.* | H. Pahari-aiel. |
| *tenuifolia.* | TAM. Kodi-vallen. |
| *procera.* | T. Pedda-patsiroo. |
| *rubicauli.* | B. Kuch-kanta. |
| *var. fœtid.* | B. Beet-khudir. |
| MIMUSOPS | |
| *Elengi.* | S. Kesura; Vukoola. B. Bukool. H. Bacul Mulsari. T. Pagada. |
| *Kauki.* | S. Ksheerika. B. Ksheerni. H. Kheeri; Chirni; M. Boasoo. |
| *hexandra.* | TAM. Paltæ. T. Palta. |
| MIRABILIS | |
| *Jalapa.* | S. Bahubami. B. Krishna-keli. H. Goolabas; Gul-abbas; Sanji. TAM. Patrashi. CYNG. Sindrikka. |
| MOACURRA | |
| *gelonoides.* | H. Moukoora. |
| MODECCA | |
| *trilobata.* | H. Akanda-phul. |
| MOLLUGO | |
| *pentaphylla.* | S. Kshetra-purputee. B. Khet-papara. T. Beri-shadrosi. |
| *triphylla.* | B. Jul-papara. |
| MOMORDICA | |
| *Carantia.* | H. Carela. B. T. Kurilla; Oochi; Poti-kakar. T. Pagul-kai. M.Pandipavel. |
| *dioica.* | S. Vahisee. TAM. Paloopaghel; Paloopagulkodi. T. Agokara; Angakara; Pooagakaratha. CYNG. Tumba-karawilla. |
| *mixta.* | H. Cancrel. S. Korkotee. H. Kakrol; Gol-kakara. |
| *monodelpha.* | H. Bhimb. S. Vimbika. B. Beembo; Tela-koocha. T. Kay-dunda; Turulli-amook-mool. |
| *muricata.* | S. Soosuvi. B. Oochya. H. Burakurella. M. Pavel. |
| *umbellata.* | B. Kosderi. H. Turulli-amoot-mool. |
| MONETIA | |
| *Barleroides.* | S. Kundali. B. Trikanta (or Tekanta-jutee). H. Kanta-goorkamae; Sukkapat. T. Sung. T. Tella-upie; |

| Gen. and Spec. | Native Names. |
|---|---|
| | Tella-vuppie ; Oopivakoo. CYNG. Katu-niyada. |
| MORÆA | |
| *Chinensis.* | B. Dush-bahoo-chundi. H. Dosbichundi. T. Belamanda. M. Sholarmini. |
| MORINDA | |
| *citrifolia.* | H. Al. |
| *umbellata.* | S. Kleeba. H. Chota-alka. T. Noonamarum. T. Moolooghoodoo-akoo. |
| *tinctoria.* | S. Uchyoota. B. H. Ach ; Aech ; Aal. T. Tagaree ; Tagaroo. |
| *exerta.* | B. Bun-ach ; Aal. |
| *multiflora.* | H. Aal. |
| MORUS | |
| *Indica.* | S. Tula. B. H. Toot. |
| *serrata.* | H. Heemoo. |
| *(sp. ? )* | H. Tuirt ; Shaitul ; Bedana. |
| MURRAYA | |
| *exotica.* | B. Kameenee. H. Bibzar. |
| MUSA | |
| *paradisiaca.* | S. Kadali. B. H. Kach-kula. H. Maoz-kella ; Kayla. TAM. Valei. T. Komaretti. CYNG. Kehl-khang. M. Vellacoy. MAH. Kail. |
| *sapientium.* | H. Mocha. S. Kudalee. H. B. Kula. T. Aretti. |
| *wild sort.* | B. H. Ram-kula ; Wully-kola. |
| *ornata.* | B. Ramaneegee-kula. |
| *Nepalensis.* | N. Gompoo-kula. |
| MUSENDA | |
| *frondosa.* | H. Bebina. |
| MYRICA | |
| *integrifolia.* | B. Suphee. |
| MYRIOPHYLLUM | |
| *verticillatum.* | TAM. Meelapa. |
| *tetrandrum.* | T. Neela-pamarum. |
| MYRISTICA | |
| *moschata.* | S. Jatiphala. B. Jaya-phula. H. Jaephal. TAM. Jadicai. T. Jajikaia. CYNG. Sadikka ; Jatipullum. |
| MYRRHIS | |
| *odorata.* | H. Bol. |
| MYRTUS | |
| *communis.* | B. Vilati-mindi. |

| *Gen. and Spec.* | *Native Names.* |
|---|---|
| **N.** | |
| NAGEIA | |
| *Putranjiwa.* | S. Pootrunjiwa. T. Poodra-juwee. |
| NAMA | |
| *Zeylanica.* | S. Languli; Kunchura. H. Kanchura |
| NAUCLEA | |
| *Cadumba.* | S. Kudumba; Neepa. B. Kudumbo. B. H. Kudum. |
| *parvifolia.* | T. Bota-kudumee. |
| *cordifolia.* | B. Keli-kudum. T. Daduga. |
| *tetrandra.* | B. Shwet-kudum. |
| *ovalifolia.* | B. Shala. |
| *purpurea.* | T. Bagada. |
| NARCISSUS | |
| *Tagetes.* | H. Nargis. |
| NASTURTIUM | |
| *officinale.* | H. Deskandar. |

| *Gen. and Spec.* | *Native Names.* |
|---|---|
| NECTANDRA | |
| *decandra.* | B. Hurindur. |
| NEERIYA | |
| *dichotoma.* | T. Neeriya. |
| NELUMBIUM | |
| *speciosum.* | S. Padmachari; Satapatra. S. B. H. Pudma-podoo. B. Komol; Ponghuj. H. Lalkamal; Kungwel; Kamal; Padam; Ambuj. TAM. Tamaray. T. Yerra-tamaray. M. Tamara; Bem-tamara. |
| *(white.)* | B. Shweta-pudma; Sada-podoo; Poontureeka. |
| *(rosy.)* | B. Rukta-pudma (or podoo). H. Lall-pudma. |
| NEPENTHES | |
| *distillatoria.* | M. Daun-gundi. CYNG. Bandura. |
| NEPETA | |
| *Malabarica.* | S. Bootankushum. TAM. Pemayrutie; Nettay-pemayruttie. T. Moga-beerakoo. M. Carim-tumba. |
| NERIUM | |
| *coronarium.* | S. Nandivriksha. TAM. Nundiavuttei. M. Nandi-ervatam. |
| *grandis.* | H. Mendasinghi. |
| *odorum (red sing.)* | S. Kuruveera; Pruteehasa. B. H. Lall-kurubee. H. Kaner. TAM. Aralivayr. T. Ghenneru-vayroo. |
| *(double red.)* | B. H. Pudma-kurube. |
| *white.* | B. H. Shwet-kurube. |
| *oleander.* | H. Karzahra. |
| *tinctorium.* | TAM. Pala. T. Chit-ankaloo. |
| *reticulatum.* | B. Karunta. T. Adivi-palla-tiga. |
| *antidysentericum.* | H. Indurjau. *See* ECHITES. |
| NICOTIANA | |
| *Tabacum.* | S. Dhumrapatra; Tamrakoota. B. H. Tumak; Tambaca. H. Bujjirbhang. TAM. Poghei. T. Poghako. CYNG. Doonkola. |
| NIGELLA | |
| *Indica.* | H. Calazira. |
| *sativa v. Indica.* | S. Krishna-jiraka; Musavi. S. H. Mugrela. B. Kala-jeera; Kreenj. |

| Gen. and Spec. | Native Names. |
|---|---|
| | H. Kolunjen. TAM. Carin-siragum. T. Nulla-gilakara. CYNG. Kaloodooroo. |
| NIPA *fruticans.* | B. Goolga; Guana; Gubna. |
| NYCTANTHES *arbor-tristis.* | S. B. Shephalika. B. Shiooli. H. Harsingahar. |
| NYMPHEA *rubra.* | S. Huluka; Ructa-sindhuka. B. Ructa-kumbula. |
| *Lotus.* | S. Koomooda. B. Shalook; Kyrob. H. Bhamber; Bhambul; Sarang; Nilofar; Kuwulgotta. T. Tella-kalwa. |
| *Nelumbo.* | H. Caul. |
| *cyanea.* | S. Khulara; Neelumbo-junma; Indeevura. B. Soondhi; Neel-podma. T. Neety-kalwa. |
| *esculenta.* | S. Koomooda; Kiruva. B. Chota-soondhi. |
| *stellata.* | B. Chota-shalook. |
| *odorata.* | S. Raktotpala. TAM. Shengalaneer. T. Kaloovagudda. |

| *Gen. and Spec.* | *Native Names.* |
|---|---|
| **O.** | |
| OCHNA | |
| *squarrosa.* | S. B. H. Kunuk-champaka. T. Yerrajuvi. |
| OCYMUM | |
| *basilicum.* | H. Pashana-bhedee. |
| *pilosum.* | H. Babai; Marua; Rahu; Nazbo; Rachan; Rihan. |
| *(sp. ? )* | H. Bantulsa; Dema; Balungoo. |
| *hirsutum.* | TAM. Koslimitan. |
| *villosum.* | B. H. Toolusee; Toolsee. |
| *sanctum.* | S. Arjaka; Parnasa. B. Kural. B. H. Kala-toolsee. H. Toolsi. TAM. Toolasee. M. Nalla-tirtava. |
| *polystachion.* | T. Neeroo-toolusee. |
| *album.* | S. Viswa-tulasi; Arjaca. H. Suffaid-toolsie. TAM. Cunja-coray. T. Kooka-tolasie. |
| *caryophyllatum.* | B. H. Goolal-toolshee. |
| *pilosum.* | S. Burbura. B. Babooi-toolshee. |
| *gratissimum.* | B. H. Ram-toolshee. |
| *basilicum.* | S. Manjirika. H. Subze; Kala-tulsee. TAM. Tirnoot-patchie. T. Vepoodipatsa. CYNG. Suwanda-tala. |
| ORNUS | |
| *rotundifolia.* | H. Shirkisht. |
| ODINA | |
| *Woodier.* | S. Jeevula; Ajasringgi. B. Jiyul. H. Kashmulla. TAM. Woodiam. T. Gumpina; Compina; Woddia. |

| *Gen. and Spec.* | *Native Names.* |
|---|---|
| OLAX | |
| *scandens.* | T. Turka-vepa. |
| *phœnicarpa.* | B. Moicha. |
| OLDENLANDIA | |
| *alata.* | S. Gundha-bhudra. B. Gundha-badalee. H. Thel-koodi. |
| *crystallina.* | B. Poonkka; Punki. |
| *biflora.* | S. Kshetra-purputea. B. Khet-papura. H. Pitpapra; Shahtara. |
| *herbacea.* | T. Veri-nella-vemos. |
| *umbellata.* | TAM. Sayawer; Imboril; Emborel. T. Cheri-veloo. |
| OLEA | |
| *dioica.* | B. Atta-jam. |
| *Emodi.* | N. Maharanga. |
| *Europea.* | H. Julpai. |
| ONOSMA | |
| *bracteata.* | H. Lalgiri. |
| OPHIOGLOSSUM | |
| *cordifolium.* | B. Danga-ghechoo; Ehteero. |
| *flexuosum.* | B. Bhootraj. |
| OPHIORHIZA | |
| *Mungos.* | CYNG. Wal-eka-weriya; Mendi. |
| OPHIOXYLON | |
| *serpentinum.* | S. Chundrika; B. H. Chundra; Chota-chand. TAM. Chivan-amelpodie. T. Patalganni. CYNG. Ratu-eka-wariya. M. Tsjovanna-amelpodi. |
| OPILIA | |
| *amentacea.* | T. Balli-kooma. |
| ORCHIS | |
| *uniflora.* | B. Kathiya-ram-ram. |
| ORIGANUM | |
| *majorana.* | H. Murwa. TAM. Marroo. |
| *(sp. ?)* | H. Satar. |
| ORNITROPHE | |
| *serrata.* | B. Rakhal-phul. T. Tantichi; Tavatiky. CYNG. Moodu-kobbœ. |
| *aporetica.* | H. Ghee-kashee. |
| ORYZA | |
| *sativa.* | S. Arunya; Ashoo-vrihi. B. H. Dhan; H. Pusuee. T. Ooori. CYNG. Ooruwee. |

| Gen. and Spec. | Native Names. |
| --- | --- |
| *(wild sort.)* | S. Neevara. B. Ooreya-dhan. |
| OSMUNDA *Zeylanica.* | B. Ekbeera. |
| OSYRIS *peltata.* | T. Bodie. |
| OVIEDA *verticillata.* | H. Bawanhatti. |
| OXALIS *corniculata.* | S. Umla-lonika; Chookrika: Amlika; Ambashta. B. H. Amrool. H. Umbuti. TAM. Pooliaray. T. Poolie-chinta; Pulla-chinta. |
| *sensitiva.* | B. Bun-narunga. H. Lushanno. M. Todda-vaddi. |

| Gen. and Spec. | Native Names. |
|---|---|
| **P.** | |
| PÆDERIA | |
| *fœtida.* | S. Ghundha-bhudra. |
| *ternata.* | B. Teoomeri ; Achelia-pata. |
| PANAX | |
| *digitatum.* | B. Soona ; Kata-soona. |
| *fragrans.* | B. Gooti-soona. |
| PANCRATIUM | |
| *triflorum.* | B. Sada-kanoor. |
| PANDANUS | |
| *odoratissimus.* | H. Ketgi ; Gagandhool. S. B. Ketukee. B. Kea. H. Keura. T. Mugali. |
| *fœtidus.* | B. Kea-kanta. H. Keur-kanta. |
| PANICUM | |
| *pilosum.* | H. Arzan. |
| *spicatum.* | H. Bujura. T. Peddi-ganti. |
| *glaucum.* | H. Pingi-nachi. T. Naka-kora. |
| *holcoides.* | B. Swati. |
| *interruptum.* | H. Nardul. T. Wolam. |
| *dactylon.* | S. Doorva. B. Doorba ; Doobla. H. Doob ; Ghaner. TAM. Arugampillee. T. Gherka ; Ghericha. |
| *ciliare.* | B. H. Makur-jali. T. Shangalli-gaddi. |
| *corymbosum.* | T. Isheepa-bora-gaddi ; Cheepa-bora-gaddi. |
| *brizoides.* | T. Woada ; Oda ; Woodoo-gaddi. |
| *fluitans.* | B. H. Petinar. T. Doosa. |
| *stagninum.* | B. H. Dula. T. Pedda-woondoo. |
| *colonum (red.)* | S. Shamaka. H. Lal-shama. T. Woondoo-gaddy. |
| *(green.)* | B. H. Shama. |
| *setigerum.* | B. H. Bura-jal-ganti. |
| *hirsutum.* | H. Jal-ganti. T. Woondoo ; Salla-woondoo. |
| *verticillatum.* | H. Dora-biaroo ; Lapta. T. Chick-lenta. |

| *Gen. and Spec.* | *Native Names.* |
| --- | --- |
| *Italicum.* | S. Kungoo; Priyungoo. B. H. Kungoo; Kangni; Kungnee. H. T. Kora; Koraloo. H. Rawla; Beertia; Kakoon. TAM. Tenney. CYNG. Tanahal. M. Tenna. MAH. Chenna. GUZ. Bajeeree. CAN. Navonay. |
| *strictum.* | B. Gang-bena. |
| *hispidulum.* | B. Bura-shama. |
| *frumentaceum.* | H. Sanwa. S. Shyamaka. B. Shama. T. Bontashama. |
| *(sp. ?)* | H. Birti; Kooduee; Kodon; Sawan. |
| *tenellum.* | H. Joopi-kunka. |
| *paludosum.* | B. Boruti. B. H. Kulusnar. T. Soda. |
| *uliginosum.* | B. Burunda. T. Gundra. |
| *miliare (var. 3.)* | T. Nella-shama. |
| *miliaceum.* | S. Vreehibheda; Unoo. B. H. Cheena. T. Worga. |
| PAPAVER | |
| *somniferum.* | S. Chosa. B. H. Post. TAM. Cassacassa. CYNG. Albin-atta. |
| PARIETARIA | |
| *Indica.* | H. Acarcarha. |
| PASTINACCA | |
| *Opoponax.* | H. Gaoshir. |
| PASPALUM | |
| *scrobiculatum.* | S. Kudruva; Korudoosha. B. Koda. H. Kodaka. T. Aruga. |
| *Kora.* | H. Koda. T. Neer-aruga. |
| PAVONIA | |
| *odorata.* | S. Bala. TAM. Peramootie. T. Chittle-bunda; Mootopalagum. |
| *Zeylanica.* | TAM. Sittamootie. T. Tsinna-mootopalagum. CYNG. Gas-bewila. |
| PAVETTA | |
| *Indica.* | *See* IXORA. |
| PEDALIUM | |
| *murex.* | S. Ghejasoodumoostra. H. Burraygokeroo. TAM. Amei-nerunshil; Ananeringie. T. Yeanugapulleroo. CYNG. Ætnerenchi. |
| PENTAPETES | |
| *Phœnicea.* | S. Ruktuka; Bundooka. B. Doopahariya. H. Duparia. |

| *Gen. and Spec.* | *Native Names.* |
|---|---|
| PENTAPTERA | |
| *tomentosa.* | S. Usuna. B. H. Usun. T. Nellamadoo. |
| *glabra.* | T. Dellamadoo. |
| *Arjuna.* | S. Urjoona; Kukhooba. B. Urjoon. H. Kahooa. |
| *coriacea.* | TAM. Anemutti. |
| *paniculata.* | TAM. Pokarakai. T. Nimmeeri. |
| PERIPLOCA | |
| *Indica.* | S. Shariva. B. Anonto-mool. H. Mugraboo. TAM. Nunnari. T. Soogundapala. CYNG. Erramassoo; Irimusu. |
| *sylvestris.* | TAM. Sirroo-corinja. |
| PHARNACEUM | |
| *cerviana v. triflora.* | S. Parpata. TAM. Purpadagum. T. Purpatakum. CYNG. Patpadagan. |
| *Mollugo.* | S. Grishmaja. B. H. Gima; Greeshmuja. H. Guma. TAM. Toora. T. Chayntara-shiakoo. CYNG. Heen-telika-pala. M. Kalpa-tsjera. |
| *pentagynum.* | B. Dhoosura; Doosera-sag. |
| PHASEOLUS | |
| *alatius.* | B. Bun-burbutee. T. Kar-alsana. |
| *sublobatus.* | B. Gora-moog. |
| *calcaratus.* | B. Ranga-moog. |
| *radiatus.* | S. Masha. B. Mash'-kulai; Ticoraikulai. H. Moong; Thikiree. |
| *Max.* | B. Kalla-moog; Krishna-moog. T. Nella-pessara. |
| *vulgaris.* | H. Bakla; Loba. |
| *Mungo.* | H. Moong. S. Moodga. B. Hali-moog; Hari-moog; Kherooya; Bulat. |
| *aureus.* | B. Sona-moog. |
| *torosus.* | N. Sweta-mas. |
| *trilobus.* | S. Moodga-purnee; Tryangguli. B. Mooganee. H. Triangguli. T. Pillipessara. |
| *aconitifolius.* | H. Moot. |
| PHELLANDRIUM | |
| *stoloniferum.* | B. Pan-trasee. |
| PHILLYREA | |
| *robusta.* | H. Bhooi-moora. |

| *Gen. and Spec.* | *Native Names.* |
|---|---|
| PHLOMIS | |
| *nepetifolia.* | H. Khujoor-churi. |
| *Zeylanica.* | B. H. Hulkussa. T. Poo-alla-toomi. |
| *cephalota.* | H. Bura-hulkussa. |
| *biflora.* | H. Shwet-busunta. |
| *esculenta.* | B. Chota-hulkussa. |
| PHŒNIX | |
| *sylvestris.* | S. Khurjjooree. H. Sendhi ; Kajur. |
| *paludosa.* | S. Hintala. B. Hental. B. H. Hintala. |
| *farinifera.* | TAM. Sirroo-eetchum. T. Chitta-eita. |
| *acaulis.* | B. Koonk. |
| *dactylifera.* | H. Khurma ; Chuhara. |
| PHRYNIUM | |
| *dichotomum.* | S. Seetula-putrika ; Vula ; Godunika ; Bhudra. H. Seetul-patee ; Moocta-patee ; Patee-patee ; Madar-patee. |
| *capitatum.* | B. Kudalee. M. Naru-killa. |
| *imbricatum.* | B. Pittuli-pata. |
| PHYLLANTHUS | |
| *Maderaspatensis.* | T. Nalla-usereki. |
| *simplex.* | T. Oochi-usereki. |
| *Niruri.* | S. Brovishirum ; Arjata. B. Sada-hazarmuni ; Kiraneli. TAM. Kilanelly. T. Nela-ooshirikeh. H. Booien-aoonlah. CYNG. Pita-wakka. M. Kirganelli. |
| *Urinaria.* | B. Hazar-muni. T. Yerra-usereki. CYNG. Bin-nelli. M. Tsieru-kerganeli. |
| *bacciformis.* | T. Rawa-salaburta-kanda. |
| *pendulus.* | T. Tella-usereki. |
| *multiflorus.* | S. Khrishna-kamboji. B. Pankooshee ; Bun-joolee. TAM. Poolavayr. T. Poolugooda ; Nella-pooroogoodoo. CYNG. Wæl-kayilla. |
| *rhamnoides.* | S. Aruni. H. Surasaruni. TAM. Pavala-pola ; Pagara-pula. CYNG. Gaskayilla. |
| *vitis-idæa.* | B. Humkata-jooli. T. Yerra-pooroogoodoo. |
| *Emblica.* | S. Amulukee; Umrita. B. Amla. H. Amlaki ; Anooli ; Aoonla ; Aoongra ; Aunwerd. TAM. Nellie-poo ; |

| *Gen. and Spec.* | *Native Names.* |
|---|---|
| | Nellie-kai. T. Usereki; Woosherike-poo. CYNG. Awusada-nelli. M. Nelli-canarum. |
| *longifolius.* | B. Lodh; Looaree. T. Rasa-usereki. |
| *tetrandra.* | B. Arjura. |
| *turbinatus.* | T. Dava-dari. |
| *cheramela.* | B. Huri-phul. H. Harfareori. |
| PHYSALIS | |
| *flexuosa.* | S. B. Ushwagundha. H. Usgund. TAM. Amkoolang-kalung. T. Penneru. |
| *Peruviana.* | H. Macao. B. Tapureea; Tepeeriya: Tophlee. |
| *minima.* | S. Lutchmee-divetiya. B. Bun-tapurea. H. Toolati-pari. T. Kupanti. |
| PIERARDIA | |
| *sapida.* | H. Lutka. |
| PIMENTA | |
| *vulgaris.* | H. Sital-chini. |
| PIMPINELLA | |
| *Anisum.* | B. Muhooree. H. Saurif; Anesum. |
| PINUS | |
| *longifolia.* | B. Surul. H. Chir; Saral; Seerul. |
| *Deodara.* | S. H. B. Deva-daroo. H. Deodwara. |
| *Neoza.* | H. Chalgoza; Chilgoza. |
| PIPER | |
| *nigrum.* | S. Vellajung; Mureechung; Kolukung. S. B. Muricha. H. Gool-murich; Felfilgird; Mirch. TAM. Mellaghoo. T. Moloovoo-kodi; Mirialoo. CYNG. Gammiris. MAH. Kalymeerchingay. |
| *trioecum.* | T. Mirial-tiga. |
| *longum.* | S. B. Pippulee. H. Pippul; Pilpul; Felfildraz. TAM. CYNG. Tipilie. T. Peepal; Pippuloo. |
| *Betel.* | S. Tamboolee; Purna. B. H. Pan. H. Nagbel. TAM. Vettilei. T. Tamalap. CYNG. Bulat-wœla. M. Betala-codi. |
| *Chuvya.* | S. Chuvya. B. H. Chuee. |
| *Cubeba.* | S. Sugandha-marichu. H. Cubab-chini; Dumke-mirchie. N. Timmue; |

| *Gen. and Spec.* | *Native Names.* |
|---|---|
| | Taiz-bul. TAM. Val-mellaghoo. T. Salavamirialoo. CYNG. Wal-gummeris. |
| *silvaticum.* | H. Puhari-pippul. |
| *dichotomum.* | TAM. Taysha. |
| PISONEA | |
| *aculeata.* | B. Bag-achera. |
| *mitis.* | T. Konki-putri. |
| PISTACCIA | |
| *officinarum.* | H. Pistu. |
| PISTIA | |
| *stratiotes.* | S. Kumbhika ; Untarei-tamara ; Varipurnee. B. Pana. H. Toka-pana ; Unterungha. TAM. Agasatamaray. T. Kodda-pail. |
| PISUM | |
| *sativum (majus.)* | S. Harenso. B. Bura-mutur. H. Buttani ; Muttir ; Muthur ; Matar. TAM. Puttanie. T. Goondoo-sanigheloo. CYNG. Vatana. MAH. Watana. |
| *viridum.* | B. H. Chota-mutur. |
| *arvense.* | H. Kirao. |
| PLADERA | |
| *decussata.* | B. Dunkoni. |
| PLANTAGO | |
| *Ispagula.* | B. H. Ispagool. |
| PLECTRANTHUS | |
| *aromaticus.* | B. Pathur-choor. H. Pat-harchur. |
| PLUMBAGO | |
| *Zeylanica.* | S. Chitruka. B. Chitra ; Chita ; Ognee-krishano. H. Chita ; Chitturmool. TAM. Cittramoolum ; Kodivaylie. T. Citra. CYNG. Elarathnetul. M. Tumba-codiveli. |
| *rosea.* | S. Rukta-chitraca. B. H. Lall-chita. TAM. Shencodie-vaylie. T. Yerracittra-moolum. CYNG. Rathnetul. M. Scheti-codiveli. |
| PLUMERIA | |
| *acuminata.* | B. Gobur-champa. H. Goolachin ; Goburchamp. |
| *alba.* | H. Gulachin. |

| *Gen. and Spec.* | *Native Names.* |
|---|---|
| POA | |
| *Chinensis.* | B. Bura-pini-nuta. |
| *cynosuroides.* | S. Koosha; Doorva. B. H. Koosha. H. Dab. T. Dorba; Dorpa. |
| *nutans.* | T. Urenka. |
| *plumosa.* | H. Puluka. |
| *unioloides.* | H. Koni. |
| *bifaria.* | T. Wooda-talum. |
| *procera.* | T. Reewona; Rewa. |
| *interrupta.* | T. Nakurnarul. |
| PODALYRIA | |
| *bracteata.* | B. Goopooree. |
| POINCIANA | |
| *pulcherrima.* | B. H. Krishna-choora. H. Kurish-churin; Gul-i-turah. CYNG. Monaramal. M. Tsietti-mandaru. |
| POLYANTHES | |
| *tuberosa.* | S. Sandhy-araga. B. Rujuni-gundha. H. Gool-shaboo. T. Undimandari. M. Andi-malleri. |
| POLYGALA | |
| *arvensis.* | B. Merradoo. |
| POLYGONUM | |
| *lanatum.* | B. Shweta-panee-murich. |
| *pilosum.* | B. Bura-panee-murich. |
| *tomentosum.* | T. Yeati-mallier. |
| *barbatum.* | TAM. Aat-alarie. T. Kunda-mallier. CYNG. Ratukimbul-wenna. |
| *flaccidum.* | B. Panee-murich. |
| *elegans.* | H. Kunuk-jhinghi. |
| *aviculare.* | S. Miromali. H. Machoti. |
| POLYPODIUM | |
| *glabrum.* | B. Chitooa-boora. |
| *taxifolium.* | M. Wellipanna-kelingoo. |
| *quercifolium.* | B. Guroor. |
| *unitum.* | B. Pan-kakrol. |
| *proliferum.* | B. Dapoo. H. Kullke-jamp. |
| *vulgare.* | H. Bisfez. |
| PONTEDERA | |
| *vaginalis.* | B. Nouka. H. Louka. T. Neeroo-cancha. |
| *hastata.* | T. Neeroo-tamana. |

| *Gen. and Spec.* | *Native Names.* |
|---|---|
| PORTULACCA | |
| *quadrifida.* | S. Oopadykee. H. Chowly ; Baclatul-humka. TAM. Passelie-keeray. T. Pedda-poil-pail-kura ; Batsalikoora. |
| *(sp ? )* | H. Candli ; Khoorfeh. |
| *oleracea (var. 3. 4.)* | S. Lonika ; Loonia. B. H. Noonya. H. Nooncha ; Lona ; Khursa ; Kurfa. TAM. Coril-keeray. CAN. Dooda-gorai. |
| *meridiana.* | B. H. Looniya ; Noonya. T. Pail-kura. |
| *pilosa.* | B. H. Bura-noonya. |
| *Posoqueria.* | *See* GARDENIA. |
| POTHOS | |
| *officinalis.* | B. Guj-pipul. |
| *Peepla.* | B. Pipul. |
| *heterophylla.* | B. H. Kanta-man. |
| *Læsia.* | B. H. Kanta-kuchoo. T. Moola-sari. |
| PRASIUM | |
| *melissifolium.* | B. Hursmun. |
| PRIMULA | |
| *denticulata.* | N. Nitaha. |
| *Stuartii.* | N. Masoo-nitaha. |
| *rotundifolia.* | N. Sapha-nitaha. |
| PREMNA | |
| *latifolia.* | T. Pedda-nella-kura. |
| *serratifolia.* | B. Bhoot-biruvee. |
| *integrifolia.* | S. Agni-mantha. TAM. Ghebboonellie. T. Moonnee. |
| *spinosa.* | S. Guree ; Gunikarika. B. Guniaree ; Kurnika. |
| *herbacea.* | S. Bhoomi-jumbooka. B. Bhooi-jamba. |
| *tomentosa.* | T. Naoroo. |
| PRENANTHES | |
| *aspenifolia.* | H. Teak-chama. |
| PROSOPIS | |
| *spicigera.* | S. T. Shumee. |
| PSIDIUM | |
| *pyriferum.* | B. Peyara ; Anjeer. H. Suffri-jam ; Amrut. |
| *pomiferum.* | B. Peyara ; Anjeer. H. Lall-suffrijam. |
| PSORALEA | |
| *corylifolia.* | S. Vakoochie. B. H. Hakooch. H. Bawchan. TAM. Karpooga-arisee. T. Kour-gestum ; Bapungie. |

| *Gen. and Spec.* | *Native Names.* |
|---|---|
| PRUNUS | |
| *Armeniacus.* | H. Zard-alu. |
| *domesticus.* | H. Alucha. |
| *cerasus.* | H. Padam. |
| PSYCHOTRIA | |
| *ophioxyloides.* | B. Basook. |
| *Asiatica v. sphærocarpa.* | B. Maisa-alada; Alada-choonari. |
| *herbacea.* | B. Kudi-munkoon. T. Karinta-kali. |
| *adenophylla.* | B. Alada-choonari. |
| PTERIS | |
| *lunulata.* | H. Kalka-jhamp; Paresiyaushan. |
| PTEROCARPUS | |
| *Santalinus.* | S. Tilaparni; Koochunduna; Ranjana. S. H. B. Rukta-chunduna. H. Lal-chundend; Undum. TAM. Segapoo-shandanum. T. Kuchandanum. CYNG. Ruct-handoon. CAN. Whonnay. |
| *marsupium.* | H. Peet-shala. T. Yeengasha. |
| *bilobus.* | CYNG. Gan-malu. |
| PTEROSPERMUM | |
| *suberifolia.* | S. B. Moochukoonda. TAM. Taddæmarum. |
| *acerifolia.* | S. Kurnikara. B. Kunuk-champa. H. Kuniyar. |
| PTERYGODIUM | |
| *sulcatum.* | B. H. Shwet-hoolee. |
| PUNICA | |
| *Granatum.* | S. Darimba. B. Dalim. S. T. Dadima. H. Darim; Anar; Gulnar. TAM. Madalum; Magilan. CYNG. Delunghedie. MAH. Dalumb. |
| — *double.* | H. Gool-anar. |
| PYRUS | |
| *communis.* | H. Amrud; Nashpati. |
| *Cydonia.* | H. Behee; Abee. |
| *Malus.* | S. Seba. H. Seb; Seo. |

| Gen. and Spec. | Native Names. |
|---|---|
| **Q.** | |
| QUERCUS | |
| *serrata.* | B. Gol-shingra. |
| *semi-serrata.* | B. Ram-katha. |
| *lancæafolia.* | B. Shingra. |
| *squamata.* | B. Bun-chukma. |
| *lappacea.* | B. Ooloo-chukma. |
| *turbinata.* | B. Bansora-batana. |
| *fenestrata.* | B. Kala-chukma. |
| *castanicarpa.* | B. Lumba-kanta-hurina-batana. |
| *ferox.* | B. Hurinea-batana. |
| *acuminata.* | B. Kanta-batana. |
| *armata.* | B. Kala-lal-batana ; Singa-hura ; Kanta-singa. |
| *(sp ?)* | H. Banj. |

| Gen. and Spec. | Native Names. |
|---|---|
| **R.** | |
| RANDIA | |
| *racemosa.* | B. Peetunga. |
| *stricta.* | H. Shwet-buruna. |
| RAPHANUS | |
| *sativus.* | S. Mooluka. B. H. Moola. H. Muli. |
| RHAMNUS | |
| *Jujuba.* | H. Birchin. |
| *circumcissus.* | S. Bhoovuduree. |
| RHEUM | |
| *palmatum.* | H. Revand-chini. |
| RHIZOPHORA | |
| *gymnorhiza.* | B. Kakra. |
| *Mangle.* | B. Bhorar. T. Upoo-punna. |
| *decandra.* | B. Guran. |
| RHODODENDRUM | |
| *ponticum.* | H. Burans. |

| Gen. and Spec. | Native Names. |
|---|---|
| *puniceum.* | H. Boorans. |
| RHOPALA | |
| *robusta.* | B. Janika. |
| RHUS | |
| *Bucki-amelam.* | N. Backi-amelo. |
| *Coriara.* | H. Sumac. |
| RICINUS | |
| *communis.* | S. Erunda. B. Bherenda. H. Arundi. T. Amadum. CAN. Haralu. M. Citnavaca. |
| ROBINIA | |
| *candida.* | B. Batas-mundulee. |
| RONDELETIA | |
| *tinctoria.* | B. Toola-lodh. |
| *longifolia.* | B. Soopari. |
| *cinerea.* | N. Goshina. |
| *coriacea.* | N. Julsi. |
| ROSA | |
| *centifolia.* | B. H. Goolab. H. Gul. T. Goolabu. |
| *Chinensis.* | B. H. Kanta-goolab. |
| *glandulifera.* | S. Sevuti. B. H. Shewuti. H. Sadbarg; Seoti. |
| ROSCOEA | |
| *pentandra.* | B. Kungeea. |
| ROTTBŒLLIA | |
| *glabra.* | B. Baksha. |
| *compressa.* | H. Pan-shiru. T. Sheroo; Sherroopanukoo. |
| *exaltata.* | B. Bura-sooti; Bura-savooate. T. Kunda-punookoo. |
| *perforata.* | B. Kurki. T. Punookoo. |
| *corymbosa.* | T. Peddoo-punookoo. |
| ROTTLERA | |
| *tinctoria.* | S. B. Poonnag; Keshoor. B. Toong. H. Camul. T. Vassuntagunda. |
| *dicocca.* | B. Akkoos. T. Conda-vettoo. |
| *tetracocca.* | B. Marlea. |
| *peltata.* | B. Seergooloolli. |
| *Indica.* | H. Pindalu. |
| ROYDSIA | |
| *suaveolens.* | H. Madhubhi-lata. |
| RUBIA | |
| *Munjistha.* | S. Vikusa; Aroona; Uroona. S. B. Munjistha. H. Munjit. TAM. Nan- |

| Gen. and Spec. | Native Names. |
|---|---|
| | jitta; Sawil-codie. T. Mandestie. CYNG. Well-madatta. M. Poo-ut. |
| *secunda.* | CYNG. Manda-mandina-wœla. |
| RUBUS | |
| *(sp?)* | H. Anchu. |
| *Gowry-phul.* | H. Gouree-phul. |
| RUELLIA | |
| *ringens.* | CYNG. Nil-puruk. M. Upu-dali. |
| *longifolia.* | S. Gokantuka. B. Kanta-koolika. H. Gochru. |
| *Pavala.* | T. Pavala. |
| *strepens.* | S. Grendie-tagarum. TAM. Kirendi-nyagum. |
| RUMEX | |
| *acutus.* | B. Bun-palung; Jol-palung. |
| *vesicarius.* | S. Chookrika; Shutuvedhee. B. Chooka-palung. H. Chukka; Chewka. TAM. Sookan-keeray. CYNG. Katoo-tumpala; Soori. |
| *acetosa.* | H. Chuka. |
| RUTA | |
| *graveolens.* | S. Brahmi; Sona-luta. H. Satoori; Allooda. TAM. CYNG. Arooda. T. Suddapoo. MAH. Suddab. |

| Spec. and Gen. | Native Names. |
|---|---|
| **S.** | |
| SABIA | |
| *lanceolata.* | B. Soobja. |
| SACCHARUM | |
| *cylindricum.* | B. Ooloo. H. Ulu. T. Barom-hiss. |
| *spontaneum.* | S. Kasha. B. Kashiya. H. Khugura; Kagara-kas. T. Billoo-gaddi; Relloo-gaddi. |
| *fuscum.* | B. H. Khuree; Pata-khuree. |
| *semi-decumbens.* | B. H. Khuree. |
| *procerum.* | B. Teng. H. Sarput; Sirki; Sarkara. |
| *officinarum.* | S. Ikshoo; Poondru; Rusala. B. Ik; Akh; Ookh; Ukyo. H. Ganna; Khulooa; Kajooli; Ich; Uch. T. Cherukoo-bodi; Cherukoo-duboo. |
| *Sara.* | S. B. H. Sara; H. Sar; Senthi. |
| *Munja.* | S. H. Munja. |
| *exaltatum.* | T. Kunda-kanumoo. |
| SAGITTARIA | |
| *cordifolia.* | B. Dal-kuchoo. |
| SALICORNIA | |
| *brachiata.* | T. Kiloo; Quoiloo. |
| *Indica.* | B. Jidoo-palung; Jadoo. TAM. Paghara-poondoo. T. Kivia-pippali. |
| SALIX | |
| *tetrasperma.* | S. Vuroona. B. Baishi. H. Pani-joma. |
| *Babylonica v. tetrandra.* | B. Baishi. H. Majnu; Betmajnu. |
| SALSOLA | |
| *nudiflora.* | TAM. Narie-oomarie. T. Rawa-kada. |
| *Indica.* | T. Ella-koora. |
| *elata.* | TAM. Oomarie-marum. |
| SALVADORA | |
| *Persica.* | H. Pilu. TAM. Ooghai. T. Pedda-waraga-winki; Ghoonie. |

| *Gen. and Spec.* | *Native Names.* |
|---|---|
| SALVIA | |
| *officinalis.* | H. Salbia. |
| *brachiata.* | B. Bhooi-toolsi. H. Bun-baburee. |
| *Bengalensis.* | H. Kafoor-ka-pawt ; Velaitie-capoor. TAM. Sayselley. T. Simie-carpoorum. CYNG. Saoohal. |
| *parviflora.* | B. Koka-buradi. |
| SALVINIA | |
| *cucullata.* | S. Akhoo-purnee. B. Indoor-kanee-pana ; Pana. |
| *imbricata.* | S. Vari-purnee. B. Pana. |
| *verticillata.* | B. Oolki-pana. |
| SANSEVERIA | |
| *Zeylanica.* | S. Moorva. B. Shoochi-mookhee ; Munga. H. Murta ; Moorga ; Moorgabie. TAM. Marool. T. Chamakada. CYNG. Maha-niyanda. |
| SANTALUM | |
| *album.* | S. Ghundasaru. S. B. H. Chunduna. |
| SAPINDUS | |
| *emarginatus.* | S. Rishta ; Arishta ; Phœnila. B. Bura-reetha. H. Ritah. TAM. Poovandie-cottay ; Manay-poongungkai. T. Kunkoodoo ; Koomuttieghenzaloo. CYNG. Gas-penela. |
| *saponaria.* | H. Reetha. |
| *detergens.* | S. Aristaphenila. B. Reetha. |
| SAPIUM | |
| *Indicum.* | B. H. Hooroos. |
| *baccatum v. bacciferum.* | B. H. Bela. |
| *cordifolium.* | T. Badeki. |
| SARCOSTEMA | |
| *viminialis.* | B. Soom. |
| SCŒVOLA | |
| *lobelia.* | H. Changara. |
| SCILLA | |
| *(sp?)* | H. Iscil. |
| SCHLEICHERIA | |
| *triga.* | TAM. May. T. Yelim-buriki. CYNG. Kunghas. |
| *pentapetala.* | B. Poora-koi. |

| Gen. and Spec. | Native Names. |
|---|---|
| SCHŒNUS | |
| *articulatus.* | T. Kunda-tunga. |
| SCHREBERA | |
| *Swietenoides.* | TAM. Mogalinga. T. Mookadi. |
| SCIRPUS | |
| *plantagineus.* | B. H. Chechka. |
| *articulatus.* | B. H. Put-puti-chechka. T. Lutti-pitta-allie. |
| *bispicatus.* | B. Kesuri-mulunga. T. Kushi-tunga. |
| *Schœnoides.* | H. Moor-moori. |
| *squarrosus.* | H. Goori. |
| *glomeratus.* | B. H. Bura-nirbisi. |
| *diphyllus.* | B. Tal-nuroo. |
| *complanatus.* | B. H. Koratiya-juvanee. |
| *tetragonus.* | B. Bura-juvani. T. Murcushalee. |
| *quinqueangularis.* | B. Juvani. |
| *anceps.* | B. Joopi. |
| *Kysoor.* | B. Kesoor; Kesooriya. |
| *dubius.* | T. Alikay. |
| *globosus.* | T. Billapa. |
| *tridentatus.* | T. Gorapa; Goraki-shaka-tunga. |
| *maximus.* | T. Booda-tunga. |
| SCLERIA | |
| *lithosperma.* | M. Kaden-pullu. |
| SCOPOLIA | |
| *aculeata.* | TAM. Molakarunnay. T. Conda-cashinda. M. Kakatoddali. |
| SCYTALIA | |
| *Litchi.* | B. Litchi. B. H. Leechee. |
| *rubra.* | H. Koi-poora. |
| *rimosa.* | B. Tinguree. |
| *Longan.* | B. Ash-phul. |
| *Danura.* | H. Danura. |
| SECURIDACA | |
| *paniculata.* | B. Furrinjur. |
| SEMECARPUS | |
| *Anacardium.* | S. Urooskura; Bhullatakee. B. H. Bhela. H. Bheela; Belawina; Bhelaman; Bhelawan. TAM. Shayng-cottay; Shayrang-cottay. T. Nellajedi; Jeedighenzadoo. |
| SERPICULA | |
| *verticillata.* | T. Poo-natsoo. |

| *Gen. and Spec.* | *Native Names.* |
|---|---|
| SERRATULA | |
| *anthelmentica.* | H. Bacchi; Somraj. |
| *cinerea.* | H. Choota-kookshima. |
| SESAMUM | |
| *orientale.* | S. Tila. B. H. Til. |
| *Indicum.* | H. Krisha-til. |
| SESBANA | |
| *grandiflora.* | B. Ogosthee; Buka; Breeka. |
| *Ægyptica.* | B. Byojainti. H. Jait. |
| SESUVIUM | |
| *Portulacastrum.* | T. Wangaredoo-koodoo. |
| SHOREA | |
| *robusta.* | S. Sala; Ushwukurnuka. B. Surj. B. H. Shal. |
| *Tumbuggia.* | TAM. Tumbuggai. |
| *Talura.* | TAM. Talura. |
| SIDA | |
| *lanceolata.* | S. Pata. TAM. Malaytanghie; A-rooa-manoo-poondoo. |
| *cuneifolia.* | T. Mutto-apullacum. |
| *acuta.* | B. Kureta. |
| *humilis.* | B. Junka. T. Nella-benda. |
| *rhomboidea.* | B. Shwet-baryala. H. Safed-baryala. |
| *rhombifolia.* | B. Rukta-baryala. H. Lal-baryala; Bala. |
| *cordifolia.* | S. Batylacca. B. Baryala. H. Biriala. |
| *Asiatica.* | B. Jhamp-petaree; Petaree; TAM. Perintoottie. |
| *populifolia.* | T. Nugoo-benda. |
| *Mauritiana.* | H. Khitmie; Coongoonie; Kungkui. TAM. Toottie; Nellie-toottie. T. Toottie-akoo. |
| *graveolens.* | H. Bura-kungee. |
| *alnifolia.* | T. Shya-nella-benda. |
| SIDEROXYLON | |
| *grandifolium.* | B. Kali-jamera; Aoa. |
| *spinosum.* | S. Obadali. M. Courou-moelli. |
| SINAPIS | |
| *Chinensis.* | S. Rajica. H. Rai; Raiy; Riey. TAM. Kadaghoo. T Avaloo. CYNG. Gan-aba. MAH. Rie. |
| *dichotoma.* | S. Surshupa. B. Surisha; Shanchi-sursha. H. Sarsori; Surshon. |

| *Gen. and Spec.* | *Native Names.* |
|---|---|
| *glauca.* | S. Rajica. B. Shwet-raee; Sada-raee. |
| *alba.* | CYNG. Rata-aba. |
| *ramosa.* | S. Rajeeka. B. Jooni-raee. H. Rai. |
| *divaricata.* | B. Bun-raee. |
| *patens.* | B. Beel-raee. |
| *(sp?)* | S. Tuverica. H. Tori. |
| SIPHONANTHUS | |
| *Indica.* | S. Brahmuna-yustika. B. Bamunhatee. |
| *hastata.* | H. Hatti-kana. |
| SIRIUM | |
| *myrtifolium.* | H. Chandan. |
| SISYMBRIUM | |
| *Nasturtium.* | H. Loot-putiyah. |
| SMILAX | |
| *China.* | B. Shook-cheena. H. Chob-chinie. TAM. Paringay. CYNG. China-alla. |
| *glabra.* | H. Hurina; Shook-china. |
| *pseudo-china.* | H. Muheesa. |
| *ovalifolia.* | B. H. Koomarika. T. Konda-garootiga. |
| *laurifolia.* | H. Koomaree. |
| *lanceofolia.* | H. Goottia-shook-china. |
| SMITHIA | |
| *sensitiva.* | T. Nalla-kashina. H. Oda-bremi. |
| *aspera.* | B. Bhat-sola. |
| SOLANUM | |
| *pubescens.* | S. Gandheera; Shweturrihutee. B. Urush; Urusa. T. Russa-ghedi. |
| *spirale.* | B. Bagooa. |
| *tuberosum.* | B. H. Bilati-aloo. TAM. Wallarai-kilangoo. T. Ooralay. CYNG. Rata-innala. |
| *rubrum.* | B. H. Goorkhi. |
| *Melongena.* | S. Vartta. S. B. Bong; Bartakoo; Mahotee; Hingolee. B. Begoon. H. Baingan; Badanjan. T. Wangkai. |
| *longum.* | S. Koolee. B. Gooli-begoon; Kooli-begoon. T. Neer-wanga. |
| *diffusum.* | S. Surputnoo. T. Nalla-mollunga. |
| *Jacquini.* | S. Nidigdhika. S. B. H. Chudra; Kanthakaree. H. Bhatcataid; Kootaye; Dorlé. TAM. Cundunghatrie. T. Vankuda; Nela-mullika. CYNG. Katuwœl-batu. |

| *Gen. and Spec.* | *Native Names.* |
|---|---|
| *hirsutum.* | S. Chundrahasa. B. Ram-bagoon; Breehuti. |
| *Indicum.* | S. Vrihutee. B. H. Byakool; Goorkamai. H. Kolsi. TAM. Moollie. T. Tèlla-mulaka. |
| *nigrum.* | H. Maco; Tulidun. |
| *trilobatum.* | S. Alarka. TAM. Toodavullay. T. Oochinta-kurra; Moondlamosteh. CYNG. Wœltil-batu. |
| *stramonifolium.* | B. Gota-begoon. |
| SONCHUS | |
| *Orixensis.* | B. Bun-palung. T. Nalla-tapata. |
| *oleraceus-lævis.* | T. Etrinta. |
| SONERILLA | |
| *maculata.* | B. Swot. |
| SONNERATIA | |
| *acida.* | B. Our-shaka. |
| *apetala.* | B. H. Kheora. |
| SOPHORA | |
| *robusta.* | B. Peeplur. |
| SORGHUM | |
| *vulgare.* | H. Joar; Karbi; Jaundri. |
| SPERMACOCE | |
| *hispida.* | S. Madana-ghanti. TAM. Nuttei-choorie. T. Mandana-burta-kada; Madana-ghenti. CYNG. Heen-moodoogœta-kola. |
| *stricta.* | T. Loukada; Sookukada. |
| SPHENOCLEA | |
| *Zeylanica.* | H. Jeel-murich. T. Neeroo-pippul-pipli. |
| SPHŒRANTHUS | |
| *mollis.* | B. Moondee; Moontee. |
| *Indicus.* | S. Mundi. H. Moondie; Mundhi. TAM. Kottang-karundei. T. Bodatarum. CYNG. Æt-muda-mahana. |
| SPILANTHUS | |
| *oleracea.* | B. Roshuniya. |
| SPINACEA | |
| *oleracea.* | H. Palak; Isfanaj. |
| *tetrandra.* | B. Pinnees. |
| SPONDIAS | |
| *mangifera.* | S. Amratuka. B. H. Amra. H. Ambara. T. Awatum. |

| *Gen. and Spec.* | *Native Names.* |
|---|---|
| *axillaris.* | N. Neema. |
| STAPELIA | |
| *adscendens.* | T. Kar-alum. |
| STALAGMITIS | |
| *Gamboja.* | H. Osam. |
| STEMODIA | |
| *ruderalis.* | B. Huldi-busunta. |
| *viscosa.* | T. Boda-sarum. |
| STERCULIA | |
| *urens.* | H. Katira; Kooli. T. Kavali. |
| *colorata.* | T. Karaka. |
| *alata.* | B. Buddha-narikela; Toola. |
| *lanceofolia.* | B. Ushlea. |
| STILAGO | |
| *tomentosa.* | B. Tenguree. |
| STREPTIUM | |
| *asperum.* | T. Ubeera. |
| STRŒMIA | |
| *tetrandra.* | TAM. Vuelie; Wėrkoodie. T. Chimoorda; Veelivie. |
| STRYCHNOS | |
| *Nux-vomica.* | S. Kulaka; Culaka; Veeshamoostie. B. H. Koochila. TAM. Yettie. T. Moostighenza; Musadi. CYNG. Kodakaddooruatta. |
| *bicirrhosa.* | T. Kousi-kandiera. |
| *colubrina.* | B. Koochila-luta. CYNG. Maha-penala. M. Modira-caniram. |
| *axillaris.* | B. Har-cuchila. |
| *potatorum.* | S. Payaprasadi; Kutaka. B. Nirmulee. H. Nell-mall; Nirmillee; Chilbinge. TAM. Tettan-kottay. T. Induga; Tsillaghenzaloo. CYNG. Ingini. M. Tettamperel. CAN. Chittu. |
| STYRAX | |
| *officinale.* | H. Asterac. |
| *Benzoin.* | H. Ban. |
| SWIETENIA | |
| *febrifuga.* | S. Rohuna; Patranga. B. H. Rohun. TAM. Womœ-marum; Shemmarum. T. Soimido. CAN. Swamy. |
| *Chickrassa.* | B. Chickrasi. |

| Gen. and Spec. | Native Names. |
|---|---|
| *chloroxylon.* | TAM. Moodooda; Vum-maray. T. Billoo. CYNG. Boorooch-gaha. |
| SYMPHOREMA *involucrata.* | T. Suroodoo. |
| SYMPLOCOS *spicata.* | B. Booree. |
| *racemosa.* | S. Lodhra. B. Lodh; Loodh; Lodro. |
| *ferruginea.* | B. Dookatiya. |

| Spec. and Gen. | Native Names. |
|---|---|
| **T.** | |
| TABERNÆMONTANA *coronaria.* | S. B. H. Tugura. H. Firki-tagar. |
| TACCA *lævis.* | B. Moti-munda. |
| TAGETES *patula.* | B. H. Gundha-jaffree. H. Gooli-jaffri. |
| *erecta.* | B. H. Gendha. |
| TAMARINDUS *Indica.* | S. Umlika; Tintiree; Tintili. B. H. Ambli. B. Amlee; Tentool. H. Imli; Tamarihindi. TAM. Pollium. T. Chinta. CYNG. Mahasi-ambala. |
| TAMARIX *Indica.* | S. Jhavooka. B. Jhawoo. H. Jhau. |
| *dioica.* | S. Pichoola. B. H. Lall-jhawoo. |
| TECTONA *grandis.* | B. H. Segoon. CAN. Jaadi. |
| TERMINALIA *Catappa.* | S. Inguddi. B. H. Budam. H. Badamie. TAM. Nattoo-vadomcottay. T. Vadomovettillo. CYNG. Cotumba. M. Adamaram. |
| *Bellerica.* | S. Vibheetukee; Buhira. B. Boyra. B. H. Buhura. H. Bulla; Beheyra. TAM. Tamkai. T. Toadi. CYNG. Boolloo. |
| *Chebula.* | S. Hureetukee. B. Huritukee. H. Hur; Har-hara; Hulda; Hura. TAM. Kadukai. T. Kudooke; Carakaia. CYNG. Araloo. CAN. Arulay. |
| *citrina.* | S. Liba. H. Harva; Harra. CAN. Alay-gara. |
| *angustifolia.* | CAN. Mungachi. |
| *alata, v. glabra, v. tomentosa.* | S. Arjuna. B. H. Arjoon; Urjoon. H. Asan. TAM. Maradum. T. Muddie. |

| Gen. and Spec. | Native Names. |
|---|---|
| TERNSTROMIA | |
| *serrata.* | B. Waloos. |
| TETA | |
| *viridiflora.* | H. Teta. |
| TETRANTHERA | |
| *nitida.* | H. Kintoni-jam. |
| *apetala.* | S. Guja-pippuli. T. Narra-alhoghi. |
| *monopetala.* | B. Kookoor-chitta. T. Narra-mamadi. |
| *quadrifolia.* | B. Sowaree. |
| *fruticosa.* | B. Oaloa. |
| *lancæofolia.* | B. Bun-mool. |
| *macrophylla.* | B. Soorea. |
| THUNBERGIA | |
| *fragrans.* | T. Yeanadari-tiga. |
| THYMUS | |
| *(sp?)* | H. Ipar. |
| TORENIA | |
| *Asiatica.* | S. Caela-dolo. CYNG. Wœl-kotala. M. Kakapu. |
| TRADESCANTIA | |
| *axillaris.* | H. Bagha-nulla; Sottraj. TAM. Nir-pulli. T. Golla-gandi. |
| *paniculata.* | T. Kunda-amadikada. |
| *Malabarica.* | M. Tali-pulli. |
| TRAGIA | |
| *involucrata.* | S. Vrischi-putree; Doost-parisha. B. Bichitee. TAM. Canchorie. T. Doo-la-ghondi. |
| *cordata, v. cordifolia.* | S. Vandari. H. Urkasi. |
| *cannabina.* | S. Casaghinnie. H. Kanchkoori. TAM. Sirroo-canchoorie; Coorundootie. T. Doolya-gunda; Tsinna-doolagundi. |
| TRAPA | |
| *bispinosa.* | S. Sringata; Sringataka. B. Panee-phul. H. Singara. |
| *natans.* | H. Singhara. |
| TREWIA | |
| *nudiflora.* | B. H. Pitoli. |
| TRIANTHEMA | |
| *obcordata (white.)* | H. Shwet-sabuni. |
| *(red.)* | H. Lall-sabuni. |
| *decandra.* | B. Gadha-buni. |
| *crystallina.* | T. Kooka-pel-koora. |

| Gen. and Spec. | Native Names. |
|---|---|
| *monogynia.* | S. Punarnavi. H. Nasurjhinghi. TAM. Sharunnay. T. Ghelijehro. |
| *(white var.)* | S. Sweta-punarnavi. TAM. Vullay-sharunnay. T. Tella-ghelijehroo. |
| *pentandra.* | H. Bisk-hupra. |
| TRIBULUS *terrestris.* | S. Soodumostra. H. Gokooroo. TAM. Neringie. T. Putleroo. |
| *(small var.)* | S. Ructa-sudomostra. TAM. Yerra-pulleroo. |
| *lanuginosus.* | S. Goshooruka. B. Gokhoor; Goo-khyoor. |
| TRICHILIA *spinosa.* | TAM. Cat-korundoo. |
| TRICHOSANTHES *anguina.* | B. Chichinga; Jijinga; Jinga. TAM. Poodalungai. CYNG. Podi-wilanga. |
| *laciniosa.* | S. Patola. TAM. Pepoodel. T. Chaynd-polla. |
| *incisa.* | H. Birmé. TAM. Sirroo-coruttei. T. Tsinna-avagooda. |
| *dioica.* | S. Putolika. B. Putol; Pulta; H. Pulwul; Parwar. |
| *cucumerina.* | T. Adavi-putla. M. Pacta-valam. |
| *lobata.* | H. Bun-chichinga. |
| *cordata.* | H. Bhooee-komra. |
| *palmata.* | B. H. Makhal. TAM. Coruttei. T. Kaki-dunda; Avagooda. |
| *heteroclita.* | H. Goolal. |
| TRIFOLIUM *Indicum.* | S. Koostha-mashinee. B. Bun-methee. |
| *officinale.* | H. Bun-piring. |
| TRIGONELLA *Fœnum-Græcum.* | S. H. Methi. B. Methee-shak; Me-thika. H. Moothee; Methee. TAM. Vendium. T. Mentluoo. CYNG. Oolowa. CAN. Mentia. |
| *corniculata.* | S. Lunkaika; Prikka. B. Piring. |
| TRIPHASIA *aurantiola.* | B. H. China-narangi. |
| TRITICUM *æstivum.* | S. Godhooma; Soomuna. B. Gom. H. Gioon |

| Gen. and Spec. | Native Names. |
|---|---|
| TRIUMFETTA *Bartramia.* | B. H. Bun-okra. |
| TROPHIS *aspera.* | S. Sakotuka ; Sprukka. B. Sheora ; Shara. H. Suhoora ; Seeura ; Nuck-chilnie. T. Barinka ; Pukkie. CYNG. Gœta-nitul. |
| *spinosa.* | T. Sukalli. |
| TYPHA *Elephantina.* | B. Hogla ; Hoogla. T. Enuga-junum. |
| *(sp ?)* | H. Gondni. |

| Spec. and Gen. | Native Names. |
|---|---|
| **V.** | |
| VALERIANA | |
| *Jatamansi.* | S. B. H. Jutamangshee. S. H. T. Jatamansi. H. Chehur; Balehar; Sunbul. |
| *officinalis.* | H. Jal-lakri. |
| VALISNERIA | |
| *octandra.* | S. Sivala. B. Sheyala; Sheola. H. Simar; Halla. |
| *alternifolia.* | B. Rusna-janji. H. Janji. |
| *spiralis.* | H. Siwar. |
| VANGUERIA | |
| *spinosa.* | S. Pindeetuka. B. H. Muyuna; Muduna; Moina. H. Mainful. |
| VATERIA | |
| *Indica.* | CAN. Pene. |
| VENTILAGO | |
| *Madraspatana.* | |
| VERBENA | |
| *nodiflora.* | S. Vashira; Unkota. B. Bhreeng; Bhreengar. H. Bhooi-okra; Tan. TAM. Podootalei. T. Nella-pippala; Bokenakoo. CYNG. Hirimandetta. |
| VERBESINA | |
| *prostrata.* | H. Biringhie-raj; Bhringraj; Bhangra. |
| *calendulacea.* | S. Pita-bhringi. B. Keshooriya. H. Peela-bhungara. TAM. Portalay-kaian-tagerei. T. Patsoopoopulataghelingerakoo. CYNG. Ram-wankee-kirindiya. |
| *scandens.* | B. Bim-raj. H. Bim-raj. |
| *sativa.* | B. Ram-til. CAN. Kutrelle. |
| VERNONIA | |
| *anthelmintica.* | S. Kanana-iraka. H. Buckchie; Kaalie-zeerie. TAM. Caat-siragum. T Adavie-zeela-kara. |

| Gen. and Spec. | Native Names. |
|---|---|
| VICIA | |
| *sativa.* | H. Chuna; Ankuri; Jhunjhuni-ankuri; Inkri. |
| VINCA | |
| *rosea.* | H. Gool-feringa; Gul-i-farang. |
| *parviflora.* | S. Sangkhi. T. Sangkhaphuli. M. Cupaveela. |
| VIOLA | |
| *odorifera.* | H. Banafsha. |
| *suffruticosa.* | S. Charati. H. Ruttun-puruss. TAM. Orilatamaray. T. Poorusharatanum. CYNG. Mahayotu-wenna. |
| *enneasperma.* | M. Nelam-parenda. |
| VISCUM | |
| *verticillatum.* | T. Soondra-woodiniki. |
| VITEX | |
| *trifolia.* | S. Jala-nirgundi; Sindwara. H. Panee-ke-shumbalie; Nisindha; Seduri; Samalu; Sinbalu. TAM. Neernochie. T. Neeta-vavilie. M. Caranosi. |
| *Haynga.* | H. Haynga. |
| *Negundo.* | S. Sindhooka; Sinduya. B. Nirgundi. H. Nisinda; Shumbalie. TAM. Noochie. T. Wayalakoo. |
| *alata.* | B. Usoola. |
| *arborea.* | T. Boosee. |
| VITIS | |
| *Indica.* | B. H. Andhouka. |
| *latifolia.* | B. Gooila; Govila. |
| *tubifolia.* | B. Rajgazee. |
| *bracteolata.* | B. Tita-gwaleeya. |
| *vinifera.* | S. B. Draksha. B. Drakhyaluta. H. Angoor. CYNG. Muddrap-palam; Wæl-midi; Oowas. |
| *barbata.* | B. Tagora. |
| VOLKAMERIA | |
| *infortunata.* | S. Bhantee. B. Bhant. |
| *odorata.* | B. Bhantee. |
| *Madœera.* | H. Madœer. |
| *inermis.* | S. Kundali. H. Sungkoopie. TAM. Shangam-cooppy. T. Nalla-oopie; Pissinghie. CYNG. Wal-boo-randa. M. Nir-notsjit. |

| *Gen. and Spec.* | *Native Names.* |
|---|---|
| **U.** | |
| ULMUS | |
| *integrifolia.* | TAM. Nauli. T. Tambachi. |
| UNCARIA | |
| *macrophylla.* | B. Luta-kudum. |
| UNONA | |
| *longiflora.* | H. Kula-kura. |
| *discolor.* | T. Chilia-durguza. |
| *dumosa.* | B. Tubee-kura. |
| URENA | |
| *lobata.* | B. H. Bun-okra. |
| *sinuata.* | B H. Kungooya. T. Palier-mankena. |
| URTICA | |
| *tuberosa.* | T. Pilla-dumpa. |
| *pentandra.* | B. Pipeera-saree. |
| *interrupta.* | B. H. Lall-bichitee. H. Bichata. |
| *Naucliflora.* | H. Luta-kudum. |
| *globulifera.* | H. Lall-luta-kudum. |
| URTICULARIA | |
| *fasciculata.* | B. H. Jhanji. T. Natsoo. |
| *stellaris.* | T. Natsoo. |
| *diflora.* | H. Chota-jhanji. |

| *Gen. and Spec.* | *Native Names.* |
|---|---|
| UVARIA | |
| *cerasoides.* | T. Chetta-duduga. |
| *tuberosa.* | B. H. Burai-chauli. T. Chetta-duduga. |
| *longifolia.* | S. Deva-daroo. B. Debdaroo. H. Asog; Deobara. |
| *macrophylla.* | B. Bagh-runga. |
| *bracteata.* | B. Jupa-bun-kula. |
| *Bada-jamba.* | B. Bada-jamba. |
| *heteroclita.* | B. Tubee-kura. |
| *dioica.* | B. Tushee. |
| *fornicata, v. bicolor.* | B. Luta-mal. |
| *lutea.* | T. Mekari. |

| Gen. and Spec. | Native Names. |
|---|---|
| # W. | |
| WALSURA | |
| *piscidia.* | TAM. Walsura. T. Wallursi. |
| *robusta.* | B. Uphing. |
| *ternata.* | TAM. Kaka-walsura. T. Chinniwallursi. |
| WEBERA | |
| *scandens.* | B. Guja-kula. |
| *corymbosa.* | S. Kurnikara. B. H. Kanura ; Kankra. T. Boma-papata. |
| *odorata.* | B. Patagruja. |
| *tetrandra.* | S. Naga-vela. TAM. Caray-cheddy ; Madoocaré. T. Balusoo-chettoo. M. Tsjerow-kara. |
| WILLOUGHBEIA | |
| *edulis.* | B. Luti-am. |
| WRIGHTEA | |
| *caryotoides.* | B. Chilputa. |

| Gen. and Spec. | Native Names. |
|---|---|
| **X.** | |
| XANTHIUM | |
| *Indicum.* | S. Urishta. H. Ghagra; Okura. T. Veri-talla-napi. |
| XANTHOCHYMUS | |
| *pictorius.* | S. Tumala. B. Dephul. |
| *ovalifolius.* | CYNG. Ambul; Goorkha. |
| XANTHOPHYLLUM | |
| *virens.* | B. Gundhi; Gundree. |
| *flavescens.* | B. Agasyak. |
| XIMENIA | |
| *Americana.* | T. Oora-nekra. |
| *Ægyptiaca.* | H. Hingun. |
| XYLOCARPUS | |
| *Granatum.* | S. Puroosha. B. H. Pusoor. T. Kandalanga. |
| XYRIS | |
| *Indica.* | S. Dadumari. B. Cheena-ghanza; Dabi-dooba. M. Kotsjilletti-pullu; Kotsjilletri. |

| *Gen. and Spec.* | *Native Names.* |
|---|---|
| **Z.** | |
| ZANTHOXYLUM | |
| *alatum.* | H. Doomur. |
| ZEA | |
| *Mays.* | B. Mokka. H. Bhotta; Bhuta. T. Moka-juna. |
| ZINZIBER | |
| *officinalis.* | S. Ardruka; Ardrukum. B. Adruk. B. H. Ada. H. Sonth. TAM. Injie. T. Ullum. CYNG. Ammooinguroo. M. Ischi. |
| *Zerumbet.* | H. Buch; Muhahuree-buch. |
| *capitatum.* | H. Junglee-adruk. |
| *Cassumunar.* | S. Vuna-ardrukum. B. H. Bun-ada. T. Kar-pooshpa. |
| *roseum.* | T. Bhooma-kachkay. |
| ZIZIPHUS | |
| *Jujuba.* | S. Koli; Kurkhunda; Vadari. B. Kool; Budree; Narikelee-kool. H. Bier; Bayr; Beri; Nazuc; Jharberi. TAM. Elandei. T. Rengha. Reyghoo. |
| *Xylopyrus.* | T. Gotti. |
| *Caracatta.* | CAN. Caracatta. |
| *scandens.* | S. Vudura. B. Shya-kool; Shyalkanta. T. Parami. |
| *Napeia.* | S. Sookshmuphula. B. Shea-kool. T. Paramie. |
| *trinervius.* | S. Vatadalla. TAM. Carookoova. T. Kakoopala. |

# PART II.

# PART II.

## SECTION 1.

### *Sanscrit, Bengalee, Hindi, and Nawar Names.*

## A.

| | | |
|---|---|---|
| Aal, .. .. | H. | Morinda *multiflora.* |
| Abbutna, .. .. | — | Artemisia *elegans.* |
| Abee, .. .. | — | Pyrus *Cydonia.* |
| Acarcarha, .. .. | — | Parietaria *Indica.* |
| Acasnim, .. .. | — | Epidendrum *(sp ?)* |
| Acaspawan, .. .. | — | Cuscuta *reflexa.* |
| Ach, or Aech, .. | B. H. | Morinda *tinctoria.* |
| Achelia-pata, .. | B. | Pœderia *ternata.* |
| Ada, or Adruck, .. | B. H. | Zinziber *officinalis.* |
| Ada-beerna (or -birni), | B. | Gratiola *Monniera.* |
| Adas, .. .. | H. | Cicer *arietinum.* |
| Adruck, .. .. | — | Zinziber *officinalis.* |
| Adulasso, .. .. | S. | Justicia *bivalvis.* |
| Agareh, .. .. | H. | Achyranthes *aspera.* |
| Agarikoon, .. .. | — | Boletus *igniarius.* |
| Agast, .. .. | — | Æschynomene *grandiflora.* |
| Agasyak, .. .. | B. | Xanthophyllum *flavescens.* |
| Agni-mantha, .. | S. | Premna *integrifolia.* |
| Agnee, .. .. | B. | Plumbago *Zeylanica.* |
| Agooroo, .. .. | — | Aquillaria (or Amyris) *Agallocha.* |
| Agosthyo, .. .. | — | Dillenia *scabrella.* |
| Agumukee, .. .. | H. | Bryonia *scabrella.* |
| Agya-ghas, .. .. | H. | Andropogon *Schœnanthus.* |
| Agya-sak, .. .. | B. | Xanthophyllum *flavescens.* |
| Ahilaykum, .. | S. | Bryonia *scabra.* |
| Ajaji, .. .. | — | Cuminum *Cyminum.* |
| Ajas-ringgi, .. | S. | Odina *Wodier.* |
| Ajmood or Ajamooda, | S. H. | Apium *involucratum.* |
| Ajouan, .. .. | B. H. | Ligusticum *Ajouan.* |

| | | |
|---|---|---|
| Ak, .. .. | H. | Asclepias *gigantea.* |
| Akanda-phul, .. | — | Modecca *trilobata.* |
| Akar-kanta, .. . | — | Allangium *hexapetalum.* |
| Akasha-vullee; Akash-bullee, .. .. | S. B. | Cassyata *filiformis.* |
| Akhoo-purnee, .. | S. | Salvinea *cucullata.* |
| Akhooroot, .. .. | B. | Aleurites *triloba.* |
| Akkoss, .. .. | — | Rottlera *dicocca.* |
| Akrot, . .. | H. | Juglans *regia.* |
| Akund, .. .. | B. | Asclepias *gigantea.* |
| Al, .. .. | H. | Morinda *citrifolia.* |
| Alada-choonari, .. | B. | Pschychotria *Asiatica,* or *adenophylla.* |
| Alarka, .. .. | S. | Solanum *trilobatum,* or Asclepias *gigantea, (white.)* |
| Algosa, .. .. | B. H. | Cuscuta *capitata.* |
| Algooch, .. .. | — | Cymbidium *tesselloides.* |
| Alkooshi, .. .. | B. | Carpopogon *pruriens.* |
| Aloo, .. .. | — | Solanum *tuberosum.* |
| Alsi, . .. | H. | Linum *usitatissimum.* |
| Alu, .. .. | — | Arum *campanulatum.* |
| Alucha, .. .. | — | Prunus *domestica.* |
| Alugnuta, .. .. | — | Cymbidium *tessalloides.* |
| Am, .. .. | B. H. | Mangifera *Indica.* |
| Amaba-huldi, .. | — | Curcuma *reclinata.* |
| Amada, . .. | B. | ——— *Amada.* |
| Amara-buruhi, .. | S. | Erythroxylon *areolatum.* |
| Ambara, .. .. | H. | Spondias *mangifera.* |
| Ambashta, .. .. | S. | Oxalis *corniculata.* |
| Ambie-huldie, .. | H. | Curcuma *Zedoaria.* |
| Ambli, .. .. | B. H. | Tamarindus *Indica.* |
| Ambuj, .. . | H. | Nelumbium *speciosum.* |
| Amdhouka, .. .. | — | Vitis *Indica.* |
| Amla, .. .. | B. H. | Phyllanthus *Emblica.* |
| Amlaki, .. .. | H. | P——— E——— |
| Amlee, .. .. | B. | Tamarindus *Indica.* |
| Amlej, .. .. | H. | Phyllanthus *Emblica.* |
| Amlika, .. .. | S. | Oxalis *corniculata.* |
| Amlukee, .. .. | B. | Mimosa *stipulata.* |
| Amoora, .. .. | — | Andersonia *cucullata.* |
| Am-puraroha, .. | B. | Loranthus *ampullaceus.* |
| Amra, .. .. | B. H. | Mangifera *Indica,* or Spondias *mangifera.* |
| Amratuka, .. .. | S. | Spondias *mangifera.* |
| Amrita, .. .. | — | Menispermum *cordifolium.* |
| Amrool, .. .. | B. H. | Oxalis *corniculata.* |

| | | |
|---|---|---|
| **Amrud,** .. .. | H. | Pyrus *communis.* |
| Amrut, .. .. | — | Psidium *pyriferum.* |
| Amshunatty-divandiva, | S. | Cassia *senna.* |
| Amultus, .. .. | H. | ——— *fistula.* |
| **Amulukee,** .. .. | S. | Phyllanthus *Emblica.* |
| Ananus, .. .. | B. H. | Bromelia *Ananas.* |
| **Anar,** .. .. | H. | Punica *Granatum.* |
| Anarush, .. .. | B. | Bromelia *Ananas.* |
| Anaspool, .. .. | H. | Illicium *anisatum.* |
| Anchu, .. .. | — | Rubus *(sp ?)* |
| Anderjow, .. .. | — | Nerium *antidysentericum.* |
| Angoor, .. .. | — | Vitis *vinifera.* |
| Anis, .. .. | — | Justicia *Adhatoda.* |
| Anjeer, .. .. | B. | Psidium *pyriferum,* or *pomiferum.* |
| Ankuri, .. .. | H. | Vicia *sativa.* |
| Anol, .. .. | B. | Arundo *bifaria.* |
| Anola, .. .. | H. | Phyllanthus *Emblica.* |
| Anonto-mool, .. | B. | Periploca *Indica,* or Asclepias *pseudosarsa.* |
| Antomoora, .. .. | — | Helicteres *Isora.* |
| Aoa, .. .. | — | Sideroxylon *grandifolium.* |
| Aongra, .. .. | H. | Phyllanthus *Emblica.* |
| **Aoonla,** .. .. | — | P——— E———. |
| Apanga, .. .. | B. | Achyranthus *aspera.* |
| Apurajita, .. .. | — | Clitorea *ternata.* |
| Aralu, .. .. | S. | Ailanthus *excelsa.* |
| Arbi, .. .. | H. | Arum *Colocasia.* |
| Ardruka ; Ardrukum, | — | Zinziber *officinalis.* |
| Arhukee, .. .. | — | Cytisus *Cajan.* |
| Arishta, .. .. | — | Sapindus *emarginatus.* |
| Arishto, .. .. | B. | Melia *Azadirachta.* |
| Aristaphenila, .. | S. | Sapindus *detergens.* |
| Arittamungayrie, .. | — | Acalypha *Indica.* |
| Arjaka, .. .. | — | Ocymum *album,* or *sanctum.* |
| Arjata, .. .. | — | Phyllanthus *Niruri.* |
| Arjuna, .. .. | — | Terminalia *alata.* |
| Arjoon, .. .. | B. | ——— *glabra.* |
| Arjura, .. .. | — | Phyllanthus *tetrandrus.* |
| Arko, .. .. | — | Calotropis *gigantea.* |
| Armatees, .. .. | B. H. | Hibiscus *diversifolius.* |
| Aroona, .. .. | B. | Rubia *Munjistha.* |
| Aruni, .. .. | S. | Phyllanthus *rhamnoides.* |
| Arundi or Arund, .. | H. | Ricinus *communis.* |
| Arus, .. .. | — | Justicia *Adhatoda.* |

| | | |
|---|---|---|
| Arushkara, .. .. | S. | Semecarpus *Anacardiun.* |
| Aruya, .. .. | — | Oryza *sativa.* |
| Arzan, .. .. | H. | Panicum *pilosum.* |
| Asaf, .. .. | — | Capparis *Spinosa.* |
| Asan, .. .. | — | Terminalia *alata, or glabra.* |
| Asgand, .. .. | — | Justicia *Adhatoda.* |
| Ashoo-kuchoo, .. | B. | Arum *Colocasia,* 1*st. var.* |
| A——vrihi, .. .. | S. | Oryza *sativa.* |
| Asog, .. .. | H. | Uvaria *longifolia.* |
| Asphota, .. .. | — | Clitoria *ternata.* |
| Ashphota, .. .. | S. B. | Jasminum *Zambac,* or Calotropis *gigantea.* |
| Ashphul, .. .. | B. | Scytalia *Longan.* |
| Ash-shoura, .. | — | Limonia *pentaphylla.* |
| Ashwutta, .. . | — | Ficus *religiosa.* |
| Asterac, .. .. | H. | Styrax *officinalis.* |
| Astma-bayda, .. | S. | Achyranthes *lanata.* |
| Ata, .. .. | B. H. | Annona *squamosa.* |
| Atasi, .. .. | S. | Linum *usitatissimum.* |
| Atoosi, . .. | B. | ( ? ) |
| Atmagoopta-murkutee, | — | Carpopogon *pruriens.* |
| Atta-jam, .. .. | B. | Olea *dioica.* |
| Auoa-champa, .. | — | Liriodendron *liliifera.* |
| Avigna, .. .. | S. | Carissa *Carundas, (black.)* |
| Avurtunnie, .. | — | Helicteres *Isora.* |
| Axka, .. .. | — | Asclepias *gigantea.* |

## SECTION 2.

### *Tamool, Telinga, Cyngalese, Malealie, Mahratta, and Canarese Names.*

## A.

| | | |
|---|---|---|
| Aat-alarie, .. .. | TAM. | Polygonum *barbatum.* |
| Abara, .. .. | CYNG. | Arum *macrorhizon.* |
| Acha or Atti, .. | TAM. | Hardwickia *binata.* |
| Ada, .. .. | T. | Bauhinia *racemosa.* |
| Adatodey, .. .. | TAM. | Justicia *Adhahota.* |
| Adalavitiloo, .. | T. | Arabis *Chinensis.* |
| Adamarum, .. .. | M. | Terminalia *Catappa.* |
| Adasara, .. .. | — | Justicia *Adhatoda.* |
| Adavi-pulla, .. .. | T. | Trichosanthes *Cucumerina.* |
| Addaleyunnay, .. | TAM. | Jatropha *glauca.* |
| Addatinapalay, .. | — | Aristolochia *bracteata.* |
| Adavie-zeela-kara, .. | T. | Vernonia *anthelmintica.* |
| Adhotoda, .. .. | CYNG. | Justicia *Adhatoda.* |
| Adiva-chama, .. | T. | Arum *sylvaticum.* |
| A——kunda, .. | — | —— *lyratum.* |
| Adive-cunda, .. | — | Dracontium *polyphyllum.* |
| A——palla-tiga, .. | — | Nerium *reticulatum.* |
| A——malle, .. .. | — | Jasminum *angustifolium.* |
| A——mulli, . .. | — | —— *latifolium.* |
| Addivitella-guddaloo, . | — | Erythronium *Indicum.* |
| Ætadiya, .. .. | CYNG. | Elephantophus *scaber.* |
| Ætora, .. .. | — | Cassia *alata.* |
| Æt-nauda-mahana, .. | — | Sphæranthus *Indicus.* |
| Æt-nerenchi, .. | — | Pedalium *murex.* |
| Agasatamaray, .. | TAM. | Pistia *stratiotes.* |
| Agati, .. .. | — | Æschynomene *grandiflora,* (*white* and *red.*) |
| Agokara, .. .. | T. | Momordica *dioica.* |
| Aguba, .. .. | — | Capparis *corymbosa.* |
| Agunda-pacoo, .. | CYNG. T. | Ammania *vesicatoria.* |
| Ahilla, .. .. | CYNG. | Cassia *fistula.* |
| Ailum-cheddy, .. | M. | Elettaria *Cardamomum.* |
| Akasagherooda-gudda, | T. | Bryonia *epigæa.* |
| Alanga, .. .. | CYNG. | Convolvolus *grandiflorus.* |

| | | |
|---|---|---|
| Alaverei, .. .. | Tam. | Ficus *Indica.* |
| Alay-gara, .. .. | Can. | Terminalia *Citrina.* |
| Albin-atta, .. .. | Cyng. | Papaver *somniferum.* |
| All, .. .. | T. | Linum *usitatissimum.* |
| Alla-batsalla, .. .. | — | Basella *alba.* |
| Alla-galli-gheetsa, .. | — | Crotalaria *verrucosa.* |
| Alle, .. .. | Tam. | Linum *usitatissimum.* |
| Allooria, .. .. | T. | Hedysarum *bupleurifolium.* |
| Alpear, .. .. | — | Grewia *didyma.* |
| Alu-bo-dan, .. .. | Cyng. | Calyptranthes *Jambolana.* |
| Amadum, .. .. | T. | Ricinus *communis.* |
| Amaun-patcheh-arisee, | Tam. | Euphorbia *pilulifera.* |
| Ambul-goorka, .. | Cyng. | Xanthochymus *ovalifolius.* |
| Amei-nerunshil, .. | Tam. | Pedalium *murex.* |
| Amkoolang, .. .. | — | Physalis *flexuosa.* |
| Ammoo-inghuroo, .. | Cyng. | Zinziber *officinalis.* |
| Ananeringie, .. | Tam. | Pedalium *murex.* |
| Anasepoo, .. .. | — | Illicium *Anisatum.* |
| Ana-shovadi, .. | M. | Elephantophus *scaber.* |
| Anasie, .. .. | Cyng.<br>Tam. | Bromelia *Ananas.* |
| Ancadoo, .. .. | R. | Leea *staphylea.* |
| Andabeerakoo, .. | — | Ballota *disticha.* |
| Angakara, .. .. | — | Momordica *dioica.* |
| Anjeli, .. .. | Mah. | Artocarpus *hirsuta.* |
| Ankados, .. .. | T. | Leea *staphylea.* |
| Annapa, .. .. | — | Dolichos *Lablab, 3d var.* |
| A—— chicureay, .. | — | —— —— *4th var.* |
| Antara-tamara, .. | — | Menyanthes *Indica, or cristata.* |
| Anykoota, .. .. | — | Combretum *decandrum.* |
| Appakovay, .. .. | — | Bryonia *rostrata.* |
| Aralivayr, .. .. | Tam. | Nerium *odorum.* |
| Araloo, .. .. | Cyng. | Terminalia *Chebula.* |
| Arasum, .. .. | T. | Ficus *religiosa.* |
| Ardel (or Adel-) odagam, .. .. | M. | Justicia *bivalvis.* |
| Areka, .. .. | Tam. | Bauhinia *parviflora.* |
| Aria-veela, .. .. | M. | Cleome *viscosa.* |
| Aria-bepou, .. .. | — | Melia *Azadirachta.* |
| Arelli, .. .. | T. | Musa *sapientum.* |
| Arrooa-manoopoondoo, | Tam. | Sida *lanceolata.* |
| Aroods, .. .. | Cyng.<br>Tam. | Ruta *graveolens.* |
| Arroe, .. .. | T. | Bauhinia *parviflora.* |
| Arry-koota, .. .. | — | Combretum *decandrum.* |

| | | |
|---|---|---|
| Arsina, .. .. | Cyng. | Curcuma *longa.* |
| Arulay, .. .. | Can. | Terminalia *Chebula.* |
| Attadi, .. .. | Cyng. | Justicia *paniculata.* |
| Attie, .. .. | Tam. | Ficus *racemosa.* |
| Attika-mamedie, .. | T. | Boerhavia *diffusa.* |
| Auroots, (or Aurooch,) | | |
| ———hangali, .. | — | Andropogon *montanum.* |
| Avagooda, .. .. | — | Trichosanthes *palmata.* |
| Avaki, .. .. | — | Æschynomene *grandiflora,* (*white* and *red.*) |
| Avaloo, .. .. | — | Sinapis *Chinensis.* |
| Avary, .. . | — | Cassia *auriculata.* |
| Avatenga-tiga, .. | — | Dioscorea *oppositifolia.* |
| Averie, .. .. | Tam. | Indigofera *tinctoria.* |
| Awatum, .. .. | T. | Spondias *mangifera.* |
| Awusada-nelli, .. | Cyng. | Phyllanthus *Emblica.* |
| Awusada-wæla-kola, .. | — | Cleome *pentaphylla.* |
| Ayapana, .. .. | — | Justicia *bivalvis.* |

## Section 1.

### *Sanscrit, Bengally, Hindi, &c.*

# B.

| | | |
|---|---|---|
| Babai, .. .. | H. | Ocymum *pilosum.* |
| Baberung or Babreng, | B. H. | Embelia *ribes.* |
| Babooi-toolshee or toolsi, .. .. | B. | Ocymum *pilosum.* |
| Babula, .. .. | B. H. | Mimosa *Arabica.* |
| Babuna, .. .. | H. | Anthemis *nobilis.* |
| Bacchi, .. .. | — | Serratula *anthelmintica.* |
| Bach, .. .. | — | Iris *germanica* or Acorus *calamus.* |
| Baclatul-humka, .. | — | Portulacca *quadrifida.* |
| Bacul, .. .. | — | Mimusops *Elengi.* |
| Bacumber, .. .. | — | Ajuga *disticha.* |
| Bada-jamba, .. .. | B. | Uvaria *Badajamba.* |
| Badam, .. .. | H. | Amygdalus *Persicus.* |
| B——gota, .. .. | — | Castanea *Indica.* |
| Badamie or Badam, .. | B. H. | Terminalia *Catappa.* |
| Badanjan, .. .. | H. | Solanum *Melongena.* |
| Badranjboyu, .. | — | Melissa *(sp?)* |
| Badyan, .. .. | — | Pimpinella *Anisum.* |
| Bag-achera, .. .. | B. | Pisonia *aculeata.* |
| B—ankra, .. .. | — | Allangium *hexapetalum.* |
| Bagh-bherenda, .. | B. H. | Jatropha *Curcas.* |
| Bagha-luta, .. .. | H. | Menispermum *polycarpon.* |
| B——nulla, .. .. | — | Tradescantia *axillaris.* |
| Bagh-nukhooa-shim, .. | B. | Dolichos *lignosus, var.* 2. |
| B——rungga, .. | — | Uvaria *macrophylla.* |
| Bagoon, .. .. | — | Solanum *spirale.* |
| Bagoon or Begoon, .. | B. H. | ——— *Melongena.* |
| Bagrendi, .. .. | H. | Jatropha *Curcas.* |
| Bahira, .. .. | S. | Terminalia *Bellerica.* |
| Bahuar, .. .. | H. | Cordia *Myxa* or *latifolia.* |
| Bahubanie, .. .. | S. | Mirabilis *Jalapa.* |
| Baingan, .. .. | H. | Solanum *Melongena.* |
| Bair, .. .. | — | Zizyphus *Jujuba.* |
| Baishee, .. . | B. | Salix *tetrasperma* or *Babylonica* or *tetrandra.* |

| | | |
|---|---|---|
| Bakas or Bakus, .. | B. H. | Justicia *Adhatoda.* |
| Bakla, .. .. | — | Phaseolus *vulgaris.* |
| Baksha, .. .. | B. | Rotbœllia *glabra.* |
| Bala, .. .. | S. | Pavonia *odorata.* |
| B—, .. .. | S. B. | Hibiscus *tortuosus.* |
| B—, .. .. | H. | Andropogon *muricatus.* |
| B—, .. .. | — | Sida *rhombifolia.* |
| Balam-cira, .. .. | — | Cucumis *sativa.* |
| Balchar, .. .. | — | Valeriana *Jatamansi.* |
| Baltar, .. .. | — | Borassus *flabelliformis.* |
| Balungoo, .. .. | — | Ocymum (*sp ?*) |
| Bamunhatee, .. | B. | Siphonanthus *Indicus.* |
| Ban, .. .. | H. | Styrax *Benzoin,* or Hyperanthera *Morunga.* |
| Banafsha, .. .. | — | Viola *odorifera.* |
| Banchan, .. .. | — | Psoralia *corylifolia.* |
| Banda, .. .. | — | Epidendrum *tessalloides.* |
| Bandhari-bet, .. | — | Calamus *tenuis.* |
| Bandhuka, .. .. | S. | Ixora *Bandhuka.* |
| Bandoor-pala, .. | B. | Aglaia *polystachya.* |
| Bandoonee, .. .. | — | Ixora *Bandhuka.* |
| Bang, .. .. | H. | Hyosciamus *niger,* or Quercus (*sp ?*) |
| Bans or Bansh, .. | B. H. | Bambusa *arundinacea.* |
| Bansoe, .. .. | H. | Hedysarum *Cephalotes.* |
| Bansputta, . .. | — | Amaranthus *atropurpureus.* |
| ——— nuteeya, .. | B. | ——— *lanceofolius.* |
| Banstara, .. .. | H. | Barleria *cærulea.* |
| Ban-pering, .. .. | — | Trifolium *officinale.* |
| Bansooa-batana, .. | B. | Quercus *turbinatus.* |
| Bantarai, .. .. | H. | Luffa *fætida.* |
| Bantulsa, .. .. | — | Ocymum (*sp ?*) |
| Baqilla, .. .. | — | Vicia (*sp ?*) |
| Bar, .. .. | — | Ficus *Bengalensis* or *Indica.* |
| Baral, .. .. | — | Artocarpus *Lacucha.* |
| Barbura, .. .. | S. | Mimosa *Arabica.* |
| Bariala, .. .. | H. | Sida *cordifolia.* |
| Barna, .. .. | — | Cratæva *Tapia.* |
| Bartakoo, .. .. | B. | Solanum *Melongena.* |
| Barur-kulai, .. .. | H. | Dolichos *scarabæoides.* |
| Baryala, .. .. | B. | Sida *cordifolia.* |
| Basoka, .. .. | — | Justicia *Adhatoda.* |
| Basontee, .. .. | — | Gærtnera *racemosa.* |
| Basook, .. .. | — | Pschychotria *ophioxyloides.* |

| | | |
|---|---|---|
| **Bastara,** .. .. | B. | Callicarpa *Americana.* |
| **Bassana,** .. .. | H. | Æschynomene *grandiflora,* (*white* and *red.*) |
| **Bastra,** .. .. | — | Callicarpa *lanata.* |
| **Basunt,** .. .. | — | Linum *trigynum.* |
| **Bat,** .. .. | — | Ficus *Indica.* |
| **Batas-mundulee,** .. | B. | Robinia *candida.* |
| **Batavi-neeboo,** .. | B. H. | Citrus *decumanus.* |
| **Bathua,** .. .. | H. | Chenopodium *album.* |
| **Batia-rung, or Beta-rung,** .. .. | B. | Justicia *tinctoria.* |
| **Batiwa,** .. .. | — | Millingtonia *pinnata.* |
| **Batoola,** .. .. | — | Cicer *arietinum.* |
| **Batyalaka,** .. .. | S. | Sida *cordifolia.* |
| **Bawanhatti,** .. .. | H. | Ovieda *verticillata.* |
| **Bebina,** .. .. | | Mussænda *frondosa.* |
| **Bed,** .. .. | — | Calamus *Rotang.* |
| **Bedana,** .. .. | — | Morus (*sp ?*) |
| **Beedul,** .. .. | B. | Bauhinia *variegata ?* |
| **Beedrukarun,** .. | — | Cissampelos *hexandra.* |
| **Beejapoora,** .. .. | S. | Citrus-*medica, var.* 1. |
| **Beel-jhun-jhun,** .. | H. | Crotolaria *retusa.* |
| **B—luta,** .. .. | — | Mentha *secunda.* |
| **B—paat,** .. .. | — | Melochia *corchorifolia.* |
| **B—raee,** .. .. | — | Sinapis *patens.* |
| **Beemboo,** .. .. | B. | Momordica *monadelpha.* |
| **Beera,** .. .. | — | Asclepias *rosea.* |
| **Beer-bruika,** .. .. | H. | Arum *curvatum.* |
| **Beertia,** .. .. | — | Panicum *Italicum.* |
| **Beerung or Berung,** .. | B. | ? |
| **Beegoon,** .. . | — | Solanum *Melongena.* |
| **Begpoora,** .. .. | B. H. | Citrus-*medica, var.* 1. |
| **Behee,** .. .. | H. | Pyrus *Cydonia.* |
| **Behoor-bansh,** .. | B. | Bambusa *spinosa.* |
| **Beheyra,** .. .. | H. | Terminalia *Bellerica.* |
| **Behooa,** .. .. | B. | Cyperus *difformis.* |
| **Bel,** .. .. { | B. H. | Ægle *Marmelos.* |
| | H. | Cratæva *religiosa.* |
| **Bela,** .. .. | B. H. | Sapium *baccatum.* |
| **B—,** .. .. | H. | Jasminum *Zambac.* |
| **Belai-chooi,** .. .. | — | Dolichos *scarabæoides.* |
| **Belawine,** .. .. | — | Semecarpus *Anacardium.* |
| **Belphool,** .. .. | B. | Jasminum *Zambac.* |
| **Bena,** .. .. | H. B. | Andropogon *muricatus.* |
| **Bena-joni,** .. .. | B. | Agrostis *diandra.* |
| **Beri,** .. .. | H. | Zizyphus *Jujuba.* |

| | | |
|---|---|---|
| Beshulyo-kurunee, .. | B. | Menispermum *cordifolium.* |
| Beta or Bet, .. .. | B. H. | Calamus *Rotang.* |
| Beta-runga or Batia-rung, .. .. | B. | Justicia *tinctoria.* |
| Betmajnu, .. .. | H. | Salix *Babylonica.* |
| Betoya or Beto-sag, .. | B. | Chenopodium *album.* |
| Bhair, .. .. | H. | Zizyphus *Jujuba.* |
| Bhalava-anga, .. | S. | Jussieua *suffruticosa.* |
| Bhallataka, .. .. | — | Semecarpus *Anacardium.* |
| Bhamber or Bhambul, | H. | Nymphæa *Lotus.* |
| Bhang, .. .. | — | Cannabis *sativa.* |
| Bhanga, .. { | B. | Indigofera *linifolia.* |
| | S. | Cannabis *sativa.* |
| Bhangra, .. .. | H. | Verbesina *prostrata.* |
| Bhant, .. .. | B. | Volkameria *infortunata.* |
| Bhantee, .. .. | S. | V——— *infortunata.* |
| Bhantee, .. .. | S. B. H. | V——— *odorata.* |
| Bharband or Bherband, | H. | Argemone *Mexicana.* |
| Bharudwajee, .. | S. | Hibiscus *vitifolius.* |
| Bhatcataid, .. .. | H. | Solanum *Jacquini.* |
| Bhat-shola, .. .. | B. | Smithia *aspera.* |
| Bheela or Bhela, .. | H. | Semecarpus *Anacardium.* |
| Bheka-purni, .. | S. | Hydrocotyle *Asiatica.* |
| Bhelaman or Bhelawan, | H. | Semecarpus *Anacardium.* |
| Bhend, .. .. | — | Æschynomene *arborea.* |
| Bherband, .. .. | — | Argemone *Mexicana.* |
| Bhimb, .. .. | — | Momordica *monadelpha.* |
| Bhinda-tori or Bhindea, | — | Hibiscus *esculentus.* |
| Bhoj, .. .. | — | Betula *Bhoorja.* |
| Bhoo-ada or Bhon-ada, | B. | Hedychium *angustifolium.* |
| Bhooee-komra, .. | H. | Trichosanthes *cordata.* |
| Bhooi-chumpa, .. | B. H. | Kæmpferia *rotunda.* |
| B——dalim, .. | B. | Careya *herbacea.* |
| B——doomoor, .. | H. | Ficus *repens.* |
| B——jam, .. .. | B. | Ardisia *Solanacea.* |
| B——jamba, .. | — | Premna *herbacea.* |
| B——koomra, .. | B. H. | Convolvulus *paniculatus*, or Trichosanthes *tuberosa.* |
| B——moora, .. | H. | Phyllyrea *robusta.* |
| B——okra, .. .. | — | Verbena *nodiflora.* |
| B——sunn, .. .. | B. | Crotolaria *prostrata.* |
| Bhoo-luvunga, .. | S. | Jussieua *exaltata.* |
| Bhoomi-chumpuka, .. | — | Kæmpferia *rotunda.* |
| B———darimba, .. | — | Careya *herbacea.* |
| B———jumboca, .. | — | Premna *herbacea.* |
| B———kuwa, .. | B. | Garcinia *Boomicowa.* |
| B———nim, .. | — | Gratiola *serrata.* |

| | | |
|---|---|---|
| Bhoomi-pat, .. .. | B. | Dentella *repens*. |
| Bhoonamtol, .. .. | H. | Dracæna *terniflora*. |
| Bhoorj, .. .. | B. | Betula *Bhoorja*. |
| Bhooroondee, .. | S. | Heliotropium *Indicum*. |
| Bhoostrina, .. .. | — | Andropogon *Schænanthus*. |
| Bhoo-toolsee, .. | B. | Salvia *brachiata*. |
| Bhoot-bhiruvee, .. | — | Premna *serratifolia*. |
| B——raj, .. . | — | Ophioglossum *flexuosum*. |
| Bhoovuduree, .. | S. | Rhamnus *circumcissus*. |
| Bhorar, .. .. | B. | Rhizophora *Mangle*. |
| Bhorenda, .. .. | — | Ricinus *communis*. |
| Bhotta, .. .. | H. | Zea *Mays*. |
| Bhramok, .. .. | B. | Helianthus *annuus*. |
| Bhreeng or Bhreenga, | — | Verbesina *calendulacea*. |
| Bhringraj, .. .. | H. | ——— *prostrata*. |
| Bhudra or Bhudra-bula, | S. | Phrynium *dichotomum*. |
| Bhudroudounee, .. | — | ——— ———. |
| Bhu-kapittham, .. | — | Feronia *Elephantum*. |
| Bhulla-takee, .. | — | Semecarpus *Anacardium*. |
| Bhumowra, .. .. | H. | Cornus *capitata*. |
| Bhunblai, .. .. | — | Fragaria *vesca*. |
| Bhuneampa, .. .. | — | Kæmpferia *rotunda*. |
| Bhungie, .. .. | — | Corchorus *olitorius*. |
| Bhuta, .. .. | — | Zea *Mays*. |
| Bhuta-ghni, .. | S. | Ballota *disticha*. |
| Bibzar, .. .. | H. | Murraya *exotica*. |
| Bichata, .. .. | — | Urtica *interrupta*. |
| Bichittie, .. .. | B. | Tragia *involucrata*. |
| Bichua, .. .. | H. | Crotolaria *juncea*. |
| Bidarie, .. .. | S. | Gmelina *Asiatica*. |
| Bier, .. .. | H. | Zizyphus *Jujuba*. |
| Bihi, .. .. | — | Cydonia *vulgaris*. |
| Bijoolee-chulack, .. | B. | Dracæna *ferræa*. |
| Bikh, .. .. | H. | Aconitum *(sp ?)* |
| Bilati-aloo, .. .. | — | Solanum *tuberosum*. |
| Bila-murich, .. .. | B. | Coffea *Arabica*. |
| Bilzar, .. .. | H. | Murraya *exotica*. |
| Bimraj, .. .. | — | Verbesina *scandens*. |
| Bina, .. .. | B. H. | Avicennia *tomentosa*. |
| Bincha, .. .. | B. | Flacourtia *sapida*. |
| Binda-gooea, .. | H. | Arum *sessiliflorum*. |
| Biniyar, .. .. | B. | Hedysarum *gyroides*. |
| Birchin, .. .. | H. | Rhamnus *Jujuba*. |
| Biriala, .. .. | — | Sida *cordifolia*. |
| Biringhie-raj, .. | — | Verbesina *prostrata*. |
| Birme, .. .. | — | Trichosanthes *incisa*. |

| | | | |
|---|---|---|---|
| Birmi, | .. .. | H. | Cratæva *Tapia*. |
| Birnak, | .. .. | — | Asphodelus *(sp ?)* |
| Birti, | .. .. | — | Panicum *(sp ?)* |
| Bis or Bish, .. | .. | B. H. | Aconitum *ferox*. |
| Bisfez, | .. .. | H. | Polypodium *vulgare*. |
| Bish-bansh, .. | .. | — | Bambusa *baccifera*. |
| B——kuchoo, | .. | — | Calla *virosa*. |
| B——man, .. | .. | B. | Arum *cucullatum*. |
| B——tarak, .. | .. | H. | Lettsomia *nervosa*. |
| Bisk-hupra, .. | .. | — | Trianthema *pentandra*. |
| Bislumba, | .. .. | — | Cucumis *Colocynthis*. |
| Biur, | .. .. | — | Zizyphus *Jujuba*. |
| Bokenakoo, .. | .. | — | Verbena *nodiflora*. |
| Bol, | .. .. | — | Myrrha *odorifera*. |
| Bola, | .. .. | B. H. | Hibiscus *tortuosus* or *tiliaceus*. |
| Bolus, | .. .. | B. | Juglans *pterococca*. |
| Bomla, | .. .. | H. | Fragaria *vesca*. |
| Bong, | .. .. | B. | Solanum *Melongena*. |
| Booien-aoonlah, | .. | H. | Phyllanthus *Niruri*. |
| ———kavite, | .. | — | Feronia *Elephantum*. |
| Boollee-sowa, | .. | N. | Androsasce *cordifolia*. |
| Boorans, | .. .. | H. | Rhododendron *arborea*. |
| Booree, | .. .. | B. | Symplocos *spicata*. |
| Boot ; Boot-kulai, | .. | B. H. | Cicer *arietinum*. |
| Bootankushum, | .. | S. | Nepeta *Malabarica*. |
| Boovishirum, | .. | — | Phyllanthus *Niruri*. |
| Bora, | .. .. | H. | Dolichos *Catjang*. |
| Bores, | .. .. | B. | Symplocos *spicata*. |
| Boruti, | .. .. | — | Panicum *paludosum*. |
| Botallapotaka, | .. | S. | Cassia *Senna*. |
| Boyra, | .. .. | B. | Terminalia *Bellerica*. |
| Bramhadurbha, | .. | S. | Ligusticum *Ajouan*. |
| Bramhie, | .. .. | — | Argemone *Mexicana*. |
| Bramhi, | .. .. | — | Ruta *graveolens*. |
| Brahmunayustica, | .. | — | Siphonanthus *Indica*. |
| Brahn-murich, | .. | — | Capsicum *frutescens*. |
| Breehuti, | .. .. | B. | Solanum *hirsutum*. |
| Brinraj or Brinraji, | .. | S. H. | Eclipta *prostrata*. |
| Buch, | .. .. | H. | Zinziber *Zerumbet*. |
| Buckchie, | .. .. | — | Vernonia *anthelmintica*. |
| Budam, | .. .. | — | Terminalia *Catappa*. |
| B——, | .. .. | S.B.H. | Amygdalus *communis*. |
| Budbuhuri, | . .. | B. | Limodorum *bicolor*. |
| Buddha-narikella, | .. | — | Sterculia *alata*. |
| Budree, | .. .. | — | Zyziphus *Jujuba*. |

| | | | |
|---|---|---|---|
| Budrunga, .. | .. | B. | Fagaria *Budrunga.* |
| Bugua, .. | .. | — | Solanum *spirale.* |
| Buhooari, .. | .. | — | Cordia *Myxa* or *latifolia.* |
| Buhoovaruka, | .. | S. | ——— *Myxa.* |
| Buhura, .. | .. | B. H. | Terminalia *Bellerica.* |
| Bujjirbhang, | .. | H. | Nicotiana *Tabacum.* |
| Bujra or Bujra-batool, | | B. H. | Corypha *elata.* |
| Bujura, .. | .. | H. | Panicum *spicatum.* |
| Buka, .. | { | B. | Æschynomene *grandiflora.* |
| | | — | Sesbana *grandifolia.* |
| Bukain, .. | .. | H. | Melia *sempervirens.* |
| Bukampadaruka, | .. | S. | Cordia *Myxa.* |
| Bukool, .. | .. | B. | Mimusops *Elengi.* |
| Bukum, .. | .. | — | Cæsalpinia *Sappan.* |
| Bulat, .. | .. | — | Phassæolus *Mungo.* |
| Bulla, .. | .. | H. | Terminalia *Bellerica.* |
| Bullum-doomoor, | .. | B. | Ficus *scabrella.* |
| Bun-ach, .. | .. | — | Morinda *exerta.* |
| B—ada, .. | .. | B. H. | Zinziber *Cassumunar.* |
| B—ajoan, .. | .. | B. | Ligusticum *diffusum.* |
| B—asarhoo, .. | .. | H. | Gossypium *herbaceum.* |
| B—baburee, | .. | — | Salvia *brachiata.* |
| B—burbutee, | ..{ | — | Dolichos *Gangeticus.* |
| | | B. H. | Phaseolus *alatus.* |
| B—challa, .. | .. | — | Leea *crispa.* |
| B—champa, .. | .. | B. | *(?)* |
| B—chandur, | .. | B.H. | Flagellaria *Indica.* |
| B—chichinga, | .. | H. | Trichosanthes *lobata.* |
| Bunda, .. | .. | — | Cymbidium *tessalloides.* |
| Bundooka, .. | .. | S. | Pentapetes *Phœnicea.* |
| Bun-dumoor, | .. | B. | Ficus *hirta.* |
| B—gab, .. | .. | H. | Diospyros *cordifolia.* |
| Bungali-elachee, | .. | B. | Amomum *subulatum.* |
| Bun-gamuk, | .. | H. | Cucumis *Maderaspatensis.* |
| Bungrah, .. | .. | — | Acorus *Calamus.* |
| Bun-harul, .. | .. | — | Hibiscus *strictus.* |
| B—huldi, .. | .. | B. H. | Curcuma *Zedoaria.* |
| B—jam, .. | .. | B. | Ardisia *Solanacea.* |
| B—jamb, .. | .. | — | Eugenia *fruticosa.* |
| B—joma, .. | .. | — | Clerodendron or Volkameria *inermis.* |
| B—joolee, .. | .. | — | Phyllanthus *multiflorus.* |
| B—julpai, .. | .. | — | Elæocarpus *rugosus.* |
| B—ka-jooli, .. | .. | H. | Hedysarum *gramineum.* |
| B—kooncha, | .. | — | Bergera *integerrima.* |
| B—kuchoo, .. | .. | B. | Arum *Colocasia.* |

| | | | |
|---|---|---|---|
| Bun-kulai, .. | .. | B. H. | Glycine *labialis*. |
| B——kupasi, .. | .. | B. | Hibiscus *vitifolius*. |
| B——kuwa or kawa, | .. | — | Coffea *Bengalensis*. |
| B——lubunga, | .. | B. H. | Ludwigia *parviflora*. |
| B——lung, .. | .. | B. | Jussieua *exaltata*. |
| B——mithee, .. | .. | — | Trifolium *Indicum*. |
| B——mool, .. | .. | — | Tetranthera *lancæofolia*. |
| B——mullika, | .. | B. H. | Jasminum *Zambac*. |
| B——murich, | .. | B. | Ammonia *vesicatoria*. |
| B——nowaree, | .. | — | Jasminum *attenuatum*. |
| B——naringa, | .. | H. | Gelonium *fasciculatum*. |
| B——narunga, | .. | B. | Oxalis *sensitiva*. |
| B——nukh, .. | .. | — | Gordonia *integrifolia*. |
| B——nurukhalee, | .. | H. | Ardisia *glandulosa*. |
| B——okra, .. | { | B. H. | Triumfetta *Bartramia*. |
| | | — | Urena *lobata*. |
| B——palang, .. | .. | B. | Sonchus *Orixensis*. |
| B——palung, .. | .. | — | Rumex *acutus*. |
| B——pat, .. | .. | — | Corchorus *olitorius*. |
| B——raee, .. | .. | — | Sinapis *divaricata*. |
| B——raj, .. | .. | B. H. | Verbesina *scandens*. |
| B——shim, .. | .. | B. | Dolichos *Lablab; var*. 1. |
| B——shulpha, | .. | H. | Fumaria *parviflora*. |
| B——sun, .. | .. | B. | Crotalaria *verrucosa*. |
| Bunt, .. | .. | H. | Cicer *arietinum*. |
| Bun-tapureeya, | .. | B. | Physalis *minima*. |
| Bur, or But, .. | .. | — | Ficus *Indica*. |
| Bura-bela, .. | .. | B. H. | Calamus *fasciculatus*. |
| B——chauli, | .. | — | Uvaria *suberosa*. |
| B——choocha, | .. | — | Cyperus *Iria*. |
| B——chooli, | .. | — | Menyanthes *Indica*. |
| B——chukma, | .. | B. | Quercus *squamata*. |
| B——gachh, | .. | H. | Croton *oblongifolium*. |
| B——gool-shaboo, | .. | — | Polyanthes *tuberosa*. |
| B——goothoobi, | .. | B. | Kyllingia *umbellata*. |
| B——hulkusa, | .. | H. | Phlomis *cephalota*. |
| B——jal-ganti, | .. | B. H. | Panicum *setigerum*. |
| B——juvani, | .. | B. | Scirpus *tetragonus*. |
| B——kanoor, | .. | B. H. | Crinum *toxicarum*. |
| B——kerooee, | .. | B. | Euphorbia *hirta*. |
| B——keshuta, | .. | — | Ageratum *aquaticum*. |
| B——koonda, | .. | — | Jasminum *arborescens*. |
| B——koosima, | .. | — | Conyza *lacera*. |
| B——kungee, | .. | H. | Sida *graveolens*. |
| B——kurella, | .. | — | Momordica *muricata*. |
| B——leesora, | .. | — | Cordia *latifolia*. |

| | | |
|---|---|---|
| **Bura-makhom-shim,** | B. | Dolichos *gladiatus ; var.* 2. *(white.)* |
| **B——munda,** .. | B. H. | Loranthus *bicolor.* |
| **B——muttur,** .. | H. | Pisum *sativum (large sort).* |
| **B——nirbishi,** .. | B. H. | Scirpus *glomeratus.* |
| **Burans,** .. .. | H. | Rhododendron *ponticum.* |
| **Bura-noonya,** .. | B. H. | Portulacca *pilosa.* |
| **B——panee-murich,** . | B. | Polygonum *pilosum.* |
| **B——phootica,** .. | — | Melastoma *Malabathrica.* |
| **B——pini-nuti,** .. | — | Poa *Chinensis.* |
| **B——reetha,** .. | — | Sapindus *emarginatus.* |
| **B——salpan,** .. | — | Flemingia *congesta.* |
| **B——shama,** .. | — | Panicum *hispidatum.* |
| **B——shial-kanta,** .. | — | Argemone *Mexicana.* |
| **B——sooti or swoate,** . | — | Rottbœllia *exaltata.* |
| **B——tugur,** .. | — | Tabernæmontana *coronaria, (double).* |
| **Burbura,** .. .. | S. | Ocymum *pilosum.* |
| **Burbutee,** .. .. | B. H. | Dolichos *Catjang.* |
| **Burethi,** .. .. | B. | Cyperus *verticillatus.* |
| **Buri-harul,** .. .. | H. | Hibiscus *strictus.* |
| **Buroon,** .. .. | B. | Capparis *trifoliata.* |
| **Bursunga,** .. .. | H. | Bergera *Kœnigii.* |
| **Burul,** .. .. | — | Artocarpus *Lacucha.* |
| **Burunda,** .. .. | B. | Panicum *uliginosum.* |
| **Buthooa,** .. .. | H. | Atriplex *hortensis (?)* |
| **Butt,** .. .. | B. H. | Ficus *religiosa.* |
| **Buti-jamb,** .. .. | B. | Eugenia *cymosa.* |
| **Buttani,** .. .. | H. | Pisum *sativum.* |
| **Butsnab,** .. .. | B. | Aconitum *ferox.* |
| **Byajainti,** .. . | — | Sesbana *Ægyptica.* |
| **Byakool,** .. .. | B. H. | Solanum *Indicum.* |
| **Bygun,** .. .. | H. | S—— *melongena.* |

## Section 2.

*Tamool, Telinga, Cyngalasse, Malealie, &c.*

# B.

| | | | |
|---|---|---|---|
| Babassa, .. | | Tam. T. | Hydrocotyle *Asiatica.* |
| Badadooma, .. | .. | T. | Erythrina *sublobata.* |
| Badala, .. | .. | — | E ——— *Indica.* |
| Badeki, .. | .. | — | Sapium *cordifolium.* |
| Bagada, .. | .. | — | Nauclea *purpurea.* |
| Baggapalla, .. | .. | — | Cyrilla *aquatica.* |
| Bagy, .. | .. | Can. | Acorus *calamus.* |
| Bahjeeree, .. | .. | Cyng. | Panicum *Italicum.* |
| Ballioorakshie, | .. | — | Arum *macrorhizon.* |
| Ballikoma, .. | .. | T. | Opilia *amentacea.* |
| Ballusookura, | .. | — | Canthium *parviflorum.* |
| Balrakis, .. | .. | — | Arum *fornicatum.* |
| Balusoo-chettoo, | .. | — | Webera *tetrandra*, or Canthium *parviflorum.* |
| Bandikoota, | .. | — | Combretum *laxum.* |
| Bandi-girgin, | .. | — | Dalbergia *volubilis.* |
| Band-mooroodoodoo, | . | — | Getonia *floribunda.* |
| Bandura, .. | .. | Cyng. | Nepenthes *distillatoria.* |
| Bapanaboori, | .. | T. | Ehretia *buxifolia.* |
| Bapungie, .. | .. | — | Psoralea *corylifolia.* |
| Baramareca, .. | .. | M. | Dolichos *cultratus.* |
| Barinka, .. | .. | T. | Trophis *aspera.* |
| Baroon-hiss, .. | .. | — | Saccharum *cylindricum.* |
| Barubutsali, .. | .. | — | Cissus *setosa.* |
| Batsala-mandu, | .. | — | Ceropægia *tuberosa.* |
| Batsalikoora, | .. | — | Portulacca *quadrifida.* |
| Belam-canda, | .. | Tam. | Moræa *Chinensis.* |
| Beli, .. | .. | Cyng. | Cratæva *religiosa.* |
| Bella-mandu, | .. | T. | Ceropægia *juncea.* |
| Belloo-labba, | .. | Cyng. | Dalbergia *Zeylanica.* |
| Belluly, .. | .. | Can. | Allium *sativum.* |
| Bemnosi, .. | .. | M. | Vitex *Negundo.* |
| Bem-tamara, | .. | — | Nelumbium *speciosum.* |
| Bena-patsja, | .. | — | Heliotropium *Indicum.* |
| Bendoo-chetoo, | .. | T. | Æschynomene *arborea.* |

| | | |
|---|---|---|
| Beri-shadrosi, | T. | Mollugo *pentaphylla*. |
| Betala-codi, | M. | Piper *Betel*. |
| Bhalkoo, | T. | Bambusa *Balcua*. |
| Bhooma-kakkay, | — | Zinziber *roseum*. |
| Biddarie-nana-beeum, | — | Euphorbia *thymifolia*. |
| Billapa, | — | Scirpus *globosus*. |
| Billoo, | — | Swietenia *chloroxylon*. |
| Billo-gaddi, | — | Saccharum *spontaneum*. |
| Bilva, | — | Cratæva *religiosa*. |
| Bin-awari, | Cyng. | Indigofera *enneaphylla*. |
| Binda, | T. | Hibiscus *longifolius*. |
| Bin-dada-keeriya, | Cyng. | Euphorbia *thymifolia*. |
| Bin-mœe, | — | Phaseolus *trilobus*. |
| B—nelli, | — | Phyllanthus *urinaria*. |
| Bobra, | T. | Dolichos *Catjang*. |
| Boda-mamadi, | — | Ficus *oppositifolia*. |
| B——sarum, | — | Stemodia *viscosa*. |
| B——tarum, | — | Sphæranthus *Indicus*. |
| Boddama-kaia, | — | Bryonia *callosa*. |
| Bodie, | — | Osyris *peltata*. |
| Bogaha, | Cyng. | Ficus *religiosa*. |
| Boma-papata, | T. | Webera *corymbosa*. |
| Bonta-jemoodoo, | — | Euphorbium *antiquorum*. |
| B——shama, | — | Panicum *frumentaceum*. |
| Booaso, | Mah. | Mimusops *Kauki*. |
| Booda-kanka-rakoo, | — | Cardiospermum *Halicacabum*. |
| B——tunga, | — | Scirpus *maximus*. |
| Boo-kadu-para, | Cyng. | Cacalia *sonchifolia*. |
| Booraga, | T. | Bombax *pentandrum*. |
| Boora-deepaki, | — | Leea *integrifolia*. |
| Boordi-tiga, | — | Lettsomia *uniflora*. |
| Boorda-goomoodoo, | — | Cucurbita *Pepo*. |
| Boorgha, | — | Bombax *heptaphyllum*. |
| Boosee, | — | Vitex *arborea*. |
| Bota-kudumee, | — | Nauclea *parviflora*. |
| Bou-gu-næ, | Can. | Gardenia *uliginosa*. |
| Brumadundoo, | Tam. | Argemone *Mexicana*. |
| Bruma-madi, | T. | Ficus *glomerata*. |
| Brumarakash, | Tam. | Argemone *Mexicana*. |
| Bugate-bunda, | T. | Athanasia *Indica*. |
| Bulat-wæla, | Cyng. | Piper *Betel*. |
| Bundaroo, | T. | Cinchona *excelsa*. |
| Bundoora, | — | ————. |
| Bura-gadam, | — | Indigofera *glandulosa*. |
| Burong, | — | Ficus *heterophylla*. |

## Section 1.

### *Sunscrit, Bengally, Hindi, &c.*

## C.

| | | | |
|---|---|---|---|
| Cachari, | .. .. | H. | Cucumis *Madraspatensis.* |
| Cacri, | .. .. | — | C ——— *utilissimus.* |
| Cacronda, | .. .. | — | Celsia *(sp ?)* |
| Cachalu, | .. .. | — | Arum *Colocasia.* |
| Cachuar, | .. .. | — | Bauhinia *variegata.* |
| Cachu, | .. .. | — | Arum *Colocasia.* |
| Cachur, | .. .. | — | Curcuma *Zerumbet.* |
| Cadu, | .. .. | — | Cucurbita *lagenaria.* |
| Cadam, | .. .. | — | Nauclea *orientalis.* |
| Caeladolo, | .. .. | S. | Torenia *Asiatica.* |
| Cafur, | .. .. | H. | Dryabalanops *Camphora.* |
| Cahu, | .. .. | — | Lactuca *sativa.* |
| Cahwa, | .. .. | — | Coffea *Arabica.* |
| Caifal, | .. .. | — | Fragaria *vesca.* |
| Caisum, | .. .. | — | Artemisia *Abrotanum.* |
| Cajur̃, | .. .. | — | Phœnix *dactylifera.* |

| | | |
|---|---|---|
| Caladana, | H. | Convolvulus *Nil.* |
| Calajira or Calazira, | — | Nigella *Indica.* |
| Calapnath, | — | Justicia *paniculata.* |
| Calatulsi, | — | Ocymum *sanctum.* |
| Calaunji, | — | Nigella *Indica.* |
| Calimarca, | S. | Guilandina (or Cæsalpinia) *Bonducella.* |
| Callia-lata, | H. | Asclepias *tunicata.* |
| Calmi, | — | Convolvulus *repens.* |
| Camal, | — | Nelumbium *speciosum.* |
| Camrha, | — | Cucurbita *Pepo.* |
| Camrhakh, | — | Averrhoa *Carambola.* |
| Camud, | — | Rottlera *tinctoria.* |
| Canac, | — | Datura *Metel.* |
| Canchari, | — | Jussieua *repens.* |
| Cancrel, | — | Momordica *mixta.* |
| Candli, | — | Portulacca *(sp ?)* |
| Canduri, | — | Cucurbita *(sp ?)* |
| Caner, | — | Nerium *odorum.* |
| Cangan or Cangni, | — | Panicum *Italicum.* |
| Capicachu, | S. | Dolichos *pruriens.* |
| Caramcalla, | H. | Brassica *oleracea* or *campestris.* |
| Caranj, | — | Dalbergia *arborea.* |
| Caraunda, or Caranda, | — | Carissa *Carandas.* |
| Carbi, | — | Sorghum *vulgare.* |
| Caril, | — | Capparis *spinosa.* |
| Carela, | — | Momordica *Charantia.* |
| Carna, | — | Citrus *medica.* |
| Carnicara, | S. | Ixora *Pavetti.* |
| Cas, | H. | Saccharum *spontaneum.* |
| Casaghimie, | S. | Tragia *cannabina.* |
| Casandi, | H. | Cassia *Sophora.* |
| Caseru, | — | Cyperus *tuberosus.* |
| Casni, | — | Cichorium *Endivia.* |
| Cataca, | S. | Strychnos *potatorum.* |
| Catara, | H. | Echinops *echinatus.* |
| Cat-caleji or Cat-caranja, | — | Cæsalpinia or (Guilandina) *Bonducella.* |
| Catira, | — | Sterculia *urens.* |
| Cathal, | — | Artocarpus *integrifolia.* |
| Cattra-bunga, | S. | Aristolochia *Indica.* |
| Caua-thenthi, | H. | Clitoria *ternata.* |
| Caul, | — | Nymphœa *Nelumbo.* |

| | | |
|---|---|---|
| Cawa, .. .. | H. | Convolvolus *Nil.* |
| Chagool-battee, .. | — | Atragene *Zeylanica.* |
| Chagul-nadi, .. | B. | Sphæranthus *Indicus.* |
| C——patee, .. | — | Asclepias *tunicata.* |
| C——putputtee, .. | H. | Euphorbia *dracunculoides.* |
| Chah, .. .. | — | Camellia *Bohea.* |
| Chakatra, .. .. | — | Citras *decumanus.* |
| Chakoolya, .. .. | B. | Hemionitis *cordifolia.* |
| Chakoonda, .. .. | — | Cassia *Tora.* |
| Chakour, .. .. | H. | C—— *obtusifolia.* |
| Chala, .. .. | — | Cicer *arietinum.* |
| Chalgoza, .. .. | — | Pinus *Neoza.* |
| Chalta, .. .. | B. H. | Dillenia *speciosa*, or *Indica.* |
| Chambak, .. .. | H. | Kæmpferia *rotunda.* |
| Chambeli-ratta, .. | — | Jasminum (*sp ?*) |
| Champa, .. .. | B. H. | Michelia *Champaka.* |
| C———nuteeya, .. | B. | Amaranthus *polygamus.* |
| Champuka, .. .. | S.B.H. | Michelia *Champaka.* |
| Chamush, .. .. | H. | Arum (*sp ?*) |
| Chandan, .. .. | — | Sirium *myrtifolium.* |
| Chansur, .. .. | — | Lepidum *sativum.* |
| Chaoolmoogra, .. | B. | Chaulmoogra *odorata.* |
| Chaplash, .. .. | H. | Artocarpus *Chaplasha.* |
| Chapulasha, .. .. | — | (as above) |
| Charati, .. .. | S. | Viola *suffruticosa.* |
| Char-kucha, .. .. | B. | Arum *colocasia; var.* 2. |
| Chasa, .. .. | S. | Papaver *somniferum.* |
| Chatin, .. .. | B. | Echites *scholaris.* |
| Chatiya-shookar, .. | H. | Epipactis *babianifolia.* |
| Chaugara, .. .. | — | Scævola *Lobella.* |
| Chaulal, .. .. | — | Amaranthus *polygamus.* |
| Chaya, .. .. | B. | Achyranthes *lanata.* |
| Chayapulla, .. .. | S. | Cucurbita *citrullus.* |
| Chayntarashiakoo, .. | — | Pharnaceum *Mollugo.* |
| Chebiera, .. .. | — | Justicia *bicalyculata.* |
| Cheeka, .. .. | B. H. | Scirpus *plantagineus.* |
| Cheelo-nuteeya, .. | B. | Amaranthus *polygonoides.* |
| Cheena, .. .. | B. H. | Panicum *miliaceum.* |
| C——ghanzi, .. | B. | Xyris *Indica.* |
| Cheer, .. .. | H. | Pinus *longifolia.* |
| Chehur, .. .. | — | Valeriana *Jatamansi.* |
| Chela, .. | B. | Allangium *tomentosum.* |
| | H. | Cicer *arietinum.* |
| Chennaka, .. .. | S. | —— ———. |
| Cherayti, Cheraita, .. | B. H. | Gentiana *Cherayta.* |

| | | |
|---|---|---|
| Cher-kanta, | B. H. | Andropogon *aciculatus*. |
| Cheretta, | B. | Gentiana *Cherayta*. |
| Chichinga, | — | Trichosanthes *anguina*. |
| Chichinda, | H. | Beta *vulgaris*. |
| Chichiria, | B. H. | Achyranthes *aspera*. |
| Chilaka-tola-kura, | H. | Amaranthus *fasciatus*. |
| Chil-binge, | — | Strychnos *potatorum*. |
| Chilia-tangi, | B. | Hedysarum *vespertilionis*. |
| Chilmaree,<br>Chilmuri, | — | Coffea *tetrandra*. |
| Chilputa, | — | Wrightea *caryotoides*. |
| China-narangie, | H. | Triphasia *Aurantiola*. |
| Chinar, | — | Platanus *(sp ?)* |
| Chincha, | — | Ficus *Chincha*. |
| Chini, | — | Melilotus *Baumetta*. |
| Chinnie, | — | Acalypha *betulina*. |
| Chir, | — | Pinus *longifolia*. |
| Chirchera, | — | Achyranthes *aspera*. |
| Chirichira, | — | Milium *sanguinale*. |
| Chironji, | — | Chironjia *sapida*. |
| Chiti, | — | Plumbago *Zeylanica*. |
| Chitcabra, | — | Hedysarum *pictum*. |
| Chitra, | B. | Plumbago *Zeylanica*. |
| C—— or Chitta, | H. | Berberis *vulgaris*. |
| C——, | S. | Anthericum *tuberosum*. |
| Chitruka, | — | Plumbago *Zeylanica*. |
| Chittoa-bera, | B. | Polypodium *glabrum*. |
| Chittra, | B. H. | Plumbago *Zeylanica*. |
| Chitturmool, | — | ——— ———. |
| Chob-chini, | H. | Smilax *China*. |
| Chooa, | B. | Celosia *argentea*. |
| Choee, | B. H. | Piper *Chuvya*. |
| Chokandar or Chukandar, | H. | Beta *vulgaris*. |
| Chooka-palung or Chooka, | B. H. | Rumex *vesicarius*. |
| Chookrika, | S. | ——— ———. |
| Chooli, | H. | Menyanthes *cristata*. |
| Choonaree, | — | Ixora *villosa*. |
| Chooncha, | B. H. | Cyperus *compressus*. |
| Choon-khuriki, | B. | Apluda *aristata*. |
| Choopri-aloo, | B. H. | Dioscorea *globosa*. |
| Choota-dood-luta, | H. | Asclepias *geminata*. |
| C—— gothoobi, | B. | Cyperus *dubius*. |
| C—— kookshima, | H. | Serratula *cinerea*. |
| C——micheta, | B. | Justicia *polysperma*. |

| | | |
|---|---|---|
| Choota-pushpa, | — | Melastoma *aspera.* |
| Chora-phootica, | S. | Andropogon *aciculatus.* |
| Chorich, | H. | Gorteria (*sp ?*) |
| Chosa, | S. B. | Papaver *somniferum.* |
| Chota-bhooi-kamadi, | B. | Columnea *tomentosa.* |
| C——bish-taruk, | B. H. | Lettsomia *speciosa.* |
| C——hulkusha, | B. | Phlomis *esculenta.* |
| C——jamb, | — | Eugenia *caryophyllifolia.* |
| C——jhanjie, | H. | Utricularia *biflora.* |
| C——kherooee, | — | Euphorbia *Chamæsyce.* |
| C——kulpa, | B. | Borago *Indica.* |
| C——kunwar, | H. | Aloe *littoralis* or *perfoliata.* |
| C——munda, | B. | Loranthus *globosus.* |
| C——muttur, | B. H. | Pisum *viridis.* |
| C——pini-nutee, | B. | Aira *filiformis.* |
| C——shalook, | — | Nymphæa *stellata.* |
| C——soondhi, | — | N—— *esculenta.* |
| Chouputeeya, | H. | Kydia *calycina.* |
| Chowly, | — | Portulacca *quadrifida.* |
| Chuchinda, | — | Cucumis ? (*sp ?*) |
| Chuee, | B. | Piper *Chuvya.* |
| Chudra, | S.B.H. | Solanum *Jacquini.* |
| Chuhara, | H. | Phœnix *dactylifera.* |
| Chukka, | — | Rumex *vesicarius,* or *acetosa.* |
| Chuka-tipatti, | — | Marica *paludosa.* |
| Chukra-murda, | S. | Cassia *Tora.* |
| Chukrasi, | H. | Swietenia *Chukrasi.* |
| Chumalipatee, | B. H. | Cyperus *Pangoorie.* |
| Chumbeli, | H. | Jasminum *grandiflorum.* |
| Chumli-sag, | — | Amaranthus *polygamus.* |
| Chuna, | B. | Lathyrus *Aphaca,* or Cicer *Arietinum,* or Vicia *sativa.* |
| Chunalata, | — | Chionanthus *Smilacifolia.* |
| Chundra, | B. H. | Ophioxylon *serpentinum.* |
| Chundra-moola, | B. | Kæmpferia *Galanga.* |
| C———moolika, | S. | ———— ——. |
| Chundree-mullika, | B. | Chrysanthemum *Indicum.* |
| Chundruhasa, | — | Solanum *hirsutum.* |
| Chundruka, | — | Ophioxylon *serpentinum.* |
| Chunduna, | S.B.H. | Santalum *album.* |
| Chun-hatlee, | H. | Abrus *precatorius.* |
| Chungira, | N. | Cornus *capitata.* |
| Chunkee, | B. | Gadelupa *Piscidia.* |
| Chunser, | H. | Lepidium *sativum.* |
| Chunuka, | S. | Cicer *arietinum.* |

| | | | |
|---|---|---|---|
| **Chutka,** | . | .. | **B.** | **Bauhinia *acuminata.*** |
| **Chuveya,** | .. | .. | **S.** | **Piper *Chuvya.*** |
| **Citnagueri,** | .. | .. | **—** | **Melastoma *aspera.*** |
| **Congoonie,** | .. | .. | **H.** | **Sida *Mauritiana.*** |
| **Crëat,** | .. | .. | **—** | **Justicia *paniculata.*** |
| **Cubab-chini,** | | .. | **—** | **Piper *Cubeba.*** |
| **Culaka,** | .. | .. | **S.** | **Strychnos *Nux-vomica.*** |
| **Curayia,** | .. | .. | **H.** | **Echites *antidysenterica.*** |
| **Curayja,** | .. | .. | **—** | **——— (or Nerium) *anti-dysentericum.*** |
| **Cussumbha,** | .. | .. | **S.** | **Carthamus *tinctorius.*** |
| **Cutaja,** | .. | .. | **—** | **Echites *antidysentericum.*** |
| **Cuveraca,** | .. | .. | **—** | **Cedrela *Tuna.*** |

## Section 2.

### *Tamool, Telinga, Cyngalese, &c.*

## C.

| | | |
|---|---|---|
| Caat-amunak, .. | Tam. | Jatropha *Cureas.* |
| C—aralie, .. .. | — | Cerbera *manghas.* |
| C—attie, .. .. | — | Bauhinia *tomentosa.* |
| C—jootie, .. .. | — | Atropa *Mandragora.* |
| C—karnay, .. .. | — | Dracontium *polyphyllum.* |
| C—kolingie, .. .. | — | Galega *purpurea.* |
| C—mallica, .. .. | — | Jasminum *angustifolia.* |
| C—morunghie, .. | — | Hedysarum *Sennoides.* |
| C—noochie, .. .. | — | Jatropha *Curcas.* |
| C—siragum, .. .. | — | Vernonia *anthelmintica.* |
| Cadala, .. .. | — | Cicer *arietinum.* |
| Cadapum, .. .. | — | Eugenia *racemosa.* |
| Cairata, .. .. | — | Justicia *paniculata.* |
| Cakay, .. .. | Can. | Cassia *fistula.* |
| Camachie-pilloo, .. | Tam. | Andropogon *Schœnanthus,* or Cyperus *odoratus.* |
| Canaga, .. .. | Can. | Dalbergia *arborea.* |
| Canapa-tiga, .. | T. | Cissus *carnosa.* |
| Canchorie, .. .. | Tam. | Tragia *involucrata.* |
| Capoor-kichlie, .. | — | Curcuma *Zerumbet.* |
| Cara-caniram, .. | M. | Justicia *paniculata.* |
| Carakaia, .. .. | T. | Terminalia *Chebula.* |
| Carambu, .. .. | M. | Jussieua *suffruticosa.* |
| Caranosi, .. .. | — | Vitex *trifoliata.* |
| Caraveela, .. .. | — | Cleome *pentaphylla.* |
| Caray-cheddy, .. | Tam. | Webera *tetrandra,* or Canthium *parviflorum.* |
| Carimpana, .. .. | — | Borassus *flabelliformis.* |
| Carin-siragum, .. | — | Nigella *sativa* or *Indica.* |
| Carookoova, .. .. | — | Zizyphus *trinervius.* |
| Caroo-noochie, .. | — | Justicia *Gandarussa.* |
| Carpoo-woolandoo, .. | — | Cytisus *Cajan.* |
| Carun-chembai, .. | — | Coronilla *picta.* |
| Cassa-cassa, .. .. | — | Papaver *somniferum.* |
| Castoorie-munjil, .. | — | Curcuma *Zedoaria.* |
| C——passapoo, .. | T. | ——— ———. |

| | | |
|---|---|---|
| Cat-korundoo, .. | TAM. | Trichilia *spinosa.* |
| Catæla-vegon, .. | M. | Aristolochia *Indica.* |
| Cattu-gasturi, .. | — | Hibiscus *Abelmoschus.* |
| C——tirpali, .. | — | Piper *longum.* |
| Cavatum-pilloo, .. | TAM. | Andropogon *Schœnanthus.* |
| Chacunda, .. .. | T. | Cassia *Tora.* |
| Chadacula, .. .. | TAM. | Chloroxylon *Dupada.* |
| Chamakada, .. .. | T. | Sanseveria *Zeylanica.* |
| Chana, .. .. | CYNG. | Cicer *arietinum.* |
| Chancheli-kura, .. | T. | Achyranthes *alternifolia.* |
| Chandanum, .. .. | TAM. | Santalum *album.* |
| Chanschena, .. .. | M. | Bauhinia *tomentosa.* |
| Chaynd-polla, .. | T. | Trichosanthes *laciniosa.* |
| Cheepa-bora-gaddi, .. | — | Panicum *corymbosum.* |
| Chendanum, .. .. | — | Santalum *album.* |
| Chenna, .. .. | M. | Panicum *Italicum.* |
| Cheppoo-neringie, .. | TAM | Indigofera *enneaphylla.* |
| Cheri-velloo, .. | T. | Odenlandia *umbellata.* |
| Cherukoo-bodi, } C————duboo, } | — | Saccharum *officinarum.* |
| Cherra-gaddam, .. | — | Indigofera *enneaphylla.* |
| Chesti-veloo, .. .. | — | Odenlandia *umbellata.* |
| Chetta-duduga, .. | — | Uvaria *Cerasoides.* |
| Chewka, .. .. | — | Tamarindus *Indica.* |
| Chick-lenta, .. .. | — | Panicum *verticillatum.* |
| Chick-linta-kura, .. | — | Marsilea *quadrifolia.* |
| Chikai, .. .. | — | Mimosa *Concina.* |
| Chilia-durguga, .. | — | Unona *discolor.* |
| Chilta-eita, .. .. | — | Phœnix *farinifera.* |
| Chimoorda, .. .. | — | Strœmia *tetrandra.* |
| China-alla, .. .. | CYNG. | Smilax *China.* |
| Chin-anam-patchy-arisee, .. .. | TAM. | Euphorbia *thymifolia.* |
| Chinamanghie, .. | T. | Lagerstræmia *parviflora.* |
| Chini-kala-bunda, .. | — | Aloe *littoralis*, or *perfoliata.* |
| Chinni-wallursi, .. | — | Walsura *ternata.* |
| Chinny-chintee, .. | — | Celastrus *emarginatus.* |
| Chinta, .. .. | — | Tamarindus *Indica.* |
| Chirra-kura, .. .. | — | Amaranthus *polygonoides.* |
| Chiruparam, .. .. | TAM. | Melochia *corchorifolia.* |
| Chit-ankaloo, .. | T. | Nerium *tinctorium.* |
| C—kinta, .. .. | — | Hedysarum *umbellatum.* |
| Chitreka, .. .. | — | Limonia *pentagyna.* |
| Chittle-bunda, .. | — | Pavonia *odorata.* |
| Chittu, .. .. | CAN. | Strychnos *potatorum.* |
| Chivan-amelpodie, .. | TAM. | Ophioxylon *serpentinum.* |

| | | | |
|---|---|---|---|
| Chumunti, .. | .. | T. | Chrysanthemum *Indicum.* |
| Cit-amerdoo, | .. | M. | Menispermum *cordifolium.* |
| Citavanaca, .. | .. | — | Ricinus *communis.* |
| Citra, .. | .. | T. | Plumbago *Zeylanica.* |
| Cittramoolum, | .. | Tam. | ——— ———. |
| Cocrinja, .. | .. | — | Cæsalpinia *Mimosoides.* |
| Codagam, .. | .. | — | Asclepias *vomitoria.* |
| Coda-wawul-ætiya, | .. | Cyng. | Cæsalpinia *Mimosoides.* |
| Coletta-veetla, | .. | M. | Barleria *Prionitis.* |
| Conda-cashina, | .. | T. | Scopolia *aculeata.* |
| C——pani, | .. | Tam. | Corypha *umbraculifera.* |
| C——pooshpoo, | .. | T. | Globba *bulbifera.* |
| C—— vettoo, | .. | — | Rottlera *dioica.* |
| Condumunnie-vayr, | .. | Tam. | Abrus *precatorius.* |
| Cooringa, .. | { | Tam.<br>T. | } Asclepias *vomitoria.* |
| Cooruvingie, | .. | Tam. | Ehretia *Buxifolia.* |
| Cooroo-vayroo, | .. | T. | Andropogon *muricatus.* |
| Cootivella, .. | .. | Tam. | Feronia *Elephantum, var.* |
| Coraloo, .. | .. | T. | Panicum *Italicum.* |
| Coril-keeray, | .. | Tam. | Portulacca *oleracea.* |
| Coruttei, .. | .. | — | Trichosanthes *palmata.* |
| Cossumba, .. | .. | Can. | Carthamus *tinctorius.* |
| Cotimbiry, .. | .. | — | Coriandrum *sativum.* |
| Cottamillie, .. | .. | Tam. | ——— ———. |
| Cotumba, .. | .. | Cyng. | Terminalia *Catappa.* |
| Cotumbaroo, | .. | — | Coriandrum *sativum.* |
| Courou-moelli, | .. | M. | Sideroxylon *spinosum.* |
| Covalam, .. | .. | Tam. | Cratæva *marmelos.* |
| Covay, .. | .. | — | Bryonia *grandis.* |
| Cundunghatrie, | .. | T. | Solanum *Jacquini.* |
| Cunja-koray, | .. | Tam. | Ocymum *album.* |
| Cupa-veela, .. | .. | M. | Vinca *parviflora.* |
| Cushelli, .. | .. | T. | Anthericum *tuberosum.* |

# D.

## Section 1.

*Sanscrit, Bengally, Hindi, Nawar, &c.*

## D.

| | | |
|---|---|---|
| Dab, .. .. | H. | Poa *cynosuroides.* |
| Dabi-dooba, .. .. | B. | Xyris *Indica.* |
| Dabra, .. .. | H. | Hedysarum *pictum.* |
| Dadima, .. .. | S. | Punica *Granatum.* |
| Dad-mari, .. .. | B. H. | Ammania *vesicatoria.* |
| Dadmari, .. .. | B. | Hastingia *scandens.* |
| Dadmerden, .. .. | H. | Cassia *alata.* |
| Dadoo-murdun, .. | B. | C—— ——. |
| Dadumari, .. .. | S. | Xyris *Indica.* |
| Dain, .. .. | H. | Aralia *digitata.* |
| Dalim, .. .. | B. | Punica *Granatum.* |
| Dal-kuchoo, .. .. | — | Sagittaria *cordifolia.* |
| Dam, .. .. | — | |
| Damana, .. .. | S. | Æschynomene *aspera,* or *arborea.* |
| Danga, .. .. | N. | Coriandrum *sativum.* |
| D——ghechoo, .. | B. | Ophioglossum *cordifolium.* |
| D——gurgar, .. | — | Coix *gigantea.* |
| Dansha, .. .. | — | Æschynomene *cannabina.* |
| Danta-sag, .. .. | — | Amaranthus *Gangeticus.* |
| Danura, .. .. | H. | Scytalia *Danura.* |
| Dapoo, .. .. | B. | Polypodium *proliferum.* |
| Dar-chini or Dal-chini, | — | Laurus *Cinnamomum,* (broad-leaved.) |
| Darim, .. .. | H. | Punica *Granatum.* |
| Darimba, .. .. | S. | ——— ————. |
| Daroositi, .. .. | — | Laurus *Cinnamomum.* |

| | | |
|---|---|---|
| Dasee, .. .. | S. | Barleria *cærulea.* |
| Daudi, .. .. | H. | Chrysanthemum *Indicum.* |
| Daudmari, .. .. | B. H. | Ammania *vesicatoria.* |
| Dauna, .. .. | H. | Artemisia *(sp ?)* |
| Dawanakaha, .. | S. | Artemisia *Austriaca.* |
| Deb-daroo, .. .. | B. | Uvaria *longifolia.* |
| Deb-dhanya, .. .. | — | Andropogon *Sorghum.* |
| Debkhotee, .. .. | H. | Celosia *argentea.* |
| Deeb-kanchun, .. | B. | Bauhinia *purpurea.* |
| Deepuk, .. .. | — | Celosia *cristata.* |
| Dela, .. .. | H. | Jasminum *multiflorum.* |
| Dengooa, .. .. | B. | Amaranthus *Gangeticus.* |
| Deodhan, .. .. | H. | Andropogon *saccharatus.* |
| Deobara, .. .. | — | Uvaria *longifolia.* |
| Deodwara, .. .. | — | Pinus *Deodara.* |
| Deogandun, .. .. | — | Secale *orientale.* |
| Deokandar, .. .. | — | Nasturtium *officinale.* |
| Deona, .. .. | — | Ocymum *(sp ?)* |
| Dephul, .. { | B. | Xanthochymus *pictorius.* |
| | — | Artocarpus *Lacucha.* |
| Deshi-mullika, .. | — | Jasminum *Zambac.* |
| Detara or Detto, .. | — | Andropogon *serratum.* |
| Deu-gullar, .. | H. | Calamus *extensus.* |
| Deva-daroo, .. { | S. H. | Pinus *Deodara.* |
| | S. | Uvaria *longifolia.* |
| Deva-tara, .. .. | — | Andropogon *serratum.* |
| Dewudar, .. .. | H. | Erythroxylon *areolatum.* |
| Dhae, .. .. | — | Grislea *tomentosa.* |
| Dhak, .. .. | — | Butea *frondosa.* |
| Dhan, .. .. | B. H. | Oryza *sativa.* |
| Dhanattar, .. .. | H. | Clitoria *ternata.* |
| Dhandain, .. .. | — | Æschynomene *(sp ?)* |
| Dhanga, .. .. | — | Coriandrum *sativum.* |
| Dhangaphul, . | B. | Grislea *tomentosa.* |
| Dhan-lunka-murich, . | — | Capsicum *minimum.* |
| D——murich, .. | — | ———— ————. |
| Dhanyaca, .. .. | S. | Coriandrum *sativum.* |
| Dhatura, .. .. | H. | Datura *Metel.* |
| Dhaulichampa, .. | — | Liriodendron *grandiflora.* |
| Dhari, .. .. | B. | Grislea *tomentosa.* |
| Dhemna, .. .. | — | Cissus *elongata.* |
| Dhena, .. .. | | ———— ————. |
| Dhenroos or Dhendus, | B. H | Hibiscus *esculentus,* or *longifolius.* |
| Dhol-sumoodra, .. | B. | Leea *macrophylla.* |
| Dhoolacherra, .. | H. | Bergia *Ammanioides.* |

| | | |
|---|---|---|
| Dhooli-bansh, .. | B. | Bambusa *Balcua.* |
| Dhoondoo, .. .. | — | Luffa *pentandra.* |
| Dhoostoora, .. .. | S. | Datura *fastuosa* (double.) |
| Dhootura, .. .. | B. | D——— *Metel.* |
| D———luta, .. | — | Büttnera *aspera.* |
| Dhub, .. .. | — | Grislea *tomentosa.* |
| Dhuivé, or Dhuwi, .. | H. | ——— ———. |
| Dhumoola, .. .. | S. | Alpinia *Galanga.* |
| Dhumrapatra, .. | — | Nicotiana *Tabacum.* |
| Dhumura, .. .. | — | Arundo *Karka.* |
| Dhuncha, .. .. | B. | Æschynomene *Cannabina.* |
| Dhunya, .. .. | S.B.H. | Coriandrum *sativum.* |
| Dier, .. .. | H. | Menispermum *hirsutum.* |
| Dirya-ka-naril, .. | — | Cocos *Maldivica*, or Lodoicea *Sechellarum.* |
| Dobutee-luta, .. | B. | Convolvulus *pes-capra.* |
| Doob, .. .. | H. | Panicum *dactylon.* |
| Doobla, .. .. | B. | ——— ———. |
| Doodeeya, .. .. | — | Asclepias *rosea.* |
| Doodha-pitulee-shim, . | — | Dolichos *lignosus, var.* 5. |
| Doodh-kulmee, .. | — | Convolvulus *Turpethum.* |
| D——luta, .. .. | — | Asclepias *rosea.* |
| Doodiya-champa, .. | — | Liriodendron *grandiflora.* |
| Dood-luta, .. .. | — | Echites *marginata.* |
| Doogahika, .. .. | S. | Asclepias *volubilis.* |
| Dooi-kesha, .. .. | B. | Amomum *sericeum.* |
| Dookateya, .. .. | S. | Symplocos *ferruginea.* |
| Dookesswa, .. .. | B. | Cluytia *oblongifolia*, or Alpinia *Cardamomum.* |
| Doolala-chumpa, .. | — | Hedychium *coronarium.* |
| Doombur, .. .. | H. | Ficus *glomerata.* |
| Doomoor, .. .. | B. | —— *Carica.* |
| Doomur, .. .. | H. | Xanthoxylum *alatum.* |
| Doopahariya, .. | B. | Pentapetes *Phœnicea.* |
| Doopatee, .. .. | — | Impatiens *Balsamina.* |
| Doorba, .. .. | — | Panicum *dactylon.* |
| Doorva, .. .. | S. | ——— ———. |
| Doost-parisha, .. | — | Tragia *involucrata.* |
| Dora-byara, .. | H. | Panicum *verticillatum.* |
| Dorlé, .. .. | — | Solanum *Jacquini.* |
| Dosbi-chundi, .. | — | Morea *Chinensis.* |
| Downah, .. .. | — | Artemisia *Austriaca.* |
| Drakhyalata, .. | B. | Vitis *vinifera.* |
| Draksha, .. .. | S. B. | —— ———. |
| Dub, .. .. | H. | Agrostis *linearis.* |

| | | |
|---|---|---|
| **Duddhi,** .. .. | H. | Euphorbia *hirta*, or *thymifolia*. |
| **D——,** .. .. | — | Asclepias *rosea*. |
| **Dudrooghna,** .. | S. | Cassia *alata*. |
| **Dula,** .. .. | B. H. | Panicum *stagninum*. |
| **Dulpai,** .. .. | B. | Elæocarpus *robustus*. |
| **Dumke-mirchie,** .. | H. | Piper *Cubeba*. |
| **Duna,** .. .. | — | Artemisia *Indica*. |
| **Duna-dana,** .. .. | S. | ——— ———. |
| **Dungura,** .. .. | B. | Ficus *hirsuta*. |
| **Dunkoni,** .. .. | — | Pladera *decussata*. |
| **Dunta-rungee,** .. | — | Millingtonia *simplicifolia*. |
| **Dunti,** .. .. | S. | Croton *Tiglium*. |
| **Duparia,** .. .. | H. | Pentapetes *phœnicea*. |
| **Durma,** .. .. | B. | Arundo *Bengalensis*. |
| **Dusha-bahoo-chundi,** . | — | Morea *Chinensis*. |
| **Duya-kuya,** .. .. | — | Achyranthes *Lappacea*. |
| **Dwiputree,** .. .. | S. | Impatiens *Balsamina*. |

## SECTION 2.

### *Tamool, Telinga, Cyngalese, &c.*

## D.

| | | |
|---|---|---|
| Dadima, .. .. | T. | Punica *Granatum.* |
| Daduga, .. .. | — | Nauclea *cordifolia.* |
| Daleemb, .. .. | M. | Punica *Granatum.* |
| Dalookgaheh, .. | CYNG. | Euphorbium *antiquorum.* |
| Darboojee, .. .. | T. | Cucurbita *citrullus.* |
| Dasanie, .. .. | — | Hibiscus *Rosa-sinensis.* |
| Daun-gundi, .. | M. | Nepenthes *distillatoria.* |
| Dava-dari, .. .. | T. | Phyllanthus *turbinatus.* |
| Dawanum, .. .. | — | Artemisia *Austriaca.* |
| Dayla-kura, .. .. | — | Amaranthus *polygamus.* |
| Della-madoo, .. | — | Pentaptera *tomentosa.* |
| Delunghedie, .. | CYNG. | Punica *Granatum.* |
| Devadarum, .. .. | TAM. | Erythroxylon *areolatum.* |
| Dewadari, .. .. | T. | ——— ———. |
| Dewadooroo, .. | CYNG. | Anethum *Panmorium,* or *fæniculatum.* |
| Dewipaghura, .. | — | Dolichos, (or Carpopogon) *pruriens.* |
| Dewul, .. .. | — | Feronia *Elephantum.* |
| Dhoonkola, .. .. | — | Nicotiana *Tabacum.* |
| Dirshena, .. .. | T. | Mimosa *Sirissa.* |
| Doda-gorai, .. .. | CAN. | Portulacca *oleracea.* |
| Donda, .. .. | T. | Bryonia *grandis.* |
| Doodi-palla, .. .. | — | Asclepias *volubilis.* |
| Doola-ghonda, .. } | — | Carpopogon, (or Dolichos) *pruriens.* |
| | — | Tragia *involucrata.* |
| Doolagovila-Eesaravay-roo, .. .. | — | Aristolochia *Indica.* |
| Doolya-gunda, .. | — | Tragia *Cannabina.* |

| | | | |
|---|---|---|---|
| Doombrasticum, | .. | T. | Alpinia *Galanga*. |
| Doonki-boora, | .. | — | Briedelia *scandens*. |
| Doosa, .. | .. | — | Panicum *fluitans*. |
| Doosera-tiga, | .. | — | Menispermum *hirsutum*. |
| Doskay, .. | .. | — | Cucumis *utilissimus*. |
| Dotury, .. | .. | CAN. | Argemone *Mexicana*. |
| Dovana, .. | .. | — | Artemisia *Maderaspatana*. |
| Dulago-vila, | .. | T. | Aristolochia *Indica*. |
| Durba, Durpa, | .. | — | Poa *cynosuroides*. |

## SECTION 1.

*Sanscrit, Bengally, Hindi, Nawar, &c.*

### E.

| | | | |
|---|---|---|---|
| Eesha-nungula, | .. | B. | Gloriosa *superba.* |
| Ekbeera, | .. .. | — | Osmunda *Zeylanica.* |
| Ela, | .. .. | S. } | Alpinia, or Amomum, or Elettaria *Cardamomum.* |
| Elaich, | .. .. | H. } | |
| Elwa, | .. .. | H. | Aloe *perfoliata.* |
| Erenda, | .. .. | S. | Ricinus *communis.* |

## Section 2.

### *Tamool, Telinga, Cyngalese, &c.*

## E.

| | | |
|---|---|---|
| Eella, .. .. | Cyng. | Callicarpa *lanata.* |
| Eerminakullie, .. | Tam. | Cacalia *Kleinia.* |
| Ek-sætiya, .. .. | Cyng. | Heliotropium *Indicum.* |
| Elagabora-gaddi, .. | T. | Fuirena *ciliaris.* |
| Elandei, .. .. | Tam. | Zizyphus *Jujuba.* |
| Ela-palol, .. .. | Cyng. | Bignonia *Chelonoides.* |
| Elarathnetul, .. | — | Plumbago *Zeylanica.* |
| Elavum, .. .. | Tam. | Bombax *pentandrum.* |
| Elekullie, .. .. | — | Euphorbia *Nereifolia.* |
| Elettaria, .. .. | M. | Elettaria *Cardamomum.* |
| Ella-koora, .. .. | T. | Salsola *Indica.* |
| Eloopei, .. .. | Tam. | Bassia *longifolia.* |
| Elum-chedi, .. .. | Can. | Alpinia *Cardamomum.* |
| Emboorel, .. .. | — | Oldenlandia *umbellata.* |
| Ensal, .. .. | Cyng. | Elettaria *Cardamomum.* |
| Enuga, .. .. | T. | Carpopogon *monospermum.* |
| Erramassoo, .. .. | Cyng. | Periploca *Indica.* |
| Errumoottie, .. | Tam. | Ballota *disticha.* |
| Etrinta, .. .. | T. | Sonchus *oleraceus—lævis.* |

## SECTION 1.

### *Sanscrit, Bengally, Hindi, Nawar, &c.*

## F.

| | | |
|---|---|---|
| Faltar, .. .. | H. | Borassus *flabelliformis, (female.)* |
| Faridbuti, .. .. | — | Menispermum *hirsutum.* |
| Falsa, .. .. | — | Grewia *Asiatica.* |
| Felfildraz, .. .. | — | Piper *longum.* |
| Felfilgird, .. .. | — | —— *nigrum.* |
| Feringie-datura, .. | — | Argemone *Mexicana.* |
| Ficki-tagar, .. .. | — | Tabernæmontana *coronaria.* |
| Firduk, .. .. | — | Corylus *Avellana.* |
| Fool-sola, .. .. | B. | Æschynomene *aspera.* |
| Furrinjeer, .. .. | — | Securidaca *paniculata.* |
| Fut, .. .. | H. | Cucumis *Momordica.* |

## SECTION 2.

### *Tamool, Telinga, Cyngalese, &c.*

## Section 1.

### *Sanscrit, Bengalee, Hindi, &c.*

## G.

| | | |
|---|---|---|
| Gab, .. .. | B. H. | Diospyros or Embryopteris *glutinosa.* |
| Gaba-nul, .. .. | B. | Arundo *Bengalensis.* |
| Gachmirch, .. .. | H. | Capsicum *annuum.* |
| Gadha-buni, .. .. | B. | Trianthema *decandra.* |
| G——poorna, .. | — | Boerhaavia *procumbens.* |
| Gagandhool, .. | H. | Pandanus *odoratissimus.* |
| Gajur, .. .. | B. H. | Daucus *carota.* |
| Gandana, .. .. | H. | Allium *Porrum.* |
| Gandar, .. .. | — | Andropogon *muricatum.* |
| Gandbel, .. .. | — | ——— *Schœnanthus.* |
| Gandhee, .. .. | B. | Xanthophyllum *virens.* |
| Gandheera, . .. | S. | Solanum *pubescens.* |
| Gandhraj, .. .. | H. | Gardenia *florida.* |
| Gangatiah, .. .. | — | Achryanthes *alternifolia.* |
| Gangbena, .. .. | B. | Panicum *strictum.* |
| Ganja, .. .. | B. H. | Cannabis *sativa.* |
| Ganjh, .. .. | H. | Andropogon *muricatum.* |
| Ganna, .. .. | — | Saccharum *officinarum.* |
| Gaynatuka, .. .. | N. | Aster *Chinensis.* |
| Gehun, .. .. | H. | Triticum *hybernum.* |
| Gela, .. .. | — | Mimosa *scandens.* |
| Genda, .. .. | — | Tagetes *erecta.* |
| Gewa, .. .. | — | Excoecaria *Agallocha.* |
| Ghagra, .. .. | — | Xanthium *Indicum.* |
| Gharicum, .. .. | — | Agaricus *(sp ?)* |
| Ghanur, .. .. | — | Panicum *dactylon.* |
| Ghata, .. .. | S. | Phrynium *dichotomum.* |
| Ghee-kashee, .. | H. | Ornitrophe *Aporetica.* |
| Ghee-nalta-pat, .. | B. | Corchorus *capsularis, (red var.)* |
| Ghejasoodumoostra, .. | S. | Pedalium *mureæ.* |
| Ghetchoo, .. .. | H. | Aponogeton *monostachyon.* |
| Ghetkool, .. .. | B. | Arum *orixense.* |

| | | |
|---|---|---|
| Ghicwar, .. .. | H. | Aloe *perfoliata.* |
| Ghinulita-pat, .. | — | Corchorus *capsularis.* |
| Ghoosh, .. .. | B. | Luffa *pentandra,* or *acutangula.* |
| Ghrita-koomaree, .. | B. H. | Aloe *perfoliata.* |
| Ghun, .. .. | B. | Cyperus *rotundus.* |
| Ghunchi, .. .. | H. | Abrus *precatorius.* |
| Ghursutum, .. .. | B. | Gossypium *(var. ?)* |
| Gundalee, .. .. | H. | Pæderia *fœtida.* |
| Ghundasaru, .. | S. | Santalum *album.* |
| Ghundha-bhudra, .. | — | Pæderia *fœtida,* or Oldenlandia *alata.* |
| Ghunta, .. .. | B. | Bignonia *suaveolens.* |
| Gilan, .. .. | H. | Menispermum *glabrum.* |
| Gilaunda, .. .. | — | Bassia *latifolia.* |
| Gima, . .. | — | Pharnaceum *Mollugo.* |
| Gindha, .. .. | B. H. | Tagetes *erecta.* |
| Gioon, .. .. | H. | Triticum *æstivum.* |
| Girmi, .. .. | B. | Chironia *Centauroides.* |
| Goaliya, .. .. | — | Andropogon *punctatus.* |
| Gooamooree, .. | — | Anethum *Panmorium.* |
| Gobhi, .. .. | H. | Cacalia *sonchifolia.* |
| Gobura, .. .. | B. H. | Ajuga *disticha.* |
| G——nuteeya, .. | B. | Amaranthus *lividus.* |
| Gobur-champa, .. | B. H. | Plumeria *acuminata.* |
| Gochru, .. .. | H. | Ruellia *longifolia.* |
| Godha-pudee, .. | S. | Cissus *pedata.* |
| Godhooma, .. .. | — | Triticum *æstivum.* |
| Godunika, .. .. | — | Phrynium *dichotomum.* |
| Gohantuka, .. .. | — | Ruellia *longifolia.* |
| Gojihwa, .. .. | — | Elephantophus *scaber.* |
| Gokantuka, .. .. | — | Ruellia *longifolia.* |
| Gokhoor, or Gokhyoor, | B. | Tribulus *lanuginosus.* |
| Gokhoroo, .. .. | H. | ——— *terrestris.* |
| Gokshura, .. .. | — | Barleria *longifolia.* |
| Goshooruka, .. | S. | ——— *lanuginosus.* |
| Gola-mohunee, .. | B. | Deeringia *Celosioides.* |
| Gol-mirch, .. .. | H. | Piper *nigrum.* |
| Gol-mulunga, .. | B. | Cyperus *elatus.* |
| Golomi, .. .. | S. | Acorus *Calamus.* |
| Gol-shingra, .. | B. | Quercus *serratus.* |
| Goluk-chakulee, .. | H. | Hedysarum *Lagopodioides.* |
| G——laroo, .. .. | B. | Johnia *salacioides.* |
| Gompoo-kula, .. | N. | Musa *Nepalensis.* |
| Gondi, .. .. | H. | Cordia *(sp ?)* |
| Gondni, .. .. | — | Typha *(sp ?)* |

| | | |
|---|---|---|
| Googgoola, .. .. | S. B. | Amyris *Agallocha.* |
| Gooila, .. .. | B. | Vitis *latifolia.* |
| Gooja, .. .. | N. | Dipsacus *inermis.* |
| Gool, .. .. | B. | Menispermum *cordifolium.* |
| Goolab, .. .. | B. H. | Rosa *centifolia.* |
| Goolabas, .. .. | H. | Mirabilis *Jalapa, var.* |
| Goolab-jamun, .. | — | Eugenia *Jambos.* |
| G——-toolshee, .. | B. | Ocymum *caryophyllatum.* |
| Goolachin, .. .. | H. | Plumeria *acuminata.* |
| Goolal, .. { | B. | Diospyros *racemosa,* or *lanceofolia.* |
| | H. | Trichosanthes *heteroclita.* |
| Goola-moothi, .. | — | Cyperus *semi-nudus.* |
| Gool-ashroopi, .. | — | Linum *trigynum.* |
| Goolga, .. .. | B. | Nipa *fruticans.* |
| Gooli-ajaib, .. .. | H. | Hibiscus *mutabilis.* |
| G——ashrafi, .. | — | Linum *trigynum.* |
| Gooli-bagoon, .. | B. | Solanum *longum.* |
| Gooli-jafri, .. .. | H. | Tagetes *patula.* |
| Gooli-khiree, or Kyru, | — | Althea *rosea.* |
| G——kesh, .. .. | — | Amaranthus *cruentus.* |
| G——mendi, .. | — | Impatiens *balsamina.* |
| G——mukhmul, .. | — | Gomphrena *globosa.* |
| G——nurgis, .. | — | Hemerocallis *fulva.* |
| G——pringa, .. | — | Vinca *rosea, (red.)* |
| G——shaboo, .. | — | Polyanthes *tuberosa.* |
| G——sham, .. | — | Eranthemum *pulchellum.* |
| G——sosun, .. | — | Lilium *(sp ?)* |
| G——suranjan, .. | — | Colchicum *Illyricum.* |
| G——turah, .. | — | Poinciana *pulcherrima.* |
| Goolum, .. .. | — | Eugenia *oblata.* |
| Gooluncha, or Golunchee, .. .. | — | Menispermum *glabrum,* or *cordifolium.* |
| Goopooree, .. .. | B. | Podalyria *bracteata.* |
| Goordal-shim, .. | — | Dolichos *Lablab.* |
| Gooree, .. .. | — | Leucocephala *graminifolia.* |
| Goor-gwaliya, .. | — | Cissus *glauca.* |
| Goori, .. .. | H. | Scirpus *squarrosus.* |
| Goor-kamai, .. .. | B. | Solanum *Indicum.* |
| Goorkha, .. .. | — | Menispermum *cordifolium.* |
| Goorkhi, .. .. | B. H. | Solanum *rubrum.* |
| G——kuchoo, .. | B. | Arum *Colocasia, var.* 1. |
| Goot, .. .. | H. | Vinca *rosea (white.)* |
| Gooti-shoora, .. | B. | Ficus *heterophylla.* |
| G——soona, .. | — | Panax *fragrans.* |

| | | |
|---|---|---|
| Gootia-shook-china, .. | H. | Smilax *lanceofolia.* |
| Goovaka, .. .. | S. | Areca *Catechu.* |
| Goowa, .. .. | B. | ——— ———. |
| Goowamooree, .. | — | Anethum *Panmorium.* |
| Gooya-babula, .. | — | Mimosa *Farnesianæ.* |
| Gora-chand, .. .. | H. | Hedysarum *gyrans.* |
| G——moog, .. | B. | Phaseolus *sub lobatus.* |
| G——neboo, .. | B. H. | Citrus *acida, var.* 3. |
| Goruckhya-chakoolya, . | B. | Hedysarum *Lagopodioides.* |
| Goorooma, .. | H. | Limodorum *virens.* |
| Gooti-soona, .. | B. | Panax *fragrans.* |
| Goruk-phuna, .. | — | ——— ———. |
| G——natha, .. | — | Hedychium *coronarium.* |
| Goruksha, .. .. | S. | Menispermum *cordifolium.* |
| Goruma, .. .. | H. | Apluda *aristata.* |
| Goshega-soa, .. | N. | Hedyotis *gracilis.* |
| Goshina, .. .. | — | Rondeletia *cinerea.* |
| Gota-begoon, .. | B. | Solanum *Stramonifolium.* |
| Gouree-phul, .. | H. | Rubus *Goury-phul.* |
| Govila, .. .. | B. | Vitis *latifolia.* |
| Gow, .. .. | H. | Triticum *æstivum.* |
| Grendie-tagarum, .. | S. | Ruellia *strepens.* |
| Grinjuna, .. .. | — | Daucus *carota.* |
| Grishmaya, .. .. | — | Pharnaceum *mollugo.* |
| Guana, .. } | B. | Nipra *fruticans.* |
| Gubna, .. } | | |
| Gudgega, .. .. | H. | Guilandina *Bonducella.* |
| Guduchi, .. .. | S. | Menispermum *cordifolium.* |
| Gugal, .. .. | H. | Amyris *agallocha.* |
| Guja-kula, .. .. | B. | Webera *scandens.* |
| Guji, .. .. | — | Hedyotis *scandens.* |
| Gul-abbas, .. .. | H. | Mirabilis *Jalapa.* |
| Gular, .. .. | — | Ficus *glomerata.* |
| Gulnar, .. .. | — | Punica *granatum.* |
| Guma, .. .. | — | Pharnaceum *mollugo.* |
| Gumbharee, .. .. | S. | } Gmelina *arborea.* |
| Gumhar, .. .. | B. H. | } |
| Gunda-gatra, .. | S. | Annona *squammosa.* |
| Gundha-bena, or Gund-beyl, .. .. | B. H. | Andropogon *Schœnanthus.* |
| Gundha-bela, .. | B. | ——— ———. |
| G———bhadalee, .. | — | Oldenlandia *alata.* |
| G———goorana, .. | — | Andropogon *glabra.* |
| Gundhi, .. .. | — | Xanthophyllum *virens.* |
| Gundhul-rungun, .. | — | Ixora *parviflora.* |
| Gundhumar, .. | H. | Artemisia *Indica.* |

| | | | |
|---|---|---|---|
| **Gundmar,** | .. .. | H. | Artemisia *Austriaca.* |
| **Gundra,** | .. .. | S. | Saccharum *Sara.* |
| **Gundree,** | .. .. | B. | Xanthophyllum *virens.* |
| **Gunikarika,** | .. .. | S. | Premna *spinosa.* |
| **Guniaree,** | .. .. | B. | |
| **Gunna,** | .. .. | H. | Saccharum *officinarum.* |
| **Guran,** | .. .. | H. B. | Rhizophorus *decandra.* |
| **Gurch,** | .. .. | H. | Menispermum *glabrum.* |
| **Gurcha,** | .. .. | — | M——— *cordifolium.* |
| **Gursoonder,** | .. .. | B. | Mimosa *Arabica.* |
| **Gwali-lata,** | .. .. | — | Cissus *vitiginea.* |
| **Gwara,** | .. .. | — | Eleagnus *conferta.* |

## Section 2.

### *Tamool, Telinga, Cyngalese, &c.*

| | | |
|---|---|---|
| **G.** | | |
| Gadi-chikurea, .. | T. | Dolichos *medicaginus.* |
| Gadiday-gudda-purra, | — | Aristolochia *bracteata.* |
| Gadi-janoo, .. .. | — | Andropogon *laxus.* |
| Gaedumba, .. .. | Cyng. | Celtis *orientalis.* |
| Gæta-demata, .. | — | Gmelina *Asiatica.* |
| Gæta-keena, .. .. | — | Calophyllum *Calaba.* |
| Gæta-nitul, .. .. | — | Trophis *aspera.* |
| Gahkatu, .. .. | — | Stalagmitis *Gambogia.* |
| Galberya, .. .. | — | Cissus *latifolia.* |
| Gammiris, .. .. | — | Piper *nigrum.* |
| Gampela, .. .. | — | Galega *purpurea.* |
| Ganda-ganeroo, .. | T. | Echites *venenata.* |
| Gangare, .. .. | — | Hibiscus *populneus.* |
| Ganja, .. | Tam. T. | Cannabis *sativa.* |
| Gardi-garapa, .. | T. | Aristolochia *bracteata.* |
| Garga, .. .. | — | Gardenia *arborea.* |
| Garikoon, .. .. | Tam. | Boletus *igniarius.* |
| Garooy-moodi, .. | T. | Eugenia *bracteata.* |
| Garu, .. .. | — | Xylocarpus *granatum.* |
| Garugo, .. .. | — | Garugo *pinnata.* |
| Garugoodoo, .. | — | Casearia *tomentosa.* |
| Gas-bewila, .. .. | Cyng. | Pavonia *Zeylanica.* |
| G—kæla, .. .. | — | Butea *frondosa.* |
| G—kayla, .. .. | — | Phyllanthus *rhamnoides.* |
| G—kural-sœbo, .. | — | Achryanthes *aspera.* |
| G—miris, .. .. | — | Capsicum *frutescens.* |
| G—nawa-handi, .. | — | Euphorbia *Tirucalli.* |
| Gazeeragedda, .. | T. | Daucus *carota.* |
| Geema, .. .. | — | Chironia *Centauroides.* |
| Getolua, .. .. | Cyng. | Maranta *paniculata.* |
| Getoakaia, .. .. | T. | Guilandina *Bonducella.* |
| Ghebbonellie, .. | — | Premna *integrifolia.* |
| Gherka, .. .. | — | Panicum *dactylon.* |
| Gheedi-moraloo, .. | — | Bryonia *Garcini.* |
| Gheelaba-tunga, .. | — | Cyperus *tenuiflorus.* |

| | | |
|---|---|---|
| Ghelegherinta, .. | T. | Crotalaria *verrucosa.* |
| Ghelijehroo, .. | — | Trianthema *monogynia.* |
| Ghella-gaddy, .. | — | Coix *barbata.* |
| Ghenasa, .. | Can. | Convolvulus *Batatas.* |
| Ghengheravie, .. | T. | Hibiscus *populneus.* |
| Ghenneru-vayroo, .. | — | Nerium *odorum.* |
| Ghericha, .. .. | — | Panicum *dactylon.* |
| Gherutti-kamma, .. | — | Conyza *cinerea.* |
| Ghoedi-soucumdi, .. | — | Asclepias *pseudosarsa.* |
| Ghœdoo-tunga, .. | — | Cyperus *semi-nudus.* |
| Ghoonie, .. .. | — | Salvadora *persica.* |
| Gilakara, .. .. | — | Cuminum *Cyminum.* |
| Gilatiga, .. .. | — | Mimosa *scandens.* |
| Goda-manel, .. | Cyng. | Amaryllis *Zeylanica.* |
| Gollagand, .. .. | T. | Tradescantia *axillaris.* |
| Gollunga, .. .. | — | Limonia *pentaphylla.* |
| Gong-kura, .. .. | — | Hibiscus *Cannabinus.* |
| Gonkadura, .. .. | Cyng. | Cerbera *Manghas.* |
| Googoolapoo-chitto, .. | T. | Boswellia *glabra.* |
| Goolal, .. .. | — | Diospyros *lanceofolia.* |
| Goolabu, .. .. | Tam. | Rosa *centifolia.* |
| Gooli, .. .. | T. | Capparis *bisperma.* |
| Goomadi, .. .. | — | Gmelina *parviflora.* |
| Goomoodoo, .. .. | — | ——— *Asiatica.* |
| Goondoo-samgheloo, . | — | Pisum *sativum.* |
| Goontaghelinjeroo, .. | — | Eclipta *prostrata.* |
| Goor-chikurkai, .. | — | Dolichos *fabæformis.* |
| Goorie-ghenza, .. | — | Abrus *precatorius.* |
| Goraki-shaka-tunga, . | — | Scirpus *tridentatus.* |
| Gorapa, .. .. | — | ——— ———. |
| Gorinta, or Gorunta, . | — | Lawsonia *inermis,* or *spinosa.* |
| Gotti, .. .. | — | Zizyphus *Xylopyrus.* |
| Gugul, .. .. | Cyng. | Amyris *Agollocha.* |
| Gugulapoo-tschettoo, . | T. | Boswellia *glabra.* |
| Gumpina, .. .. | — | Odina *Woodier.* |
| Gundra, .. .. | — | Panicum *uliginosum.* |

## Section 1.

*Sanscrit, Bengallee, Hindi, Nawar, &c.*

# H.

| | | | |
|---|---|---|---|
| Hachittee, .. | .. | B. | Artemisia *sternutatoria.* |
| Haimavatee, .. | .. | S. | Acorus *Calamus (white var)* |
| Hakooch, .. | .. | B. H. | Psoralea *Corylifolia.* |
| Hakooee, .. | .. | — | Croton *polyandrum.* |
| Haleem, .. | .. | H. | Arabis *Chinensis.* |
| Halim, .. | .. | B. H. | Lepidium *sativum.* |
| Hali-moog, .. | .. | — | Phaseolus *Mungo.* |
| Haliun, .. | .. | H. | Asparagus *(sp ?)* |
| Halla, .. | .. | — | Valisneria *octandra.* |
| Hapur-malee, | .. | — | Echites *dichotoma.* |
| Har, or Hara, | .. | H. | Terminalia *Chebula.* |
| Har, or Harchara, | .. | B. | Cissus *quadrangularis.* |
| Harchara, .. | .. | H. | Flagellaria *Indica.* |
| Har-cuchila, .. | .. | B. | Strychnos *Colubrina.* |
| Harenso, .. | .. | S. | Pisum *sativum.* |

| | | |
|---|---|---|
| Harfareori, | H. | Phyllanthus *Cheramela.* |
| Hari, | S. | Aristolochia *Indica.* |
| Harikussa, | — | Acanthus *Ilicifolius.* |
| Hari-moog, | B. | Phaseolus *Mungo.* |
| Har-jorah, | B. H. | Cissus *quadrangularis.* |
| Harkat, | H. | Acanthus *illicifolius.* |
| Harkee, | B. | Echites *macrophylla.* |
| Harkuch-kanta, | H. | Acanthus *Ilicifolius.* |
| Harpar, | — | Cleome *viscosa.* |
| Harpoolli, | B. | Harpullia *Cuponioides.* |
| Harpung, | H. | Arum *gracile.* |
| Harra, | — | Terminalia *citrina.* |
| Harsingahar, | — | Nyctanthes *arbor-tristis.* |
| Harva, | — | Terminalia *citrina.* |
| Hasti-carni, | S. | Arum *macrorhizon.* |
| Hata-jori, | B. | Lycopodium *imbricatum.* |
| Hatta-kuna, | H. | Siphonanthus *hastata.* |
| Haynga, | — | Vitex *Haynga.* |
| Hazar-muni, | B. | Phyllanthus *Urinaria.* |
| Heabooka, | H. | Adelia *nereifolia.* |
| Heemoo, | — | Morus *serrata.* |
| Helencha, | B. | Hingcha *repens.* |
| Heluncha, | B. H. | ——— ———. |
| Hema-pooshpika, | S.B.H. | Jasminum *Chrysanthemum.* |
| H——sagura, | S. | Cotyledon *laciniata.* |
| Hemsagur, | B. H. | ——— ———. |
| Hental, | B. | Phœnix *paludosa.* |
| Hier, | H. | Menispermum *hirsutum.* |
| Hijul, | B. | Barringtonia *acutangula.* |
| Hijulee-budam, | — | Anacardium *occidentale.* |
| H——mindee, | H. | Eugenia *bracteata.* |
| Hilumochika, | S. | Hingcha *repens.* |
| Hina, | H. | Lawsonia *inermis.* |
| Hing, | S.H.B. | Ferula *Assafœtida.* |
| Hingcha, | B. | Hingcha *repens.* |
| Hingoo, | S. | Ferula *Assafœtida.* |
| Hingoolee, | B. | Solanum *Melongena.* |
| Hingun, | H. | Ximenia *Ægyptica.* |
| Hintal, | B. H. | Phœnix *paludosa.* |
| Hintala, | S. | ——— ———. |
| Hirina, | H. | Smilax *glabra.* |
| Hogla, | B. | Typha *Elephantina*, or *angustifolia.* |
| Hooeet, | — | Achryanthes *centrostachys.* |
| Hoogla, | — | Typha *Elephantina.* |
| Hoolhool, | H. | Cleome *pentaphylla.* |

| | | |
|---|---|---|
| Hoor-hooriya, .. | B. H. | Cleome *viscosa*. |
| Hoorooa, .. .. | — | Sapium *Indicum*. |
| Huding-nioong-mari, . | B. | Berberis *pinnata*. |
| Hulda, .. .. | H. | Terminalia *Chebula*. |
| Huldi, .. .. { | B. | Gardneria *ovata*. |
| | B. H. | Curcuma *longa*. |
| H——algosi-luta, .. | B. | Cuscuta *reflexa*. |
| H——busunta, .. | — | Stemodia *ruderalis*. |
| H——lunka-murich, | — | Capsicum *frutescens*. |
| H——moorga, .. | — | Celosia *cristata*. |
| H——murich, .. | — | Capsicum *frutescens*. |
| Hulkusi, .. | B. H. | Phlomis *Zeylanica*. |
| Hulsi, .. .. | B. | Ægiceras *majus*. |
| Humkata-joolee, .. | — | Phyllanthus *Vitis-Indica*. |
| Humula, .. .. | B. | Kæmpferia *Galanga*. |
| Hur or Hura, .. | H. | Terminalia *Chebula*. |
| Hurbhury, .. | — | Cicer *Arietinum*. |
| Hureetukee, .. | S. | Terminalia *Chebula*. |
| Hurhuria, .. | H. | Cleome *viscosa*. |
| Huri, .. .. | — | Casuarina *muricata*. |
| Huri-kekra, .. | — | Erythrina *ovalifolia*. |
| Huridra, .. | S. B. | Curcuma *longa*. |
| Hurindur, .. | B. | Nectandra *decandra*. |
| Hurineea-batana, .. | — | Quercus *ferox*. |
| Hurin-hura, .. | H. | Andersonia *Rohita*. |
| Huri-phul, .. | B. | Phyllanthus *Cheramela*. |
| Huritukee, .. | S. B. | Terminalia *Chebula*. |
| Hurivilasinee, .. | — | Curcuma *longa*. |
| Hurmur-gullar, .. | H. | Calamus *quinquenervius*. |
| Hursmun, .. | B. | Prasium *melissifolium*. |
| Huttian, .. | H. | Bombax *pentandrum*. |

## Section 2.

*Tamool, Telinga, Cyngalese, &c.*

# H.

| | | |
|---|---|---|
| Habarala, .. .. | Cyng. | Arum *macrorhizon.* |
| Hæmarago, .. | — | Jussieua *suffruticosa.* |
| Haradul, .. .. | — | Curcuma *longa.* |
| Haralu, .. .. | Can. | Ricinus *communis.* |
| Heen-bowitiya, .. | Cyng. | Melastoma *aspera.* |
| H—— gotu-kala, .. | — | Hydrocotyle *Asiatica.* |
| H—— monara-kudimbya, .. .. | — | Conyza *lacera.* |
| Heento labo, .. | — | Crinum *Asiaticum.* |
| Heen-yak-wenassa, .. | — | Ballota *disticha.* |
| Hingo, .. .. | — | Ferula *Asafœtida.* |
| Hingul-kura, .. | — | Melochia *Corchorifolia.* |
| Hinhooroo-pecalliculla, | — | Curcuma *Zerumbet.* |
| Hirimandetta, .. | — | Verbena *nodiflora.* |
| Hulud, .. | Mah. | Curcuma *longa.* |

## Section 1.

*Sanscrit, Bengallee, Hindi, Nawar, &c.*

# I.

| | | |
|---|---|---|
| Ibharunkusha, .. | B. H. | Andropogon *Iwarancusa.* |
| Igir, .. .. | H. | Acorus *Calamus.* |
| Ijjul, .. .. | S. | Barringtonia *Acutangula.* |
| Ik, .. .. | H. | Saccharum *officinale.* |
| Ikshoo, .. .. | — | ——— ——— |
| Ikshugandha, . | — | Barleria *longifolia.* |
| Ilachi, .. .. | — | Amomum *Aromaticum,* or *Cardamomum.* |
| Imli, .. .. | — | Tamarindus *Indica.* |
| Indoor-kanee-pana, .. | B. | Salvinia *cucullata.* |
| Indradroog, .. .. | S. | Lagerstræmia *grandiflora.* |
| Indraini or Indrayan, . | H. | Cucumis *Colocynthis.* |
| Indra-varonee, .. | S. | (Cucumis *Colocynthis.*) |
| Indurjaw, .. .. | H. | Nerium *antidysentericum.* |
| Indurjob, .. .. | B. | ——— ——— |
| Inguddi, .. .. | S. | Terminalia *Catappa.* |
| Inkri, .. .. | H. | Vicia *sativa.* |
| Ipar, .. .. | — | Thymus *(sp.?)* |
| Irsa, .. .. | — | Iris *Florentina.* |
| Isarmel or Isarmal, Ishurmool, | B. H. | Aristolochia *Indica.* |
| Iscil or Iskil, | — | Scilla *(sp.?)* |
| Isfanaj, .. .. | H. | Spinacia *oleracea.* |
| Isch-pecha, .. .. | — | Ipomæa *Quamoclit.* |
| Ishwari, .. .. | S. | Aristolochia *Indica.* |
| Ispagool, .. .. | B. H. | Plantago *Ispagul,* or *Psyllium.* |
| Isriwayl, .. .. | H. | Aristolochia *Indica.* |
| Iwarankoosa, .. | — | Andropogon *nardus,* or *Iwarancusa.* |

## Section 2.

### *Tamool, Telinga, Cyngalese, &c.*

## I.

| | | | |
|---|---|---|---|
| Illipee, .. | .. | Tam. | Bassia *longifolia.* |
| Imboril, .. | .. | — | Oldenlandia *umbellata.* |
| Induga, .. | .. | T. | Strychnos *potatorum.* |
| Ingoova, .. | .. | — | Ferula *Assafœtida.* |
| Injee, .. | .. | Tam. | Zinziber *officinalis.* |
| Ippee, Ippa, | .. | T. | Bassia *latifolia.* |
| Irimusu, .. | .. | Cyng. | Periploca *Indica.* |
| Irminakullie, | .. | Tam. | Cacalia *Kleinia.* |
| Irumbilli-marum, | .. | — | Ferriola *buxifolia.* |
| Ischi, .. | .. | M. | Zinziber *officinalis.* |
| Isheepa-bora-gaddi, | .. | T. | Panicum *corymbosum.* |
| Isora-murri, | .. | M. | Helicteres *Isora.* |
| Itoo-monghy-tiga, | .. | T. | Dolichos *falcatus.* |

## SECTION 1.

### *Sanscrit, Bengallee, Hindi, Nawar, &c.*

# J.

| | | |
|---|---|---|
| Jaci, .. .. | H. | Jasminum *grandiflorum.* |
| Jadwar, .. .. | — | Curcuma *Zedoaria.* |
| Jafari, .. .. | — | Linum *trigynum.* |
| Jaephal, .. .. | — | Myristica *moschata.* |
| Jait, .. .. | — | Sesbania *Ægyptica.* |
| Jainti, .. .. | B. H. | Æschynomene *Sesban.* |
| Jala-brinni, .. | S. | Gratiola *Monniera.* |
| J—nirgundi, .. | — | Vitex *trifolia.* |
| Jal-lakri, .. .. | H. | Valeriana *officinalis.* |
| Jalpai, .. .. | — | { Elæocarpus *serratas.*<br>{ Olea *Europea.* |
| Jamalgota, .. | — | Croton *Tiglium.* |
| Jaman, .. | — | Eugenia *Jambulana.* |
| Jamb, .. .. | B. H. | E——— *aquea.* |
| Jambu, .. .. | S. | E——— *Jambu.* [*folia.* |
| Jamoon, .. .. | H. | Calyptranthes *caryophylli-* |
| Jamoun, .. .. | — | C ——— ——— *Jambolana.* |
| Jamrool, .. .. | B. | Eugenia *alba.* |
| Janeka, .. .. | — | Rhopala *robusta.* |
| Janewa, .. .. | H. | Agrostis *linearis.* |
| Janteyana, .. | — | Gentiana *officinalis.* |
| Jarool; Jarul, .. | B. H. | Lagerstræmia *Regina*, v. 1. or 2. |
| Jarye, .. .. | H. | Valisneria *alternifolia.* |
| Jasoon, .. .. | — | Hibiscus *Rosa-sinensis.* |
| Jatadhari, .. | — | Celosia *cristata.* |
| Jatamansi, .. | S.B.H. | Valeriana *Jatamansi.* |
| Jatee, .. .. | — | Jasminum *grandiflorum.* |
| J——phala, .. .. | S. | Myristica *moschata.* |
| Jaundri, .. .. | H. | Sorghum *vulgare.* |
| Jawa, .. .. | — | Hibiscus *Rosa-sinensis.* |
| Jawasi, .. .. | — | Hedysarum *Alhagi.* |
| Jawi, .. .. | — | Melia *Azadirachta.* |
| Jaya-phula; Jayphul;<br>Jaiphal, .. | B. H. | Myristica *moschata.* |
| Jeebuna, .. .. | B. | Celtis *orientalis.* |
| Jeel-murich, .. | H. | Sphenoclea *Zeylanica.* |
| Jeemota, .. .. | S. | Andropogon *serratum.* |

| | | | |
|---|---|---|---|
| Jeera, | .. .. | B. H | Cuminum *Cyminum.* |
| Jeeruka, | .. .. | S. | ——— ——— |
| Jeevula, | .. .. | — | Odina *Wodier.* |
| Jeevunee, | .. .. | — | Celtis *orientalis.* |
| Jethi-mudh, | .. .. | H. | Glycirrhiza *glabra.* |
| Jhampe-petaree, | .. | B. | Sida *Asiatica.* |
| Jhanj, | .. .. | — | } Utricularia *fasciculata.* |
| Jhanji, | .. .. | H. | |
| J——, | .. .. | B. | Chara *involucrata.* |
| J——, | .. .. | H. | Ceratophyllum *verticillatum.* |
| Jharberi, | .. .. | — | Zizyphus *Jujuba.* |
| Jhaw, | .. .. | — | Tamarix *Indica.* |
| Jhavooka, | .. .. | S. | ——— ——— |
| Jhawoo, | .. .. | B. | ——— ——— |
| Jhinga, | .. .. | H. | Luffa *acutangula.* |
| Jhinjhora, | .. .. | — | Bauhinia *parviflora.* |
| Jhintee, | .. .. | S. B. | Barleria *cristata,* (purple.) |
| Jhunjhun, | .. .. | B. | Crotalaria *Sericea.* |
| Jhunjhuni-ankuri, | .. | H. | Vicia *sativa.* |
| Jidoo-palung, | .. | B. | Salicornia *Indica.* |
| Jijinga, | .. .. | — | Trichosanthes *anguina.* |
| Jinga, | .. .. | — | Luffa *acutangula.* |
| J——, | .. .. | — | Trichosanthes *anguina.* |
| Jingee, | .. .. | S. | Rubia *Munjistha.* |
| Jipala, | .. .. | — | Croton *Tiglium.* |
| Jira, | .. .. | H. | Cuminum *Cyminum.* |
| Jitee, | .. .. | B. H. | Asclepias *tenacissima.* |
| Jivaka, | .. .. | S. | Bryonia *grandis.* |
| Jiyul, | .. .. | B. | Odina *Wodier.* |
| Joar, | .. .. | H. | Sorghum *vulgaris.* |
| Jodoo-palung, | .. | B. | Salicornia *Indica.* |
| Joffiah, | .. .. | — | Croton *Jouffiah.* |
| Jol-palung, | .. .. | — | Rumex *acutus.* |
| Jooar, | .. .. | B. H. | Andropogon *Sorghum, v.* 3. |
| Jooi, | .. .. | — | Ixora *tomentosa.* |
| J—, | .. .. | B. | Jasminum *auriculatum.* |
| J—-pana, | .. .. | — | Justicia *nasuta.* |
| Jooni-raee, | .. .. | — | Sinapis *ramosa.* |
| J——ugur, | .. .. | — | Combretum *pilosum.* |
| Joopi, | .. .. | — | Scirpus *anceps.* |
| J——kunka, | .. .. | — | Panicum *tenellum.* |
| Joothipooshpika, | .. | B. H. | Jasminum *auriculatum.* |
| Jow, | .. .. | H. | Hordeum *hexastichon.* |
| J—, | .. .. | B. | Casuarina *muricata.* |
| Jub; Juba, | .. .. | — | Hordeum *hexastichon.* |
| Juba, | .. .. | B. H. | Hibiscus *Rosa-sinensis,* or *Syriacus.* |

| | | | |
|---|---|---|---|
| Jugut-mudun, | .. | B. | Justicia *Gandarussa.* |
| Jugya-doomoor, | .. | — | Ficus *glomerata.* |
| Jul-gurgur, | .. | B. H. | Coix *lacryma.* |
| Julpai, .. | .. | — | Elæocarpus *serratus.* |
| Jul-papara, | .. | B. | Mollugo *triphylla.* |
| Julsi, .. | .. | N. | Rondeletia *coriacea.* |
| Jumalgota, . | .. | B. H. | Croton *Tiglium.* |
| Jumbeera,... | .. | S. | Citrus *acida.* |
| Junglai-kandi, | .. | H. | Dracontium *polyphyllum.* |
| J——moonghie, | .. | — | Hedysarum *Sennoides.* |
| J——adruk, | .. | — | Zinziber *capitatum.* |
| J——pat, | .. | — | Uvaria *bracteata.* |
| J——huldee, | .. | B. | Curcuma *Zedoaria.* |
| J——piaz, | .. | H. | Erythronium *Indicum.* |
| Junka, .. | .. | B. | Sida *humilis.* |
| Junki-jam, | .. | — | Dalrympelia *pomifera.* |
| Juo-chahee | .. | H. | Hordeum *hexastichon ?* |
| J—kakee,, | .. | — | ——— ———*sp. (?)* |
| Jupa, .. | .. | S. B. | Hedysarum *Rosa-sinensis.* |
| J—bun-kula, | .. | B. | Uvaria *bracteata.* |
| Jupal-saynd, | .. | H. | Cactus *Indica.* |
| Jurad-bangra, | .. | — | Conyza *trifoliata.* |
| Jurud-kulmee, | .. | — | Convolvolus *bicolor.* |
| Juta-kanshira, | .. | B. | Commelina *commuis.* |
| Jutamangshee, | .. | S.B.H. | Valeriana *Jatamansi.* |
| Juta-shalpanee, | .. | B. | Hedysarum *pulchellum.* |
| Juva, .. | .. | S. | Hibiscus *Rosa-sinensis.* |
| Juvanee; Juwanee, | .. | B. H. | Ligusticum *Ajouan.* |
| Juwani, .. | .. | B. | Scirpus *quinqueangulaais.* |
| Juwasi, .. | .. | H. | Hedysarum *Alhagi.* |
| Juya-phootica, | .. | B. | Melastoma *(sp. nov.)* |
| Juyuntee, .. | .. | S.B.H. | Æschynomene *Sesban.* |
| Jyosthi-madhoor, | .. | B. H. | Glycirrhiza *glabra.* |
| Jyotish-mutee, | .. | S. | Cardiospermum *Halicacabum* |

## Section 2.

### *Tamool, Telinga, Cyngalese, &c.*

## J.

| | | | |
|---|---|---|---|
| Jadicai, | .. .. | Tam. | Myristica *moschata.* |
| Jajikaiai, | .. .. | T. | |
| Janiki, | .. .. | — | Adelia *nereifolia.* |
| Jatamansi, | .. .. | — | Valeriana *Jatamansi.* |
| Jatipullum, | .. .. | Cyng. | Myristica *moschata.* |
| Javellaka, | .. .. | T. | Grewia *hirsuta.* |
| Jeeraga, | .. .. | Can. | Cuminum *Cymiuum.* |
| Judu-kata-patuk, | .. | Cyng. | Cactus *Indicus.* |
| Jutuga, | .. .. | T. | Asclepias *echinata.* |
| Jyapala, | .. .. | Can. | Croton *Tiglium.* |

## SECTION 1.

### *Sanscrit, Bengallee, Hindi, Nawar, &c.*

# K.

| | | | |
|---|---|---|---|
| Kabuter-ke-jar, | .. | H. | Justicia *nasuta*. |
| Kachura-dam, | .. | — | Jussieua *repens*. |
| Kadali, .. | .. | B. | Musa *Paradisiaca*. |
| Kafoor-ka-pawt, | .. | S. | Salvia *Bengalensis*. |
| Kaffri-murich, | .. | H. | Capsicum *grossum*. |
| Kagugee-neebo, | .. | — | Citrus *acida* (var. 2.) |
| Kagura, | .. | B. H. | Saccharum *spontaneum*. |
| Kahoowa, | .. | H. | Pentaptera *Arjuna*. |
| Kai-nim, | .. | — | Gratiola *amara*. |
| Kajeerah, | .. | B. | Carthamus *tinctorius*. |
| Kajur ; Khajur, | .. | — | Phœnix *dactylifera*, or *sylvestris*. |
| Kaka-chinchi, | .. | H. | Abrus *precatorius*. |
| K——doomboorica, | . | S. | Ficus *oppositifolia*. |
| K——doomoor, | .. | — | F——— ——— |
| K——jambu, | .. | B. | Calyptranthes *caryophyllifolia*. |
| K——jungha, | .. | S. | Leea *hirta*. |
| Kakamari, | .. | B. | Menispermum *cocculus*. |
| Kakangee, | .. | S. | Leea *hirta*. |
| K———, | .. | S. | Aponogeton *monostachyon*. |
| Kaka-pulla, | .. | H. | Asclepias *asthmatica*. |
| K——thontee, | .. | B. | Ardisia *solanacea*. |
| Kakhur, | .. | H. | Curcuma *Zerumbet*. |
| Kakindoo, | .. | S. | Diospyros *melanoxylon*. |
| Kakmari, | .. | H. | Menispermum *cocculus*. |
| Kakoon, | .. | H. | Panicum *Italicum*. |
| Kakra, | .. | B. | Rhizophora *gymnorhiza*. |
| Kakrol, | .. | H. | Momordica *mixta*. |
| Kala-buchnak, | .. | — | Cinchona *excelsa*. |
| K—chuckma, | .. | B. | Quercus *fenestratus*. |
| K—deodhanya, | .. | — | Andropogon *bicolor*. |
| K—dhootura, | .. | B. H. | Datura *fastuosa*. |
| K—jatee, | .. | B. | Eranthemum *pulchellum*. |
| K—jeera, | .. | — | Nigella *Indica*, or *sativa*. |
| K— -kalkashonda, | .. | — | Cassia *purpurea*. |
| K—kuchoo, | .. | — | Arum *colocasia*. |

| | | | |
|---|---|---|---|
| Kala-kurpoo, | .. | H. | Capraria *gratissima.* |
| K—-kustooree, | .. | — | Hibiscus *Abelmoschus.* |
| K—-megh, | .. | B. | Justicia *paniculata.* |
| K—-oja, | .. | — | Ehretia *serrata.* |
| K—-shim, | .. | B. H. | Dolichos *virosus.* |
| Kalee-toolsee, | .. | H. | Ocymum *Basilicum.* |
| K——-koura, | .. | B. | Guarea *paniculata.* |
| K——-shumbali, | .. | H. | Justicia *Gandarussa.* |
| Kalikeker, | .. | — | Mimosa *Arabica.* |
| Kalizer, | .. | — | Clitoria *ternata.* |
| Kaliezeerie, | .. | H. | Vernonia *Anthelmintica.* |
| Kalka-jhamp, | .. | — | Pteris *lunulata.* |
| Kalla-soa, | .. | N. | Houttuynia *cordata.* |
| Kalu-kera, | .. | H. | Capparis *acuminata.* |
| Kalumishika, | .. | S. | Rubia *Mungistha.* |
| Kamal, | .. | H. | Nelumbium *speciosum.* |
| Kam-aloo, | .. | B. H. | Dioscorea *alata.* |
| Kamalottara, | .. | S. | Carthamus *tinctorius.* |
| Kama-luta, | .. | S.B.H. | Ipomœa *Quamoclit.* |
| Kamana, | .. | S. | Hedysarum *Sennoides.* |
| Kamaral-neeboo, | .. | B. H. | Citrus *acida* (var. 5.) |
| Kama-runga, | .. | — | Averrhoa *Carambola.* |
| Kameenee, | .. | B. | Murraya *exotica.* |
| Kanana-canda, | .. | S. | Dracontium *polyphyllum.* |
| K———-iraka, | .. | — | Vernonia *anthelmintica.* |
| K———-kerundum, | .. | — | Jatropha *Curcas.* |
| K———-mallika, | .. | — | Justicia *angustifolium.* |
| Kanara, | .. | B. H. | Webera *corymbosa.* |
| Kana-raj, | .. | H. | Bauhinia *candida.* |
| Kanchkoori, | .. | — | Tragia *Cannabina.* |
| K————, | .. | — | Dolichos (or Carpopogon) *pruriens.* |
| Kanchun, | .. | B. | Bauhinia *acuminata.* |
| Kanchura, | .. | H. | Nama *Zeylanica.* |
| Kanda, | .. | H. | Erythronium *Indicum.* |
| Kanduli, | .. | B. | Commelina *nudiflora.* |
| Kaner, | .. | H. | Nerium *odorum* (single). |
| Kangni, | .. | B. H. | Panicum *Italicum.* |
| Kanjam-boora, | .. | H. | Kæmpferia *angustifolia.* |
| Kanka-juriya, or Kan-koojooriya, | .. | — | Milium *filiforme.* |
| Kankoor, | .. | B. | Cucumis *utilissimus.* |
| Kankra-eesh-langula, | . | — | Nama *Zeylanica.* |
| Kankhura, | .. | — | Urtica *tenacissima.* |
| Kanta-aloo, | .. | B. H. | Dioscorea *pentaphylla.* |
| K——batana, | .. | B. | Quercus *acuminata.* |

| | | |
|---|---|---|
| Kanta-goolab, .. | B. H. | Rosa *Chinensis.* |
| K——goor-kamaee, .. | B. | Capparis *sepiaria.* |
| K————— .. | H. | Monetia *Barleroides.* |
| K——jatee, .. | — | Barleria *prionitis.* |
| K—— koolika, .. | — | Ruellia *longifolia.* |
| K——kutchoo, .. | B. H. | Pothos *Læsia.* |
| K——lal-batana, .. | B. | Quercus *armata.* |
| K——man, . | B. H. | Pothos *heterophylla.* |
| K——nuteeya, .. | B. | Amaranthus *spinosus.* |
| Kantchi-shim, .. | — | Dolichos *lignosus.* |
| Kanth-mullika, .. | — | Jasminum *Zambac.* |
| Kantha-karee, .. | B. H. | Solanum *Jacquini.* |
| K——karika, .. | S. | S—— *J*——. |
| Kanuraca, .. | B. H. | Commelina *Bengalensis.* |
| Kapas, .. | B. | Gossypium *herbaceum.* |
| Kapicachlie, .. | S. | Dolichos, (or Carpopogon) *pruriens.* |
| Karak-bet, .. | B. | Calamus *latifolius.* |
| Karambha, .. | S. | Antirrhinum *Cymbalaria.* |
| Karanja, .. | — | Dalbergia *arborea.* |
| Kara-vela, .. | — | Cleome *pentaphylla.* |
| Karavi, .. | — | Cardiospermum *Halicacabum.* |
| Karbi, .. | H. | Sorghum *vulgare.* |
| Karela, .. | B. H. | Cleome *pentaphylla.* |
| Karia-phool, .. | B. | Bergera *Kœnigii.* |
| Kariari, .. | H. | Gloriosa *superba.* |
| Karkhura, .. | S. | Curcuma *Zerumbet.* |
| Karpassa, .. | B. | Gossypium *herbaceum.* |
| Karpassee, .. | S. | G—— *h*—— |
| Karan-phul, .. | H. | Amyris *heptaphylla.* |
| Kas, .. | H. | Saccharum *spontaneum.* |
| Kasha, .. | S. | S—— —— |
| Kashiya, .. | B. | S—— —— |
| Kashmulla, .. | H. | Odina *Wodier.* |
| Kasmirajanma, .. | S. | Crocus *sativus.* |
| Kas-murdun, .. | B. | Cassia *esculenta.* |
| Kasoori, .. | N. | Euonymus *tingens.* |
| Kastha, .. | B. | Curcuma *xanthorhiza.* |
| Kasya-pat, or Kasyapal, .. | H. | Hibiscus *macrophyllus.* |
| Katch-kula, .. | B. H. | Musa *paradisiaca.* |
| Katha-mulli, .. | B. | Canthium *angustifolium.* |
| Kathaee-bun-jhoopie, . | B. | Dendrobium *veratrifolium.* |
| Katha-moolie, .. | — | Canthium *angustifolium.* |
| Kathbel, .. | — | Jasminum *pubescens.* |

| | | |
|---|---|---|
| Kathya-ram-ram, .. | B. | Orchis *uniflora*. |
| Kat-kulija, .. | H. | Cæsalpinia *Bonducella*. |
| Kattia-jorung, .. | B. | Kæmpferia *secunda* or *linearis*. |
| Kattia-laffia or Laphya, | B. | Hedychium *gracile*. |
| K——lung-mutti, .. | — | H—— *speciosum*. |
| K——ram-rait, .. | — | H—— *villosum*. |
| K——rit-yam, .. | — | H—— *flavum*. |
| K——tilook-seer, .. | — | H—— *fl*——. |
| Katira, .. | H. | Sterculia *urens*. |
| Kawa-hurinee, .. | — | Mimosa *heterophylla*. |
| Kayla, .. | H. | Musa *Paradisiaca*. |
| Kea, or Kea-phool, .. | B. | Pandanus *odoratissimus*. |
| K—kanta, .. | — | P—— *fœtidus*. |
| Keco, .. | B. H. | Costus *speciosus*. |
| Kedora, .. | B. | Urtica ? (*sp. ?*) |
| Keéra, .. | H. | Cucumis *sativus*. |
| Keerat, .. | B. | Gentiana *Cheyrata*. |
| Kela, .. | H. | Musa *paradisiaca*. |
| Kemboo, .. | S. | Costus *speciosus*. |
| Kemooka, .. | S. | C—— *s*——. |
| Kendoo, .. | B. | Diospyros *melanovylon*. |
| Kendru, .. | — | Commelina *nudiflora*. |
| Kental, .. | — | Artocarpus *integrifolius*. |
| Kentoni-jam, .. | H. | Tetranthera *nitida*. |
| Keralee, .. | B. | Ambrosinia *ciliata*. |
| Keril, .. | H. | Capparis *aphylla*. |
| Kerula, .. | — | Luffa *amara*. |
| Kesa-proom, .. | B. | Ceratostema *vaccinacea*. |
| Kesari, .. | H. | Lathyrus *sativus*. |
| Keshinee, .. | S. | Andropogon *aciculatum*. |
| Keshoor, .. | B. | Rottlera *tinctoria*. |
| Keshooriya, .. | B. H. | Eclipta *prostrata*. |
| K——, .. | B. | Verbesina *calendulacea*. |
| Kesoor ; Kesoorea, .. | B. H. | Scirpus *Kysoor*. |
| Kesura-vukoola, .. | S. | Mimusops *Elengi*. |
| Kesuri-mulunga, .. | B. | Scirpus *bispicatus*. |
| Ket, .. | H. | Feronia *elephantum*. |
| Ketalee, .. | B. | ? |
| Ketgi, .. | — | Pandanus *odoratissimus*. |
| Ketukee, .. | B. S. | P—— *o*——. |
| Keura-keora, .. | H. | P—— *o*——. |
| Keysur, .. | — | Crocus *sativus*. |
| Khadira, .. | S. | Acacia or Mimosa *Catechu* or *ferruginea*. |
| Khair, .. | H. | Acacia *Catechu* or *ferruginea* |

| | | | |
|---|---|---|---|
| Khajoor, | .. | B. H. | Phœnix *sylvestris.* |
| Khajora, | .. | H. | Saccharum *spontaneum.* |
| Khali-jamera, | .. | B. | Sideroxylon *grandifolium.* |
| Khamach, | .. | H. | Carpopogon *niveum.* |
| Kharj-jooree, | .. | S. | Phœnix *sylvestris.* |
| Khas-zahra, | .. | H. | Nerium *oleander.* |
| Khas-khas, | .. | — | Andropogon *muricatum.* |
| Kheeri, | .. | B. | Mimusops *Kanki.* |
| Kheora, | .. | B. H. | Sonneratia *apetala.* |
| Kherooya, | .. | B. | Phaseolus *Mungo.* |
| Khesaree, | .. | — | Lathyrus *sativus.* |
| Khet-papara, | .. | — | Mollugo *pentaphylla.* |
| K——-papura, | .. | — | Oldenlandia *biflora.* |
| Khikhri, | .. | H. | Zizyphus *Jujuba.* |
| Khira, | .. | — | Cucumis *utilissimus.* |
| Khirni, | .. | — | Mimusops *Kanki.* |
| Khishniz, | .. | — | Coriandrum *sativum.* |
| Khitmie, | .. | H | Sida *Mauritiana.* |
| Khoobanie, | .. | B. H. | Prunus *Armeniaca.* |
| Khoodi-jam, | .. | — | Antidesma *paniculata.* |
| K———-okra, | .. | — | Croton *plicatum.* |
| Khoojlee, | .. | B. | Hibiscus *pistus.* |
| Khoorfeh, | .. | H. | Portulacea *(sp ?)* |
| Khor, | .. | B. | Andropogon *serratum* or *muricatum.* |
| Khrishanoo, | .. | — | Plumbago *Zeylanica.* |
| Khrishna, | .. | H. | Sesamum *Indicum.* |
| K————-choora, | .. | B. H. | Poinciana *pulcherrima.* |
| Khrishnacula-goonga, | . | S. | Abrus *precatorius.* |
| Khrishna-dhattura, | .. | S. H. | Datura *fastuosa.* |
| K————-jiraka, | .. | S. | Nigella *sativa* or *Indica.* |
| K————-kamboji, | .. | — | Phyllanthus *multiflorus.* |
| K————-keli, | .. | B. | Mirabilis *Jalapa.* |
| K————-phula, | .. | S. | Carissa *Carandas.* |
| K————-rajam, | .. | S. | Coronilla *picta.* |
| Khuera, | .. | B. H. | Mimosa *Catechu.* |
| Khugura, | .. | B. | Saccharum *spontaneum.* |
| Khujoor-choori, | .. | H. | Phlomis *nepitifolia.* |
| Khul, | .. | — | Achryanthes *lanata.* |
| Khunkui, | .. | — | Sida *Mauritiana.* |
| Khura, | .. | S. | Andropogon *serratum.* |
| Khurbooja, | .. | B. H. | Cucumis *Melo.* |
| Khuree, | .. | — | Saccharum *semidecumbens* or *fuscum.* |
| Khurma, | .. | H. | Phœnix *dactylifera.* |
| Khursa, | .. | — | Asphodelus *(sp ?)* |

| | | | |
|---|---|---|---|
| Kiew, | .. | B. | Diospyros *melanoxylon.* |
| Kingshookha, | .. | S. B. | Butea *frondosa.* |
| Kinsuka, | .. | S. | B—— *f*——. |
| Kintun, | .. | B. | Laurus *obtusifolia.* |
| Kiraneli, | .. | B. | Phyllanthus *Niruri.* |
| Kiras, | .. | H. | Lathyrus *sativus.* |
| Kiraticta, | .. | S. | Gentiana *Cherayti.* |
| Kiruwa, | .. | S. | Nymphea *esculenta.* |
| Kispetra-purputee, | .. | S. | Mollugo *pentaphylla.* |
| Kiwach, | .. | B. H. | Carpopogon (or Dolichos) *pruriens.* |
| Kleeba, | .. | S. | Morinda *umbellata.* |
| Koamoora, | .. | B. H. | Callicarpa *lanata.* |
| Koda, | .. | H. | Paspalum *Kora.* |
| Koda, | .. | B. | Paspalum *scrobiculatum.* |
| K——ka-chaul, | .. | H. | |
| Kodaleya, | .. | H. | Hedysarum *triflorum.* |
| Koduee, | .. | H. | Panicum *(sp ?)* |
| Koi-poora, | .. | H. | Scytalia *rubra.* |
| Koka-buradi, | .. | B. | Salvia *parviflora.* |
| Kokhura-shoonga, | .. | B. | Conyza *lacera.* |
| Kokra, | .. | H. | Alnus *dioica.* |
| Koli, | .. | S. | Zizyphus *Jujuba.* |
| Kolshia, or Kolshi, | .. | B. | Leersia *aristata.* |
| Kolsi, | .. | H. | Solanum *Indicum.* |
| Kolunjen, | .. | — | Nigella *sativa* or *Indica.* |
| Komla-neeboo, | .. | B. | Citrus *aurantium.* |
| Komol, | .. | B. | Nelumbium *speciosum.* |
| Koni, | .. | H. | Poa *unioloides.* |
| Kooa, | .. | — | Curcuma *angustifolia.* |
| Koobayratchie, | .. | S. | Guilandina *Bonducella.* |
| Koobedar, | .. | B. | Bauhinia *variegata.* |
| Koochee-kanta, | .. | B. | Mimosa *octandra.* |
| Koochila, | .. | B. H. | Strychnos *Nux-vomica.* |
| K————luta, | .. | B. | S———— *colubrina.* |
| Koochunduna, | .. | S. H. | Adenanthera *pavonina.* |
| Koochuri, | .. | B. | Exacum *tetragonum.* |
| Koodum-bet, | .. | — | Calamus *polygamus.* |
| Koogroom, | .. | — | Dalbergia *ramosa.* |
| Kooka-vaivinta, or Vu-nitie, | .. | S. | Cleome *viscosa.* |
| Kookoora-choora, | .. | B. | Ixora *Pavetta.* |
| K————neja, | .. | — | Gloriosa *superba.* |
| Kookoor-aloo, | .. | B. H. | Dioscorea *anguina.* |
| K————chitta, | .. | B. | Tetranthera *monopetala.* |
| K————jeewa, | .. | — | Leea *staphylea.* |

| | | | |
|---|---|---|---|
| Kookshima, | .. | B. | Celsia *Coromandeliana.* |
| Kookunduna, | .. | S. | Pterocarpus *Santalinus.* |
| Kool, | .. | B. | Zizyphus *Jujuba.* |
| Koolunjuna, | .. | S. | Alpinia *Galanga.* |
| Koolanyoga, | .. | S. | A.—— *G*——. |
| Koolee, | .. | — | Solanum *longum.* |
| Kooli, | .. | H. | Sterculia *urens.* |
| K——begoon, | .. | B. | Solanum *longum.* |
| Koolthee, | .. | B. H. | Dolichos *biflorus.* |
| Kooluttha, | .. | S. | Dolichos *biflorus.* |
| Koomaree, | .. | — | Aloe *perfoliata.* |
| K——, | .. | H. | Smilax *laurifolia.* |
| Koomooda, | .. | S. | Nymphæa *Lotus.* |
| K——, | .. | — | Menyanthes *Indica.* |
| Koomoodinee ; Koomoodwutee, | .. | — | M—— *I*—— or *cristata.* |
| Koomra, | .. | B. H. | Cucurbita *pepo.* |
| Koomurka, | .. | — | Smilax *ovalifolia.* |
| Koonch, | .. | B. | Abrus *precatorius.* |
| Koonda, | .. | S. B. | Jasminum *pubescens.* |
| Koondoorie, | .. | H. | Bryonia *grandis.* |
| Koondroo, | .. | H. | Trichosanthes ? *(sp ?)* |
| Koonk, | .. | B. | Phœnix *acaulis.* |
| Kooppie, | .. | H. | Acalypha *Indica.* |
| Koorchi, | .. | — | Echites *antidysenterica.* |
| Koosha, | .. | S.B.H. | Poa *cynosuroides.* |
| Kooshoom, | .. | H. | Carthamus *tinctorius.* |
| Koosth-nashinee, | .. | S. | Trifolium *Indicum.* |
| Koostoola, | .. | H. | Justicia *verticillata.* |
| Koosum, | .. | — | Carthamus *tinctorius.* |
| Koosumbha, | .. | S.B.H. | C—— *t*——. |
| Kootaya, | .. | H. | Solanum *Jacquini.* |
| Kootuja, | .. | S. | Echites *antidysenterica.* |
| Kooveruka, | .. | — | Cedrela *Toona.* |
| Kopee, | .. | B. H. | Brassica *oleracea.* |
| Kora, Koraloo, | .. | H. | Panicum *Italicum.* |
| Koratiya-juvanee, | .. | B. H. | Scirpus *complanatus.* |
| Koriya-doombar, | .. | H. | Ficus *oppositifolia.* |
| Korkotee, | .. | S. | Momordica *mixta.* |
| Korna-neeboo, | .. | B. H. | Citrus *medicus.* |
| Korudoosha, | .. | S. | Paspalum *scrobiculatum.* |
| Korunkoosha, | .. | B. | Andropogon *Nardus* or *Ivarancusa.* |
| Kosapulla, | .. | S. | Dolichos *cultratus.* |
| Kosderi, | .. | B. | Momordica *umbellata.* |
| Kosh-amra, | .. | S. | Mangifera *sylvatica.* |

| | | |
|---|---|---|
| Koshnanto, .. | B. | Cucurbita *pepo.* |
| Koshta, .. | — | Corchorus *capsularis* or *olitorius.* |
| Koto-mulli, .. | — | Canthium *angustifolium.* |
| Kotoo, .. | — | Michelia *Champaca.* |
| Kotta-paharia, .. | B. H. | Hippocratia *arborea.* |
| Kovi-dara, .. | S. B. | Bauhinia *variegata.* |
| Kowa-luta, .. | B. | Combretum *rotundifolium.* |
| Kramuca, .. | S. | Areca *Catechu.* |
| Kreenj, .. | B. | Nigella *Indica.* |
| Krishna, .. | H. | Sesamum *Indicum.* |
| K——dhattura, .. | S. | Datura *fastuosa.* |
| K——jiraka, .. | — | Nigella *sativa* or *Indica.* |
| K——kamboja, .. | — | Phyllanthus *multiflorus.* |
| K——keli, .. | B. | Mirabilis *Jalapa.* |
| K——neeboo, .. | S. | Bergera *Kœnigii.* |
| K——rajam, .. | S. | Coronilla *picta.* |
| Krishnula-goonja, .. | S. | Abrus *precatorius.* |
| Kroee, .. | B. | Dalbergia *ferruginea.* |
| Krowee, .. | H. | D—— *robusta.* |
| Kshetra-purputee, .. | S. | Mollugo *pentaphylla.* |
| Kuchiree, .. | B. | Arum *fornicatum.* |
| Kuch-kanta, .. | — | Mimosa *rubicaulis.* |
| Kuchoo, .. | S. | Arum *Colocasia.* |
| K——gundhubee, .. | H. | Calla *aromatica.* |
| Kuchoora, .. | — | Curcuma *Zerumbet.* |
| Kuchree, .. | — | Cucumis *Maderaspatamus?* |
| Kuchwee, .. | S. | Arum *Colocasia.* |
| Kudalee, .. | — | Musa *sapientium.* |
| Kudali, .. | B. | Phrynium *capitatum.* |
| Kuddema, .. | — | Cucurbita *(sp?)* |
| Kudi-munkoon, .. | — | Psychotria *herbacea.* |
| Kudoo, .. | — | Cucurbita *lagenaria* or *Pepo.* |
| Kudumba, .. | S. | Nauclea *Cadumba.* |
| Kudrusha; Kudruva, . | — | Paspalum *scrobiculatum.* |
| Kudum, .. | B. H. | Nauclea *Cadumba.* |
| Kuhlara, .. | S. | Nymphæa *cyanea.* |
| Kukree, .. | H. | Cucumis (?) *(sp?)* |
| Kula, .. | B. H. | Musa *sapientium.* |
| Kulaee, .. | H. | Dolichos *pilosus (?)* |
| Kulaka, .. | S. | Strychnos *Nux-vomica.* |
| Kulu-kura, .. | H. | Unona *longiflora.* |
| K——moocha, .. | — | Andropogon *laxum.* |
| Kulinjam, .. | — | Alpinia *Galanga.* |
| Kulkashinda, .. | B. | Cassia *Sophora.* |
| Kulke-jamp, .. | H. | Polypodium *proliferum.* |

| | | | |
|---|---|---|---|
| Kullum, | .. .. | N. | Houttuynia *cordata.* |
| Kulmie-luta, | .. | B. | Lettsomia *bona-nox.* |
| K——-shak, | .. | — | Convolvolus *reptans.* |
| Kuloos, | .. .. | H. | Saccharum *officinarum.* |
| Kulpa-vroochum, | . | S. | Hyphæne *coriacea* (?) |
| Kulumbee, | .. .. | S. | Convolvolus *reptans.* |
| Kulusnar, | .. .. | B. H. | Panicum *paludosum.* |
| Kulyamnee, | .. | S. | Phrynium *dichotomum.* |
| Kumari, | .. .. | — | Aloe *littoralis* or *perfoliata.* |
| Kumbhika, | .. .. | — | Pistia *Stratiotes.* |
| Kumla, | .. .. | B. | Citrus *aurantium.* |
| Kumula, | .. .. | — | Kæmpferia *Galanga.* |
| Kunchun, | .. .. | — | Bauhinia *acuminata.* |
| Kunda, | .. .. | S. | Arum *Campanulatum.* |
| Kundali, | .. .. | — | Monetia *Barleroides.* |
| K——, | .. .. | — | Volkameria *inermis.* |
| Kungeea, | .. .. | B. | Roscoea *pentandra.* |
| Kungir, | .. .. | H. | Cynara *Scolymus.* |
| Kungnee; Kungoo, | .. | S. H. | Panicum *Italicum.* |
| Kungooya, | .. .. | B. H. | Urena *sinuata.* |
| Kungwel, | .. .. | B. | Nelumbium *speciosum.* |
| Kuniyar, | .. .. | — | Pterospermum *acerrifolium.* |
| Kunja-luta, | .. .. | — | Asclepias *odoratissima.* |
| Kunkoora, | .. .. | B. | Urtica *tenacissima.* |
| Kunkuma, | .. .. | S. | Crocus *sativus.* |
| Kunsa, | .. .. | H. | Asphodelus (*sp ?*) |
| Kuntala, | .. .. | S. | Agave *Cantala.* |
| Kunuka, | .. .. | B. | Ehretia *umbellulata.* |
| Kunuk-champa, | .. | — | Pterospermum *acerrifolium.* |
| K——-champuka, | .. | S.H.B. | Ochna *squarrosa.* |
| K——-jhingi, | .. | H. | Polygonum *elegans.* |
| Kupittha, | .. .. | S. | Feroni *Elephantum.* |
| Kural, | .. .. | B. | Ocymum *sanctum.* |
| K—— | .. .. | — | Hemisdemus *Indicus.* |
| Kurboor, | .. .. | — | Curcuma *reclinata.* |
| Kurelli, | .. .. | H. | Commelina *Bengalensis.* |
| Kurendra, | .. .. | — | Garcinia *lanceafolia.* |
| Kureta, | .. .. | B. | Sida *acuta.* |
| Kurfa, | .. .. | H. | Portulacea *oleracea.* |
| Kurilla, | .. .. | B. H. | Momordica *Carantia.* |
| Kurish-churin, | .. | H. | Poinciana *pulcherrima.* |
| Kurkaroo, | .. .. | S. | Cucurbita *Pepo.* |
| Kurki, | .. .. | B. | Rottbællia *perforata.* |
| Kurktie, | .. .. | — | Cucumis *utilissimus.* |
| Kurma, | .. .. | H. | Phœnix *dactylifera.* |
| Kurkunda, | .. .. | S. | Zizyphus *Jujuba.* |

| | | | |
|---|---|---|---|
| Kurnika, .. | .. | B. | Premna *spinosa.* |
| Kurnikara, .. | .. | S. | Webera *corymbosa.* |
| K———, .. | .. | — | Pterospermum *acerrifolium.* |
| Kurpoor, .. | .. | B. | Columnea *balsamica.* |
| Kurpoora, .. | .. | S. | Laurus *camphorifera.* |
| Kurubee, .. | .. | B. | Nerium *odorum.* |
| Kurumcha, .. | .. | — | Carissa *Carandas (black).* |
| Kurumurdika, | .. | S. | C—— *diffusa.* |
| Kurunda, .. | .. | H. | C—— *Carandas.* |
| Kurundur, .. | .. | B. | Hibiscus *fragrans.* |
| Kurunja, .. | .. | H. | Dalbergia *arborea.* |
| Kuruntuka, .. | .. | S. | Barleria *Prionitis.* |
| Kuruvuka, .. | .. | — | B——— *ciliata.* |
| Kuruveera, .. | .. | — | Nerium *odorum.* |
| Kurvoora, .. | .. | S. | Curcuma *Zerumbet.* |
| Kuseroo, .. | .. | H. | *(?)* |
| Kuskus, .. | .. | B. | Andropogon *muricatus.* |
| Kusmeer, .. | .. | — | Ficus *elastica.* |
| Kusrunt, .. | .. | H. | Hedysarum *alatum.* |
| Kussa-gila, .. | .. | B. | Dolichos *hexandrus.* |
| Kusseb-bewa, | .. | H. | Acorus *Calamus.* |
| Kutaka, .. | .. | S. | Strychnos *Nux-Vomica.* |
| Kuthbel, .. | .. | B. H. | Feronia *Elephantum.* |
| Kuth-goolurea, | .. | H. | Ficus *Golooria.* |
| Kutoo-toombee, | .. | S. | Cucurbita (?) (bitter species.) |
| Kutul-but, .. | .. | B. | Ficus *bacciferus.* |
| Kuwa, .. | .. | — | Coffea *Arabica.* |
| Kuwulgotta, | .. | H. | Nymphæa *Lotus?* |
| Kuya-duya, .. | .. | — | Achyranthes *lappacea.* |
| Kyeeree, .. | .. | — | Euphorbia *hirta* or *thymifolia.* |
| K——, .. | .. | — | E——— *Chamæsyce.* |
| Kyrob, .. | .. | — | Nymphæa *Lotus.* |

## Section 2.

*Tamool, Telinga, Cyngalese, &c.*

# K.

| | | |
|---|---|---|
| Kaat-toottie, .. .. | Tam. | Hibiscus *obtusifolia*. |
| Kadaghoo, .. .. | — | Sinapis *Chinensis*. |
| Kadami, .. } | T. | Bombax *pentandrum*. |
| K——, .. } | — | Barringtonia *acutangula*. |
| Kaden-pullu, .. | M. | Scleria *lithosperma*. |
| Kaddil-tayngai, .. | Tam. | Cocos, (or Lodoicea) *Sechellarum*. |
| Kadukai, .. .. | — | Terminalia *Chebula*. |
| Kæn-kækiri, .. | Cyng. | Bryonia *grandis*. |
| Kaha, .. .. | — | Kæmpferia *rotunda*. |
| Kaiantagerie, .. | Tam. | Eclipta *prostrata*. |
| Kail, .. .. | Mah. | Musa *Paradisiaca*. |
| Kakacollie-verei, .. | Tam. | Menispermum *cocculus*. |
| Kakapu, .. .. | M. | Torenia *Asiatica*. |
| Kaka-walsura, .. | Tam. | Walsura *ternata*. |
| Kakichempoo-vittiloo, | T. | Menispermum *cocculus*. |
| Kakoopala, .. .. | — | Zizyphus *trinervius*. |
| Kalichikai, .. .. | — | Guilandina *Bonducella*. |
| Kalighotoo, .. .. | — | Begonia *Chelonoides*. |
| Kaloo-attana (or antenna,) .. | Cyng. | Datura *fastuosa*. |
| Kaloodooro, .. | — | Nigella *sativa* or *Indica*. |
| Kaloovagudda, .. | T. | Nymphæa *odorata*. |
| Kalpa-tsjera, .. | M. | Pharnaceum *Mollugo*. |
| Kalu-wæra-miya, .. | Cyng. | Justicia *Gandarussa*. |
| K——wawul-ætiya, .. | — | Guilandina *Bonducella*. |

| | | | |
|---|---|---|---|
| Kaly-meerchingay, | .. | Mah. | Piper *nigrum*. |
| Kamachie-kussoo, | .. | T. | Andropogon *Schœnanthus*. |
| Kana-kidaram, | .. | Cyng. | Dracontium *polyphyllum*. |
| Kanchi-chikurkai, | .. | T. | Dolichos *prostratus*. |
| Kanda-langa, | .. | Tam. | Xylocarpus *Granatum*. |
| Kanitee, .. | .. | T. | Eugenia *racemosa*. |
| Kanoogamnoo, | .. | — | Dalbergia *arborea*. |
| Kanrew, | .. | — | Flacourtia *sepiaria*. |
| Kany, | .. | — | Cytisus *Cajan*. |
| Kapu-kinaissa, | .. | Cyng. | Hibiscus *Abelmoschus*. |
| Karaka, .. | .. | T. | Sterculia *colorata*. |
| Karakar-booda, | .. | — | Ficus *asperrima*. |
| Karakatta, .. | .. | Can. | Zizyphus *Caracatta*. |
| Kar-alsana, .. | .. | T. | Phaseolus *alatus*. |
| K—alum, .. | .. | — | Stapelia *adscendens*. |
| Karinga, .. | .. | Tam. | Gardenia *arborea*. |
| Karinta-kali, | .. | T. | Pschychotria *herbacea*. |
| Kari-vepa, .. | .. | T. | Bergera *Kœnigii*. |
| Kariwila, .. | .. | Cyng. | Momordica *Carantia*. |
| Karkakartan-vayr, | .. | T. | Clitoria *ternata*. |
| Kar-kandi, .. | .. | — | Dolichos *glutinosus*. |
| K—nelee, .. | .. | — | Indigofera *cerulea*. |
| Karoo-oomatay, | .. | Tam. | Datura *fastuosa*. |
| K——velum, | . | — | Mimosa *Arabica*. |
| Karpooga-arisee, | .. | — | Psoralea *corylifolia*. |
| Karpoorawullie, | { | Tam.<br>T. | { Borago *officinalis*, or<br>Lavendula *carnosa*. |
| Kar-pooshpa, | .. | — | Zinziber *Cassumunar*. |
| Karraway-pillay, | .. | Tam. | Bergera *Kœnigii*. |
| Karrivaympakoo, | .. | T. | B—— —— |
| Karruwa, .. | .. | Tam. | Laurus *Cinnamomum*. |
| Kar-sodi, .. | .. | T. | Eleusine *Indica*. |
| Karu-indu, .. | .. | Tam. | Pisonia *aculeata*. |
| Karunta, .. | .. | T. | Nerium *reticulatum*. |
| Kasa-gaha, .. | .. | Cyng. | Casuarina *equisitifolia*. |
| Kasavoo, .. | .. | Tam. | Andropogon *muricatus*. |
| Katoo-tumpala, | .. | Cyng. | Rumex *vesicarius*. |
| Katsu-kadali, | .. | Tam. | Melastoma *aspera*. |
| Katsjula-kelengu, | .. | — | Kæmpferia *rotunda*. |
| Katt-atteraee, | .. | — | Adelia *Nereifolia*. |
| Katu-karna, .. | .. | M. | Laurus *cinnamomum*. |
| Katu-karandu, | .. | Cyng. | Barleria *prionitis*. |
| K—karna, | .. | M. | Convolvolus *Malabaricus*. |
| K—niyada, | .. | Cyng. | Monetia *Barleroides*. |
| K—wæl-batu, | .. | — | Solanum *Jacquini*. |
| Kavali, .. | .. | T. | Sterculia *Urens*. |

| | | | |
|---|---|---|---|
| Kawoolimera, | .. | T. | Diospyros *cordifolia.* |
| Keechlie, .. | .. | — | Curcuma *Zerumbet.* |
| Keen-gal-kura, | .. | CYNG. | Melochia *corchorifolia.* |
| Kelwarajoo, .. | .. | TAM. | Eleusine *Coracana.* |
| Kembally, .. | .. | CAN. | Allium *cepa.* |
| Khehiree, .. | .. | CYNG. | Mimosa *Catechu.* |
| Khohoon, .. | .. | — | Crocus *sativus.* |
| Khoongoomapoo, | .. | TAM. | C—— —— |
| Khoonkhoomapohoo, | .. | T. | C—— —— |
| Khristna-tamara, | .. | — | Canna *Indica* (*red*, var. 1). |
| K———toolusu, | .. | — | Ocymum *gratissimum.* |
| Kiery, .. | .. | CYNG. | Amaranthus *frumentaceus.* |
| Kilanelly, .. | .. | TAM. | Phyllanthus *Niruri.* |
| Kiligilippe, .. | .. | — | Crotalaria *verrucosa.* |
| Kiloo, .. | .. | T. | Salicornia *brachiata.* |
| Kimda-tunga, | .. | — | Schænus *articulatus.* |
| Kirendmyagum, | .. | TAM. | Ruellia *strepens.* |
| Kirganeli, .. | .. | M. | Phyllanthus *Niruri.* |
| Kivia-pippala, | .. | T. | Salicornia *Indica.* |
| Koa-kaita, .. | .. | — | Lettsomia *nervosa.* |
| Kodaga-saleh, | .. | TAM. | Justicia *repens.* |
| Kodakadooruatta, | .. | CYNG. | Strychnos *Nux-vomica.* |
| Kodda-pail, .. | .. | T. | Pistia *stratiotes.* |
| Kodibudinga, | .. | — | Cucumis *Madraspatanus.* |
| Kodie-palay, .. | .. | TAM. | Asclepias *Volubilis.* |
| Kodaivaylie, | .. | — | Plumbago *Zeylanica.* |
| Kodisha, .. | .. | T. | Cluytia *collina.* |
| Kodi-vallen, | .. | — | Mimosa *ternifolia.* |
| K——veloe, .. | .. | TAM. | M—— *tomentosa.* |
| Koida-cheeka, | .. | M. | Bromelia *Annanas.* |
| Kokta, .. | .. | T. | Nymphæa *esculenta.* |
| Kokuna, .. | .. | CAN. | (?) |
| Kolungie, .. | .. | TAM. | Galega *purpurea.* |
| Kolung-kovay-kalung, | | — | Bryonica *epigæa.* |
| Komaretti, .. | .. | T. | Musa *Paradisiaca.* |
| Konda-gong, | .. | — | Hibiscus *collinus.* |
| K——-jajara, | .. | — | Mentha *quadrifolia.* |
| K——-korinta, | .. | — | Mimosa *Cæsina.* |
| K——-mayoor, | .. | — | Ardisia *Solanacea.* |
| K——-rakis, | .. | — | Arum *montanum.* |
| Kond-garoo-tiga, | .. | — | Smilax *ovalifolia.* |
| Kond-tangheroo, | .. | T. | Mimosa *Xylocarpa.* |
| Konki-putri, | .. | — | Pisonia *metis.* |
| Konnekai, .. | .. | TAM. | Cassia *fistula.* |

| | | |
|---|---|---|
| **Kooa,** .. .. | M. | Curcuma *angustifolia.* |
| **Kooamaoo,** .. .. | Tam. | C—— —— |
| **Kooda-juvee,** .. | T. | Ficus *tuberculata.* |
| **Kooghei,** .. .. | M. | Curcuma *angustifolia.* |
| **Kooka-pel-koora,** .. | T. | Trianthema *crystallina.* |
| **K——tolasie,** .. | — | Ocymum *album.* |
| **Koolimitan,** .. .. | Tam. | O—— *hirsutum.* |
| **Koollu-ka-vaylie,** .. | — | Galega *purpurea.* |
| **Koomatha,** .. .. | Can. | Gmelina *parviflora.* |
| **Koomooda,** .. .. | T. | Nymphæa *esculenta.* |
| **Koomutti-ghenzaloo,** .. | — | Sapindus *emarginatus.* |
| **Koona-galli-getsa,** .. | — | Crotalaria *Orixensis.* |
| **Koopaymaynie,** .. | Tam. | Acalypha *Indica.* |
| **Koopamenya,** .. | Cyng. | A—— —— |
| **Koosumba-chettoo,** .. | T. | Carthamus *tinctorius.* |
| **Kora,** .. .. | — | Panicum *Italicum.* |
| **Koraloo,** .. .. | — | P—— —— |
| **Koralli,** .. .. | — | Corallia *lucida.* |
| **Kora-maun,** .. | — | Briedelia *spinosa.* |
| **Koray-kalung,** .. | Tam. | Cyperus *juncifolius* or *pertenuis.* |
| **Korenta,** .. .. | T. | Mimosa *Intsia.* |
| **Korita,** .. .. | — | Batis *spinosa.* |
| **Kosambiliwail,** .. | Cyng. | Dolichos (or Carpopogon) *pruriens.* |
| **Kottang-karundei,** .. | Tam. | Sphæranthus *Indicus.* |
| **Kotsjelleti-pullu,** .. / **Kotsjilletri,** .. | M. | Xyris *Indica.* |
| **Kour-gestum,** .. | T. | Psoralia *Corylifolia.* |
| **Kousi-kandiera,** .. | — | Strychnos *bicirrhosa.* |
| **Kreata,** .. .. | Tam. | Justicia *paniculata.* |
| **Kristmatamara,** .. | T. | Canna *Indica.* |
| **Kuchandanum,** .. | — | Pterocarpus *Santalinus.* |
| **Kudookee,** .. .. | — | Terminalia *Chebula.* |
| **Kukuma-dunda,** .. | — | Bryonia *pilosa.* |
| **Kull-pashie,** .. .. | Tam. | Lichen *rotundatus.* |
| **Kumbi,** .. .. | T. | Careya *arborea.* |
| **Kumbuk,** .. .. | Cyng. | Terminalia *alata.* |
| **Kumoo-mundoo,** .. | T. | Ceropegia *acuminata.* |
| **Kunda-amadoo,** .. | — | Croton *polyandrum.* |
| **K——amadikada,** .. | — | Tradescantia *paniculata.* |
| **K——gullungoo,** .. | — | Limonia *arborea.* |
| **Kunda-jeri,** .. .. | — | Andropogon *punctatus* or *fascicularis.* |

| | | | |
|---|---|---|---|
| Kunda-jungira, | .. | T. | Casearia *esculenta.* |
| K——kanumoo, | .. | — | Saccharum *exaltatum.* |
| K——kashinda, | .. | — | Cassia *purpurea.* |
| K——mallier, | .. | — | Polygonum *barbatum.* |
| K——pana, | .. | Tam. | Bentinckia *Condapana.* |
| K——punookoo, | .. | T. | Rottbællia *exaltata.* |
| K——putta, | .. | T. | Hibiscus *tetralocularis.* |
| Kunghas, .. | .. | Can. | Schleichera *triga.* |
| Kunkoodoo, .. | .. | T. | Sapindus *emarginatus.* |
| Kupanti, .. | .. | — | Physalis *minima.* |
| Kuppei-kirei, | .. | Tam. | Amaranthus *tristis.* |
| Kuringyan, .. | .. | Cyng. | Asclepias *vomitoria.* |
| Kuror-soloo, | .. | T. | Eleusine *Indica.* |
| Kurra-tunga, | .. | — | Cyperus *spinulosus.* |
| Kursalankunnie, | .. | Tam. | Eclipta *prostrata.* |
| Kurundu, .. | .. | Cyng. | Laurus *Cinnamomum.* |
| Kuruwehloo, | .. | T. | Lavendula *carnosa.* |
| Kushee-tanga, | .. | — | Scirpus *bispicatus.* |
| Kustoori, .. | .. | — | Mimosa *Farnesiana.* |
| Kutrelloo, .. | .. | Can. | Verbesina *sativa.* |
| Kuttalay, .. | .. | Tam. | Aloe *littoralis* or *perfoliata.* |

## Section 1.

### *Sanscrit, Bengallee, Hindi, &c.*

| L. | | |
|---|---|---|
| Labera, .. .. | H. | Cordia *Myxa.* |
| Ladan, .. .. | — | Cistus *Creticus.* |
| Lahara, .. . | — | Holcus *spicatus.* |
| Lahoree-shuboo, .. | — | Cheiranthus *Cheiri.* |
| Lajalu, .. .. | — | Mimosa *natans.* |
| Lajoolshya, .. .. | B. | M—— —— |
| Lajuk, .. .. | — | M—— *pudica.* |
| Lajwanta, .. .. | H. | M—— *adhenanthera.* |
| Lajwanti, .. .. | — | M—— *natans.* |
| Lal-baryala, .. .. | B. | Sida *rhombifolia.* |
| L—bichitee, .. .. | B. H. | Urtica *interrupta.* |
| L—chandan, .. | H. | Juniperus *Cedrus.* |
| L—chirchiri, .. | — | Plumbago *rosea.* |
| L—chita, .. .. | B. H. | P—— —— |
| L—chundend, .. | H. | Pterocarpus *Santalinus.* |
| L—giri, .. .. | — | Onosma *bracteata.* |
| L—ghurree, .. | B. H. | Epipactis *plicata.* |
| L—gool-mukhmul, .. | H. | Gomphrena *globosa (red).* |
| L—guranya, .. | B. | Dioscorea *purpurea.* |
| L—jam, .. .. | — | Ardisia *anceps.* |
| L—jhawoo, .. .. | B. H. | Tamarix *dioica.* |
| L—kamal, .. .. | H. | Nelumbium *speciosum.* |
| L—kamaluta, .. | B. | Ipomœa *Quamoclit (red).* |
| L—keshura, .. .. | B. H. | Bergia *verticillata.* |
| L—kurubee, .. | — | Nerium *odorum (sing. red).* |
| L—lunka-murich, .. | B. | Capsicum *frutescens.* |
| L—luta-kudum, .. | H. | Urtica *globulifera.* |
| L—moorga, .. .. | B. H. | Celosia *cristata (red).* |
| L—pudma, .. .. | B. | Nelumbium *speciosum.* |
| L—sabuni, .. .. | H. | Trianthema *obcordata.* |
| L—sag, .. .. | — | Amaranthus *Gangeticus.* |
| L—serinchee, .. | — | Achryanthes *ferruginea.* |
| L—shukurkund-aloo, | B. H. | Convolvulus *Batatas (red.)* |
| L—subujuya, .. | H. | Canna *Indica.* |
| L—suffriam, .. | — | Psidium *pomiferum.* |
| L—turoo-luta, .. | B. H. | Ipomœa *Quamoclit (red).* |

| | | | |
|---|---|---|---|
| Langul, | .. .. | B. | Gloriosa *superba.* |
| L——, | .. .. | — | Commelina *salicifolia.* |
| Langulee, | .. .. | S. | C—— *s*——. |
| L——, | .. .. | — | Justicia *repens.* |
| L——luta, | .. | B. | Ipomœa *Pis-tigridæ.* |
| Languli, | .. .. | S. | Nama *Zeylanica.* |
| Laoo, | .. .. | B. | Cucurbita *lagenaria.* |
| Lapta, | .. .. | H. | Panicum *verticillatum.* |
| Lasan ; Lashan, | .. | — | Allium *sativum.* |
| Lasora, | .. .. | — | A—— *cepa.* |
| Latarka, | .. .. | S. | Cordia *latifolia.* |
| Latchmie-divitiya, | .. | — | Physalis *minima.* |
| Lauca, | .. | H. | Cucurbita *lagenaria.* |
| Launa, | .. | — | Annona *reticulata.* |
| Laug, | .. | — | Eugenia *caryophyllata.* |
| Leechee, | .. | B. | Scytalia *Lichi.* |
| Lemoo ; Limu, | .. | H. | Citrus *acida.* |
| Lesoora ; Lisora, | .. | — | Cordia *Myxa.* |
| Liba, | .. .. | S. | Terminalia *citrina.* |
| Lichi, | .. .. | H. | Dimocarpus or Scytalia *Lichi.* |
| Lipta-busunt, | .. | — | Flemingia *nana.* |
| Lisanul-calb, | .. | — | Cynoglossum *(sp ?)* |
| Lisanus-saur, | .. | | Borago *officinalis.* |
| Lisoora, | .. .. | H. | Cordia *Myxa.* |
| Loba, | .. .. | — | Phaseolus *vulgaris.* |
| Loban, | .. .. | — | Boswellia *serrata.* |
| Lobia, | .. .. | — | Dolichos *sinensis.* |
| Lodh, | .. .. | B. | Phyllanthus *longifolius.* |
| Lodh ; Lodhra, | .. | S. B. | Symplocos *racemosa.* |
| Lokat, Loquat, | .. | H. | Mespilus *Japonica.* |
| Lona, | .. .. | — | Portulacca *oleracea.* |
| Loaree, | .. .. | B. | Phyllanthus *longifolius.* |
| Looari, | .. .. | H. | Andropogon *scandens.* |
| L——, | .. .. | B. | A—— *Bladhii.* |
| Looduka, | .. .. | H. | Ficus *Looduca.* |
| Loona, | .. .. | B. | Annona *squammosa.* |
| Loonia ; Loonika, | .. | S. B. | Portulacea *oleracea.* |
| Loorjoor, | .. . | B. | Casearia *glomerata.* |
| Loot-putiyah, | .. | H. | Sisymbrium *Nasturtium.* |
| Loshoon, | .. .. | B. | Allium *sativum.* |
| Louka, | .. .. | — | Pontedera *vaginalis.* |
| Loung-phool, | .. | — | Lonicera *quinquelocularis.* |
| Louralee, | .. .. | B. | Limodorum *Tankervillia.* |
| Lubah ; Luban, | .. | — | Boswellia *thurifera.* |
| Lubung, | .. .. | — | Eugenia *caryophyllata.* |
| L——lota, | .. | — | Limonia *scandens.* |

| | | |
|---|---|---|
| Luchannoo, .. | H. | Oxalis *sensitiva.* |
| Luckmuna-luckmunni, | — | Atropa *Mandragora.* |
| Lujjaloo, .. .. | S. B. | Mimosa *pudica.* |
| Lukoocha, .. .. | S. | Artocarpus *Lacucha.* |
| Lukshmee-am, .. | B. | Mangifera *sylvatica.* |
| Lumba-kanta-hurina-batana, .. .. | — | Quercus *Castanicarpa.* |
| Lung, .. .. | B. H. | Eugenia *caryophyllata.* |
| Lunkaika, .. .. | S. | Trigonella *corniculata.* |
| Lunka-shij, .. .. | B. | Euphorbia *terecaulis* or *Tirucalli.* |
| Luoka; Luokee, .. | H. | Cucurbita (*sp ?*) |
| Lushanno, .. .. | — | Oxalis *sensitiva.* |
| Luta-bichittee, .. | — | Erycibe *paniculata.* |
| L——doomoor, .. | — | Ficus *vagans.* |
| L——kudum, .. .. | H. | Urtica *Naucliflora.* |
| L——k——, .. .. | B. | Uncaria *macrophylla.* |
| L——mal, .. .. | — | Uvaria *bicolor* or *fornicata.* |
| L——muhooia, .. | — | Achyranthes *alternifolia.* |
| L——purkutti-doomoor, | — | Ficus *hederacea.* |
| Lutha, .. .. | H. | Pierardia *sapida.* |
| Lutiam, .. .. | B. | Willughbeia *edulis.* |
| Lutka, .. .. | H. | Pierardia *sapida.* |
| Lut-kun, .. .. | — | Bixa *Orellana.* |
| Lutman, .. .. | — | Deeringia *Celosoides.* |
| Luvunee, .. .. | S. | Annona *reticulata.* |
| Luvunga, .. .. | — | Eugenia *caryophyllata.* |
| L————-luta, .. | — | Limonia *scandens.* |

## SECTION 2.

### *Tamool, Telinga, Cyngalese, &c.*

## L.

| | | | |
|---|---|---|---|
| Lewærella, .. | .. | CYNG. | Conyza *balsamifera*. |
| Liniya-gaha, . | .. | — | Helicteris *Isora*. |
| Lolu, .. | .. | — | Cordia *Myxa*. |
| Loonoo, .. | .. | — | Allium *cepa*. |
| Loukada, .. | .. | T. | Spermacoce *stricta*. |
| Lunu-warna, . . | .. | CYNG. | Cratæva *religiosa*. |
| Lutti-pitta-allie, | .. | T. | Scirpus *articulatus* |

## Section 1.

### *Sanscrit, Bengallee, Hindi, &c.*

## M.

| | | |
|---|---|---|
| Macao, .. .. | H. | Physalis *Peruviana.* |
| Machana, .. .. | — | Euryale *ferox.* |
| Machoti, .. .. | — | Polygonum *aviculare.* |
| Maco, .. .. | — | Solanum *nigrum.* |
| Macoe, .. .. | — | Smilax *(sp ?)* |
| Madaer, .. .. | — | Volkameria *Madaera.* |
| Madana-ganti, .. | S. | Spermacoce *hispida.* |
| Madar, .. .. | B. | Erythrina *fulgens.* |
| M——, .. .. | H. | Asclepias *gigantea.* |
| M——-patee, .. | — | Phrynium *dichotomum.* |
| Madhubee-luta, .. | S.B.H. | Gærtnera *racemosa.* |
| Madhubita-luta, .. | H. | Roydsia *suaveolens.* |
| Madhu-malati, .. | S. | Asclepias *volubilis.* |
| Madooka, .. .. | — | Bassia *latifolia.* |
| Madoorkati, .. .. | B. H. | Cyperus *tegetus.* |
| Madu-nirbisha, .. | — | Kæmpferia *angustifolia.* |
| Maghya or Maghyun, | S. | Jasminum *pubescens.* |
| Magrela, .. .. | H. | Nigella *Indica.* |
| Maharanga, .. .. | N. | Onosma *Emodi.* |
| Mahua-wowa, .. | H. | Bassia *latifolia.* |
| Mainful, .. .. | — | Vangueria *spinosa.* |
| Maisa-alada, .. .. | B. | Psychotria *Asiatica.* |
| Mairrua, .. .. | H. | Cynosurus *cristatus.* |
| Maiuri, .. .. | — | Anethum *Sowa.* |
| Majith, .. .. | — | Rubia *Munjistha.* |
| Majnu, .. .. | — | Salix *Babylonica.* |
| Majoor-kati, .. .. | B. | Cyperus *tegetus.* |
| Makhal, .. .. | B. H. | Trichosanthes *palmata.* |
| M——, .. .. | B. | Cucumis *Colocynthis.* |
| Makhun-shim, .. | — | Dolichos *gladiatus (sm. white).* |
| Makri-shala, .. .. | — | Gordonia *integrifolia.* |
| Makura-gila, .. .. | — | Dalbergia *emarginata.* |
| Makura-jali, .. .. | B. | Eleusine *Ægyptiaca.* |
| Makurjal, .. .. | H. | Gordonia *integrifolia.* |
| Makurjali, .. . | B. | Panicum *ciliare.* |

| | | |
|---|---|---|
| Malacca-jamrool, .. | B. | Eugenia *Malaccensis.* |
| Malatrinukung, .. | S. | Andropogon *Schœnanthus.* |
| Malkangni, .. .. | H. | Celastrus *(sp?)* |
| Malutee, .. .. | S. B. | Jasminum *grandiflorum.* |
| M——, .. .. | — | Echites *caryophyllata.* |
| M——, .. .. | — | Gærtnera *racemosa.* |
| Man or Man-kuchoo, . | B. H. | Arum *Indicum.* |
| Manduka-parni, .. | S. | Hydrocotyle *Asiatica.* |
| Manjiraka, .. .. | — | Ocymum *Basilicum.* |
| Manok, .. .. | B. | Arum *Indicum.* |
| Maoz-kula, .. .. | H. | Musa *Paradisiaca.* |
| Mapoori-bet, .. | B. | Calamus *gracilis.* |
| Marchoba, .. .. | H. | Asparagus *(sp?)* |
| Marlea, .. .. | B. | Rottlera *tetracocca.* |
| Marliya, .. .. | — | Marlea *begonifolia.* |
| Maroos, .. .. | B. H | Eleusine *Coracana.* |
| Marorfali, .. .. | H. | Helicteres *Isora.* |
| Marsa, .. .. | — | Amaranthus *oleraceus.* |
| Marua, .. .. | — | Artemisia *vulgaris.* |
| M——, .. .. | — | Ocymum *pilosum.* |
| Masha, .. .. | S. | Phaseolus *radiatus.* |
| M——kulai, .. | B. | Dolichos *pilosus.* |
| Mashanee, .. .. | H. | Glycine *debilis.* |
| Mashandari, .. .. | S. | Callicarpa *incana.* |
| Masha-purnee, .. | — | Glycine *debilis.* |
| Mash-kulai, .. .. | B. | Phaseolus *radiatu.* |
| Masoo-nitaha, .. | N. | Primula *Stuartii.* |
| Massandari, .. .. | B. | Callicarpa *lanata.* |
| Mastaki, .. .. | H. | Pistacea *lentiscus.* |
| Masur, .. .. | — | Ervum *Lens.* |
| Mat-ankuri, .. .. | — | Eleusine *Indica.* |
| Matar, .. .. | — | Pisum *sativum.* |
| Mattia-chanda, .. | B. | Ixora *Rosea.* |
| Matura, .. .. | — | Callicarpa *incana.* |
| Matusee, .. .. | S. | Linum *usitatissimum.* |
| Maud, .. .. | H. | Eleusine *Coracana.* |
| Maulseri, .. .. | — | Mimusops *Elengi.* |
| Mawal, .. .. | — | Bauhinia *racemosa.* |
| Mayharie, .. .. | S. | Cassia *auriculata.* |
| Maykanada, .. .. | — | Amaranthus *campestris.* |
| Mayura-shikunda, .. | — | Adiantum *melanocaulon.* |
| Mayuri, .. .. | H. | Anethum *Panmorium* or *fœniculum.* |
| Meba, .. .. | B. | Annona *squammosa.* |
| Meetha-kamarunga, .. | — | Averrhoa *Carambola (sweet).* |

| | | | |
|---|---|---|---|
| Meetha-neeboo, | .. | B. H. | Citrus *acida (var. 9).* |
| Meethee-shak, | .. | B. | Trigonella *fœnum-græcum.* |
| Mehndi, .. | .. | H. | Lawsonia *inermis.* |
| Meluncha, .. | .. | B. | Ischæmum *aristatum.* |
| Mendasinghi, | .. | H. | Nerium *grandis.* |
| Merowrie, .. | .. | — | Helicteres *Isora.* |
| Merradoo, .. | .. | B. | Polygala *arvensis.* |
| Mesta-pat, .. | .. | — | Hibiscus *cannabinus.* |
| Metha, .. | .. | H. | Melilotus *nigellosa.* |
| Methee ; Methi, | .. | S. H. | Trigonella *fœnum-græcum.* |
| Metta-tootie, | .. | B. | Ipomœa *sepiaria.* |
| Miarmee, .. | .. | — | Limodorum *candidum.* |
| Mindee, .. | .. | B. H. | Lawsonia *inermis.* |
| Mirch, .. | .. | H. | Piper *nigrum.* |
| Mircha, .. | .. | — | Capsicum *frutescens.* |
| Mirch-sookh, . | .. | — | C——— *annuum.* |
| Miromali, .. | .. | S. | Polygonum *aviculare.* |
| Misreya, .. | .. | — | Anethum *Sowa* or *graveolens.* |
| Mista-pat, .. | .. | B. H. | Hibiscus *cannabinus.* |
| Moath, .. | .. | H. | Dolichos *(?) (sp ?).* |
| Mocha, .. | .. | — | Musa *sapientium.* |
| Moduyuntee, | .. | B. | Ligusticum *diffusum.* |
| Mogra ; Mogri, | .. | H. | Jasminum *Zambac.* |
| Mohe, .. | .. | — | Bassia *longifolia.* |
| Mohoushoodha, | .. | S. | Allium *sativum.* |
| Moicha, .. | .. | B. | Olax *phœnicarpa.* |
| Moina, .. | .. | — | Vangueria *spinosa.* |
| Mokka, .. | .. | — | Bryonia *scabra.* |
| Mooa, .. | .. | — | Bassia *longifolia.* |
| Moocta-patee, | .. | — | Phrynium *dichotomum.* |
| M——-juree, | .. | — | Acalypha *Indica.* |
| Moodga, .. | .. | S. | Phaseolus *Mungo.* |
| M———-purnee, | .. | — | P——— *trilobus.* |
| Moog, .. | . | B. | Bignonia *suaveolens.* |
| Mooganee, .. | .. | — | Phaseolus *trilobus.* |
| Moola, .. | .. | B. H. | Raphanus *sativus.* |
| Mooluka, .. | .. | S. | R——— *s———.* |
| Mool-muriya, | .. | B. | Bœobotrys *nemoralis.* |
| Moondee ; Moontee, | . | — | Sphæranthus *mollis.* |
| Moondi, .. | .. | H. | S———*Indicus.* |
| Moongay, .. | .. | — | Hyperanthera *Morunga.* |
| Moong-phulloa, | .. | — | Arachis *hypogea.* |
| Moonjiwra, .. | .. | B. | Hedysarum *orbiculatum.* |
| Moonsa-kanta, | .. | — | Cactus *Indicus.* |
| Moorga, .. | .. | — | Jasminum *Zambac (wild).* |

| | | |
|---|---|---|
| Moorgabie, .. .. | H. | Sanseveria *Zeylanica.* |
| Mooree; Mouree, .. | B. | Anethum *Panmorium.* |
| Moor-moori, .. .. | H. | Scirpus *Schœnoides.* |
| Moorva, .. .. | S. | Sanseveria *Zeylanica.* |
| Moosta, .. .. | — | Cyperus *rotundus.* |
| Moosnee, .. .. | B. | Linum *usitatissimum.* |
| Moot, .. .. | H. | Phaseolus *aconitifolius.* |
| Moota-bela, .. .. | B. | Jasminum *Zambac.* |
| Mootha, .. .. | B. H. | Cyperus *rotundus.* |
| Moothee, .. .. | H. | Trigonella *fœnum-græcum.* |
| Morung-elachee, .. | — | Amomum *aromaticum.* |
| Motea, .. .. | — | Jasminum *Zambac.* |
| Moti-munda, . .. | B. | Tacca *lævis.* |
| Mow-loo, .. .. | B. H. | Dioscorea *aculeata.* |
| Moukoora, .. .. | H. | Moacurra *Gelonioides.* |
| Moula, .. .. | B. H. | Bassia *latifolia.* |
| Mous-jat, .. .. | H. | Humea *elata.* |
| Mowng or Moong, .. | — | Phaseolus *radiatus.* |
| Mucha-koonda, .. | S. | Pterospermum *suberifolia.* |
| Mudar, .. .. | H. | Asclepias *gigantea.* |
| Mudhooka, .. .. | S. | Bassia *latifolia.* |
| Mudhoorika, . .. | — | Anethum *Panmorium* or *fœniculum.* |
| Muduna, .. .. | — | Vangueria *spinosa.* |
| Mugeena, .. .. | B. H. | V——— *s*———. |
| Mugraboo, .. .. | H. | Periploca *Indica.* |
| Mugri, .. .. | — | Jasminum *Zambac.* |
| Muha-tita, .. .. | — | Justicia *paniculata.* |
| Muheesa, .. .. | — | Smilax *pseudo-China.* |
| Muhooree, .. .. | B. | Pimpinella *Anisum.* |
| Muhootee, .. .. | — | Solanum *Melongena.* |
| Mukana, .. .. | — | Anneslea *spinosa.* |
| Mukhum-shim, .. | — | Dolichos *gladiatus.* |
| Mukoo, .. .. | H. | Andropogon *bicolor.* |
| Mukuee, .. .. | — | Zea *Mays.* |
| Mukurundoo, .. | B. | Jasminum *pubescens.* |
| Muli, .. .. | H. | Raphanus *sativus.* |
| Mulhattie, .. .. | — | Glycirrhiza *glabra.* |
| Mullie, .. .. | S. | Bombax *pentandrum.* |
| Mullika, .. .. | S. B. | Jasminum *Zambac.* |
| Mulmooriya, . .. | B. | Bœobotrys *ramentacea.* |
| Mulsari, .. .. | S. | Mimusops *Elengi.* |
| Muna, .. .. | B. | Crotalaria *laburnifolia.* |
| Mundara, .. .. | S. | Erythrina *suberosa.* |
| Mundaruka, .. .. | B. | E-——— *fulgens.* |
| Mundi; Mundhi, .. | S. H. | Sphæranthus *Indicus.* |
| Mung, .. .. | H. | Phaseolus *Mungo.* |

| | | |
|---|---|---|
| Munga, .. .. | B. | Sanseveria *Zeylanica.* |
| Mungfalli, .. .. | — | Arachis *hypogea.* |
| Munja, .. .. | S. H. | Saccharum *Munja.* |
| Mun-kokoshi, .. | N. | Hovenia *dulcis.* |
| Munjit, .. .. | H. | Rubia *Munjistha.* |
| Munjista, .. .. | S. B. | R—— *M——.* |
| Munta, .. .. | B. H. | Ischæmum *aristatum.* |
| Murich ; Muricha, .. | S. B. | Piper *nigrum.* |
| Muricha, .. .. | — | Capsicum *frutescens.* |
| Murichung ; Mureechung, .. .. | S. | Piper *nigrum.* |
| Murta, .. .. | H. | Sanseveria *Zeylanica.* |
| Murooa, .. .. | B. | Eleusine *Coracana.* |
| Mursa, .. .. | H. | Spinacia ? *(sp ?)* |
| Murwa, .. .. | — | Origanum *Majorana.* |
| Musavi, .. .. | S. | Nigella *Indica.* |
| Musina ; Musnee, .. | B. | Linum *usitatissimum.* |
| Musmusa, .. .. | H. | Bryonia *scabra.* |
| Mussoor, .. .. | B. | Ervum *hirsutum.* |
| M——, .. .. | — | Cicer *lens.* |
| Mussoora, .. .. | S. | Ervum *hirsutum.* |
| Musta, .. .. | — | Cyperus *juncifolius* or *pertenuis.* |
| Mustaroo, .. .. | H. | Artemisia *Indica* or *Maderaspatana.* |
| Muthur, .. .. | — | Pisum *sativum.* |
| Muttia-lata, .. .. | B. | Hedyotis *Auricularia.* |
| Muttir, .. .. | H. | Pisum *sativum.* |
| Myn-phul, .. .. | — | Gardenia *dumetorum.* |

## Section 2.

### *Tamool, Telinga, Cyngalese, &c.*

## M.

| | | |
|---|---|---|
| Mabera, .. .. | T. | Ajuga *disticha.* |
| Madalum, .. .. | Tam. | Punica *Granatum.* |
| Madana-burta-kada, .. | T. | Spermacoce *hispida.* |
| Madana-ghenti, .. | — | S—— *h*—— |
| Madoocare, .. .. | Tam. | Webera *tetrandra.* |
| Maduga, .. .. | T. | Butea *frondosa.* |
| Maha-bowitiya, .. | Cyng. | Melastoma *Malabathrica.* |
| Mahadiya-siyambala, . | — | Æschynomene *aspera.* |
| Maha-dumuda, .. | — | Convolvulus *speciosus.* |
| M——kakawœna, .. | — | Hedysarum *diphyllum.* |
| M——kalooa, .. | — | Alpinia *Galanga.* |
| M——nelu, .. .. | — | Justicia *bicalyculata.* |
| M——niyanda, .. | — | Sanseveria *Zeylanica.* |
| M——penala, .. | — | Strychnos *colubrina*, or Cardiospermum *Halicacabum.* |
| Mahasi-ambala, .. | — | Tamarindus *Indicus.* |
| Maha-timbiri, .. | — | Diospyros *glutinosa.* |
| M—— tolabo, .. | — | Crinum *toxicarum.* |
| Mahayotu-weenna, .. | — | Viola *suffruticosa.* |
| Mala-kœkuna, .. | — | Canarium *balsamicum.* |
| Malay-tanghie, .. | Tam. | Sida *lancœolata.* |
| Mallam-todalie, .. | M. | Celtis *orientalis.* |
| Malleamothe, .. .. | — | Ixora *Indica.* |
| Mamadi, .. .. | T. | Mangifera *Indica.* |
| Manayi, .. .. | Cyng. | Justicia *procumbens.* |
| Manay-poongung-kai, | Tam. | Sapindus *emarginatus.* |
| Manchi-jeelooga, .. | T. | Æschynomene *procumbens.* |
| Manda-mandina-wœla, | Cyng. | Rubia *secunda.* |
| Mandestie, .. .. | T. | R—— *Munjistha.* |
| Manelli, .. .. | M. | Aspalathus *Indica.* |
| Manga, .. .. | T. | Gardenia *dumetorum.* |
| Mangellacua, .. | M. | Curcuma *longa.* |
| Mangyokka, .. | Cyng. | Jatropha *Manihot.* |
| Manjittie, .. .. | Tam. | Rubia *Munjistha.* |
| Manoopala, .. .. | T. | Echites (or Nerium) *antidysentericum.* |

| | | |
|---|---|---|
| **Manseni-kotta,** .. | T. | Adenanthera *pavonina.* |
| **Mansiadi,** .. .. | Cyng. | A——— *p*——— |
| **Maradum,** .. .. | Tam. | Terminalia *alata.* |
| **Mara-haralu,** . .. | Can. | Jatropha *Curcas.* |
| **Maravullie,** .. .. | Tam. | J——— *Manihot.* |
| **Maredoo,** .. .. | T. | Ægle *Marmelos.* |
| **M———,** .. .. | — | Cratæva *Tapia.* |
| **Marikolindoo,** .. | Tam. | Artemisia *Austriaca.* |
| **Maritondi,** .. .. | Cyng. | Lawsonia *spinosa* or *inermis.* |
| **Marool,** .. .. | Tam. | Sanseveria *Zeylanica.* |
| **Marri,** .. .. | T. | Ficus *Indica.* |
| **Marroo,** .. .. | Tam. | Origanum *Majorana.* |
| **Marroodamie,** .. | — | Lawsonia *spinosa* or *inermis.* |
| **Marukarung-kai,** .. | — | Gardenia *dumetorum.* |
| **Mashipattiri,** . .. | — | Artemisia *Maderaspatana.* |
| **Mashiputri,** .. .. | — | A ——— *Indica.* |
| **Matta-pal-tiga,** .. | T. | Convolvolus *paniculatus.* |
| **Mavilinghum,** .. | Tam. | Cratæva *Tapia.* |
| **May,** .. .. | T. | Schleichera *trija.* |
| **Maydi,** .. .. | — | Ficus *racemosa.* |
| **Maydipoondi,** .. | — | F—— *Carica.* |
| **Meelapa,** .. .. | Tam. | Myriophyllum *verticillatum.* |
| **Mekari,** .. .. | T. | Uvaria *lutea.* |
| **Mellaghoo,** .. .. | Tam. | Piper *nigrum.* |
| **Mendi,** .. .. | Cyng. | Ophiorrhiza *Mungos.* |
| **Meneshena,** .. .. | Can. | Capsicum *frutescens.* |
| **Menta-soppu ; Mentia,** | — | Trigonella *Fœnum Græcum.* |
| **Mentuloo,** .. .. | T. | T-——— *F*——— *G*———. |
| **Merapakaia,** .. .. | — | Capsicum *frutescens.* |
| **Merikoolu,** .. .. | Cyng. | Hyperanthera *Morunga.* |
| **Metta-tamara,** .. | T. | Cassia *alata.* |
| **Mirialoo,** .. .. | — | Piper *nigrum.* |
| **Mirial-tiga,** .. .. | — | P—— *trioicum.* |
| **Modira-caniram,** .. | M. | Strychnos *colubrina.* |
| **Mogalinga,** .. .. | Tam. | Schrebera *Swietenoides.* |
| **Moka-juna,** .. .. | T. | Zea *Mays.* |
| **Molakar,** .. .. | Tam. | Scopolia *aculeata.* |
| **Molam,** .. .. | — | Cucumis *Melo.* |
| **Mollaghai,** .. .. | — | Capsicum *frutescens.* |
| **Molooghoodoo-akoo,** . | T. | Morinda *umbellata.* |
| **Moloovoo-kodi,** .. | Tam. | Piper *nigrum.* |
| **Monara-mal,** .. | Cyng. | Poinciana *pulcherrima.* |
| **Mondlamoosteh,** .. | T. | Solanum *trilobatum.* |
| **Mooda-cottam,** .. | Tam. | Cardiospermum *Halicacabum.* |
| **Moo-kobbæ,** . .. | Cyng. | Ornitrophe *serrata.* |

| | | |
|---|---|---|
| Moodooda, .. .. | T. | Swietenia *chloroxylon.* |
| Mooga-beerakoo, .. | — | Nepeta *Malabarica.* |
| Mookadi, .. .. | — | Schrebera *Swietenoides.* |
| Mookarutty, .. .. | Tam. | Boerhavia *diffusa.* |
| Mookavullie, . .. | — | Galega *spinosa.* |
| Moola-sari, .. .. | T. | Pothos *læsia.* |
| Moollie, .. .. | Tam. | Solanum *Indicum.* |
| Moolloogorunteh, .. | T. | Barleria *Prionitis.* |
| Moonaga, .. . | — | Hyperanthera *Morunga.* |
| Moonga, .. .. | — | Crotalaria *stricta.* |
| Mooni-gangari, .. | — | Hibiscus *Populneoides.* |
| M——maduga, .. | — | Erythrina *suberosa.* |
| Moonnee, .. .. | Tam. | Premna *integrifolia.* |
| Moonooghoo-tamara, . | T. | Mimosa *pudica.* |
| Moorunghy, . .. | Tam. | Hyperanthera *Morunga.* |
| Moostighenza, .. | T. | Strychnos *Nux-vomica.* |
| Mootamy, .. .. | M. | Eleusine *Coracana.* |
| Mootopolagum, .. | Tam. | Pavonia *odorata.* |
| Moroeda, .. .. | T. | Buchanania *latifolia.* |
| Morunga, .. .. | — | Hyperanthera *Morunga.* |
| Moryoora, .. .. | — | Ardisia *Solanacea.* |
| Mosumooski, .. | Tam. | Zea *Mays.* |
| Moulle-quede, .. | T. | Lonicera *Leschenaultia.* |
| Muddie, .. .. | — | Terminalia *alata.* |
| Muddi-ruba, . .. | — | Eleusine *stricta.* |
| Muddrap-palam, .. | Cyng. | Vitis *vinifera.* |
| Muel-schevy, .. | M. | Cacalia *sonchifolia.* |
| Mugali, .. .. | T. | Pandanus *odoratissimus.* |
| Muka-janoo, . .. | — | Andropogon *bicolor.* |
| Mulla-yampali, .. | — | Galega *spinosa.* |
| Muncha-kunda, .. | — | Arum *campanulatum.* |
| Munchi-coodi-munda, | — | Ceropegia *bulbosa.* |
| Munda-valli, . .. | M. | Convolvulus *grandiflorus.* |
| Mungil-oomatay, .. | Tam. | Datura *Metel.* |
| Murcushalee, .. | T. | Scirpus *tetragonus.* |
| Murial-tiga, .. .. | — | Piper *trioicum.* |
| Murri, .. .. | — | Ficus *Indica.* |
| Musadi, .. .. | — | Strychnos *Nux-vomica.* |
| Mutto-apullacum, .. | — | Sida *cuneifolia.* |
| Myle-conday, . .. | Tam. | Adiantum *melanocaulon.* |

## Section 1.

### *Sanscrit, Bengallee, Hindi, &c.*

## N.

| | | |
|---|---|---|
| Nafirma, .. ... | H. | Delphinium *Ajacis.* |
| Naga, .. .. | B. | Cyperus *pertenuis.* |
| N——dana, .. .. | S.B.H. | Artemisia *vulgaris.* |
| N——keshura, .. | S. | Mesua *ferrea.* |
| N——phullee, .. | B. | Heliotropium *Coromandelianum.* |
| N——vala, .. .. | S. | Webera *tetrandra,* or Canthium *parviflorum.* |
| Nagar-motha, .. | H. | Cyperus *pertenuis.* |
| Nagbel, .. .. | — | Piper *betel.* |
| Nagdauna, .. .. | — | Artemisia *vulgaris.* |
| Nagdaur, .. .. | — | Asparagus *(sp?)* |
| Nagfani, .. .. | — | Cactus *Indicus.* |
| Nagkeshur, .. .. | B. H. | Mesua *ferrea.* |
| Nagkeshura-jamba, .. | — | Eugenia *Zeylanica.* |
| Nag-phunee, . .. | — | Cactus *Indicus.* |
| N——poot, .. .. | B. | Bauhinia *anguina.* |
| Nagree, .. .. | — | Euphorbia *antiquorum.* |
| Nagrunga, .. .. | S. | Citrus *Aurantium.* |
| Nagur-mootha, .. | B. | Cyperus *juncifolius,* or *pertenuis.* |
| Najbo, .. .. | H. | Glechoma *erecta.* |
| Najooka, .. .. | B. | Mimosa *pudica.* |
| Nak-daun, .. .. | H. | Asparagus *officinalis.* |
| Naktamala, .. .. | S. | Dalbergia *arborea.* |
| Nal, ... .. | H. | Arundo *Karka.* |
| Nala-kashina, . .. | B. | Smithia *sensitiva.* |
| Nalkee, .. .. | — | Hibiscus *cannabinus.* |
| Nalta-pat, .. .. | B. | Corchorus *capsularis.* |

| | | |
|---|---|---|
| Nana-wita, .. .. | B. | Gnetum *scandens.* |
| Nandi-vriksha, .. | S. | Nerium *coronarium.* |
| Narang; Naranji, .. | H. | Citrus *Aurantium.* |
| Nara-shij, .. .. | B. H. | Euphorbia *antiquorum.* |
| Narcat, .. .. | H. | Arundo *tibialis.* |
| Nardul, .. .. | — | Panicum *interruptum.* |
| Naree, .. .. | — | Spinacia *(sp ?)* |
| Nargio, .. .. | — | Narcilus *tagites.* |
| Narikeelee-kool, .. | B. | Zizyphus *Jujuba.* |
| Narikel; Naril; Narjel, | B. H. | Cocos *nucifera.* |
| Narunjee, .. . | H. | Citrus *Aurantium.* |
| Naryel, .. .. | B. H. | Cocos *nucifera.* |
| Nasa-bagha, .. . | B. | Justicia *bicalyculata.* |
| Nashpati, .. .. | H. | Pyrus *communis.* |
| Nasurjinghi, . .. | — | Trianthema *monogynia.* |
| Nata; Nata-kanta, .. | B. | Cæsalpinia *Bonducella.* |
| N——caranja, .. | H. | C—— *B*——. |
| Nazbo, .. .. | — | Ocymum *pilosum.* |
| Nazuc, .. .. | — | Zizyphus *Jujuba.* |
| Neboo, .. .. | B. | Citrus *acida.* |
| Neel, .. .. | B. H. | Indigofera *tinctoria.* |
| Neela-gheerie-kurnee, . | S. | Clitoria *ternata.* |
| Neelee, .. .. | — | Indigofera *tinctoria.* |
| Neel-juba, .. .. | H. | Hibiscus *Syriacus.* |
| N—kantha, .. .. | B. | Curcuma *Cæsia.* |
| N—kulmee, . .. | H. | Ipomœa *cærulea.* |
| N—pudmie, . .. | B. | Nymphæa *cyanea.* |
| N—vasooka, . .. | — | Eranthemum *strictum.* |
| Neema, .. .. | N. | Spondias *axillaris.* |
| Neepa, .. .. | S. | Nauclea *Cadumba.* |
| N——, .. .. | — | Eugenia *racemosa.* |
| Nell-mall, .. .. | H. | Strychnos *potatorum.* |
| Nepala, .. .. | S. | Jatropha *Curcas.* |
| N——, .. .. | — | Croton *Tiglium.* |
| Nicchikri, .. .. | H. | Artemisia *sternutatoria.* |
| Nidigdhika, .. .. | S. | Solanum *Jacquini.* |
| Nigala, .. .. | H. | Arundo *Karka.* |
| Nikochuka, .. .. | S. | Allangium *hexapetalum.* |
| Nikumba, .. .. | — | Jatropha *glauca.* |
| Nilaveghei; Nilaverei, | Tam. | Cassia *Senna.* |
| Nilaverie, .. .. | Cyng. | C—— *S*——. |
| Nila-nirgandi, .. | — | Justicia *gandarussa.* |
| Nillur, .. .. | H. | Cissus *quadrangularis.* |
| Nilofar, .. .. | — | Nymphæa *Lotus.* |
| Nim, .. .. | B. H. | Melia *Azadirachta.* |
| Nimba, .. .. | S. | M—— *A*——. |

| | | |
|---|---|---|
| Nimda, .. .. | B. H. | Buddleia *Nimda.* |
| Nimookka, .. .. | H. | Cissampelos *hexandra.* |
| Nirbisee, .. .. | B. | Kyllingia *monocephala.* |
| N———, .. .. | H. | Curcuma *Zedoaria.* |
| Nircha, .. .. | — | Corchorus *capsularis.* |
| Nirgundi, .. .. | B. | Vitex *Negundo.* |
| Nirmullee ; Nirmillies, | B. H. | Strychnos *potatorum.* |
| Nisinda, .. .. | S. H. | Vitex *Negundo.* |
| Nisot, .. .. | H. | Convolvolus *Turpethum.* |
| Nita ; Nitaha, .. | N. | Androsace *sarmentosa.* |
| Nitaha, .. .. | — | Primula *denticulata.* |
| Noa-luta, .. .. | B. | Dalbergia *scandens.* |
| Nona, .. .. | B. H. | Annona *reticulata.* |
| Noncha, .. .. | H. | Portulacea *oleracea.* |
| Noonya, .. .. | B. H. | P——— *o*——— (3 or 4 var.) |
| N-———, .. .. | | P-——— *meridiana.* |
| Nouka, .. .. | B. | Pontedera *vaginalis.* |
| Nuckchilinie, . .. | H. | Trophis *aspera.* |
| Nukchiknie, .. .. | — | Asclepias *volubilis.* |
| Nul, .. .. | — | Arundo *Karka.* |
| Nula, .. .. | B. | A-——— *K*———. |
| Nuwa-mullika, .. | S. B. | Jasminum *arborescens.* |

## Section 2.

### *Tamool, Telinga, Cyngalese, &c.*

## N.

| | | |
|---|---|---|
| Naga-dunda, . . . | T. | Bryonia *glabra.* |
| N——galli-gheetsa, . . | — | Crotalaria *trifoliastrum.* |
| N——kali, . . . . | Tam. | Cactus *Indicus.* |
| N——mulli, . . . . | T. T. | Justicia *nasuta.* |
| Nagara-mookutty-kai, | T. | Convolvulus *grandiflorus.* |
| Naga-sara-madantoo, . | — | Arundo *Karka.* |
| N——talie-kullie, . . | Tam. | Cactus *Indicus.* |
| Nagha-mooghatei-kai, | — | Convolvulus *grandiflorus.* |
| Nahiooroovie, . . | — | Achyranthes *aspera.* |
| Nai-corana, . . . . | M. | Dolichos (or Carpopogon) *pruriens.* |
| Naka-kora, . . . . | T. | Panicum *glaucum.* |
| N——pootta-chittoo, . . | — | Justicia *procumbens.* |
| Nakur-narul, . . . | — | Poa *interrupta.* |
| Nala-tapata, . . . . | — | Sonchus *Orixensis.* |
| Nali-poonookoo, . . | — | Manisurus *Myurus.* |
| N—pootika, . . . . | — | Aristidia *depressa.* |
| Nalla-golivinda, . . | — | Cardiospermum *Halicacabum.* |
| N——kavina or Kavario, | — | Hedysarum *biarticulatum.* |
| N——mandu, . . | — | H—— *styracifolium* or *glumaceum.* |
| N——mollunga, . . | — | Solanum *diffusum.* |
| N——oopie, . . . . | — | Volkameria *inermis.* |
| N——paleroo, . . | — | Indigofera *echinata.* |
| N——sera-kada, . . | — | Hedysarum *Sororiun.* |
| N——tady, . . . . | — | Curculis *Orchioides.* |
| N——tapata, . . . | — | Sonchus *Orixensis.* |
| N——tirtava, . . . | M. | Ocymum *sanctum.* |
| N——teclooga, . . | T. | Cassia *prostrata.* |
| N——useriki, . . . | — | Phyllanthus *Maderaspatensis.* |
| Namma, . . . . | — | Aponogeton *monostachyon.* |
| Nam-papoota, . . . | — | Ixora *tomentosa.* |
| Nandi-ervatam, . . | M. | Nerium *coronarium.* |
| Nanjera-moorchuni, . . | — | Asclepias *prolifera.* |

| | | |
|---|---|---|
| Nanjera-panjan, .. | TAM. | Asclepias *prolifera*. |
| Naoroo, .. .. | T. | Premna *tomentosa*. |
| Narie-oomarie, .. | TAM. | Salsola *nudiflora*. |
| Narikadam ; Narjeele, | T. | Cocos *nucifera*. |
| Narra-alhogi, . .. | — | Tetranthera *apetala*. |
| N——mamadi, .. | — | T———— *monopetala*. |
| Narrha, .. .. | — | Laurus *involucrata*. |
| Narru-killa, .. .. | M. | Phrynium *capitatum*. |
| Natsoo, .. .. | T. | Utricularia *fasciculata* or *stellaris*. |
| Nattoo-vadomcottay, . | TAM. | Terminalia *Catappa*. |
| Navonay, .. .. | CAN. | Panicum *Italicum*. |
| Nauli, .. .. | T. | Ulmus *integrifolia*. |
| Naum-papata, .. | — | Ixora *tomentosa*. |
| N——p——, .. | — | Canthium *didymum*. |
| Nawel, .. .. | TAM. | Calyptranthes *caryophyllifolia*. |
| Nayavaylie, .. .. | — | Cleome *viscosa*. |
| Naylatunghadoo, .. | T. | Cassia *Senna*. |
| Naypalum-vittiloo, .. | TAM. | Croton *Tiglium*. |
| Neekra, .. .. | T. | Cordia *Myxa*. |
| Neela-comul, . .. | — | Gmelina *Asiatica*. |
| N——ooshirikeh, . | — | Phyllanthus *Niruri*. |
| N——pamarum, .. | — | Myriophyllum *tetrandrum*. |
| Neelum, .. .. | TAM. | Indigofera *Anil*. |
| Neepalum, .. .. | T. | Jatropha *Curcas*. |
| Neer-aruga, .. .. | — | Paspalum *Kora*. |
| N—batsola, .. .. | — | Jussieua *repens*. |
| N—ganaroo, . .. | | Impatiens *natans*. |
| N—goobi, .. .. | — | Ruellia *longifolia*. |
| N—g——, .. .. | — | Barleria *longifolia*. |
| Neeriya, .. .. | — | Neeria *dichotoma*. |
| Neer-moollie, .. | TAM. | Barleria *longifolia*. |
| N——nochie, .. .. | — | Vitex *trifolia*. |
| Neeroo-aghiondraparoo, | T. | Jussieua *exaltata*. |
| N———-cancha, .. | — | Pontedera *vaginalis*. |
| N———-pavali, .. | — | Bergia *verticillata*. |
| N———-tamana, .. | — | Pontedera *hastata*. |
| N———-toolusee, .. | — | Ocymum *pilosum*. |
| N———-pippul or pipli, | — | Sphenoclea *Zeylanica*. |
| Neer-pirimie, . .. | TAM. | Gratiola *Monniera*. |
| Neerugalli-ghetsa, .. | T. | Crotalaria *quinquefolia*. |
| Neer-wanga, .. .. | — | Solanum *longum*. |
| Neety-kalwa, . .. | — | Nymphæa *cyanea*. |
| Nekra, .. .. | — | Cordia *Myxa*. |
| Nela-ameda, .. .. | — | Jatropha *glauca*. |

| | | |
|---|---|---|
| Nelam-mari, . . .. | M. | Hedysarum *diphyllum.* |
| Nela-mullika,. . .. | T. | Solanum *Jacquini.* |
| Nelam-parenda, .. | M. | Viola *enneasperma.* |
| Nela-ponna, . . .. | T. | Cassia *Senna.* |
| N——ooshirikeh, .. | — | Phyllanthus *Niruri.* |
| Nelam-velaga, .. | M. | Feronia *Elephantum.* |
| Nelepannay, . . .. | Tam. | Curculigo *Orchioides.* |
| Nella-benda, .. .. | T. | Sida *humilis* or Crotalaria *uniflora.* |
| N——budinga, .. | — | Cucumis *turbinatus.* |
| N——dintona, .. | — | Clitoria *ternata.* |
| N——gulli, . . .. | — | Gentiana *verticillata.* |
| N——gurri-galli-ghetsa, | — | Crotalaria *cespitosa.* |
| N——jeleeroo, .. | — | Asclepias *gigantea.* |
| N——jodi, . . .. | — | Semecarpus *Anacardium.* |
| N——kakisha, .. | — | Gardenia, (or Posqueria) *uliginosa.* |
| N——madoo, . .. | — | Pentaptera *tomentosa.* |
| N——mandu, . .. | | Hedysarum *styracifolium* or H—— *glumaceum.* |
| N——pessara, . .. | — | Phaseolus *Max.* |
| N——pippala, . .. | — | Verbena *nodiflora.* |
| N——renga, . . .. | — | Mimosa *amara.* |
| N——shama, . .. | — | Panicum *miliare* (3 *var.*) |
| N——tada, . . .. | — | Curculigo *Orchioides.* |
| N——tooma, . . .. | — | Mimosa *Arabica.* |
| N——upie, . . .. | — | Capparis *sepiaria.* |
| N——vemoo, . .. | — | Justicia *paniculata.* |
| N——useriki, . .. | — | Phyllanthus *Niruri.* |
| N——woolli-mera, .. | — | Diospyros *chloroxylon.* |
| Nellie, .. .. | T. T. | Clerodendrum *Phlomoides.* |
| N——kai, .. .. | Tam. | Phyllanthus *Emblica.* |
| N——poo, .. .. | — | P—— *E*——. |
| N——toottie, . .. | — | Sida *Mauritiana.* |
| Nelli-kamarum, .. | M. | Phyllanthus *Emblica.* |
| Nemilie-shega, .. | T. | Adiantum *melanocaulon.* |
| Nepalam, .. .. | Cyng. | Croton *Tiglium.* |
| Nereddie, .. .. | T. | Calyptranthes *caryophyllifolia.* |
| Nereipoottie, . .. | — | Justicia *procumbens.* |
| Neringie, .. .. | Tam. | Tribulus *terrestris.* |
| Nervalum-cottay, .. | — | Croton *Tiglium.* |
| Nettay-pcmayruttie, . . | — | Nepeta *Malabarica.* |
| Netty-cheddie, .. | — | Æschynomene *arborea.* |
| Nil, .. .. | Cyng. | Indigofera *Anil.* |
| Nil-adana-hiriya, .. | — | Crotalaria *verrucosa.* |

| | | |
|---|---|---|
| Nilavoolla, .. .. | TAM. | Feronia *Elephantum.* |
| Nil-puruk, .. .. | CYNG. | Ruellia *ringens.* |
| Nimmeeri, .. .. | T. | Pentaptera *paniculata.* |
| Nir-notsjit, .. .. | M. | Volkameria *inermis.* |
| Nirpulli, .. .. | TAM. | Tradescantia *axillaris.* |
| Nitty-cashinda-kura, . | T. | Cassia *esculenta.* |
| Noochie, .. .. | TAM. | Vitex *Negundo.* |
| Noodhosa, .. .. | T. | Bryonia *scabra.* |
| Noona-marum, .. | TAM. | Morinda *umbellata.* |
| Nooni-paprota, .. | T. | Ixora *Pavetta.* |
| Nugga, .. .. | CAN. | Hyperanthera *Morunga.* |
| Nugoo-benda, .. | T. | Sida *populifolia.* |
| Nulla-ghentana, .. | — | Clitoria *ternata.* |
| N——ghilakara, .. | — | Nigella *sativa*, or *Indica.* |
| N——somuttie, .. | — | Coronilla *picta.* |
| N——tooma, .. | — | Mimosa *Arabica.* |
| N——vavilie, .. | — | Justicia *Gandarussa.* |
| Nullerootingeh, .. | — | Cissus *quadrangularis.* |
| Nullie, .. .. | — | Grewia *Carpinifolia.* |
| Nulloopoo-moostikaia, | — | Andrachne *Cadishaw.* |
| Nundiavuttei, .. | TAM. | Nerium *coronarium.* |
| Nuni-beera, .. .. | T. | Luffa *pentandra.* |
| Nunnara, .. .. | TAM. | Periploca *Indica.* |
| Nurri-vungyum, .. | — | Erythronium *Indicum.* |
| Nurriala, .. .. | CYNG. | E——— —— *I*-———. |
| Nuttei-choorie, .. | TAM. | Spermacoce *hispida.* |
| Nuvala, .. .. | M. | Cratœva *religiosa.* |

## Section 1.

### *Sanscrit, Bengallee, Hindi, &c.*

# O.

| | | | |
|---|---|---|---|
| Oaloa, .. | .. | B. | Tetranthera *fruticosa.* |
| Oaour-baberung, | .. | — | Embelia *vestita.* |
| Obadali, .. | .. | S. | Sideroxylon *spinosum.* |
| Ochooyot, .. | .. | B. | Morinda *tinctoria.* |
| Ochhya, .. | .. | — | Momordica *muricata.* |
| Oda-bremi, .. | .. | H. | Smithia *sensitiva.* |
| Ognee, .. | .. | B. | Plumbago *Zeylanica.* |
| Ogooroo, .. | .. | — | Amyris *Agallocha.* |
| Oknee, .. | .. | H. | Gadelupa *marginata.* |
| Okura, .. | .. | — | Xanthium *Indicum.* |
| Ol, .. | .. | B. H. | Arum *campanulatum.* |
| Oocha-soa, .. | .. | N. | Gardenia *ovata.* |
| Oodbeg, .. | .. | B. | Areca *Catechu.* |
| Odoo-jatee, .. | .. | H. | Justicia *Ecbolium.* |
| Oodoombura, . | .. | S. | Ficus *glomerata.* |
| Oojootee, .. | .. | B. | Barleria *ciliata.* |
| Ookunchi, .. | .. | — | Ageratum *cordifolium.* |
| Oolkipanna, .. | .. | — | Salvinia *verticillata.* |
| Ooloo, .. | .. | — | Saccharum *cylindricum.* |
| O——chukma, | .. | — | Quercus *lappacea.* |
| Oolut-kumbul, | .. | — | Abroma *augusta.* |
| Ooma, .. | .. | S. | Linum *usitatissimum.* |
| Oopadykee, .. | .. | — | Portulacca *quadrifida.* |
| Oord, .. | .. | H. | Dolichos *pilosus (?)* |
| Ootaso-braba, . | .. | B. | Echites *cymosa.* |
| Orjoon, .. | .. | — | Terminalia *alata*, or *glabra.* |
| Orol, .. | .. | — | Cytisus *Cajan.* |
| Orook, .. | .. | — | Laurus *glaucescens.* |
| Osam, .. | .. | H. | Stalagmitis *Gamboja.* |
| Osir, .. | .. | — | Andropogon *muricatum.* |
| Our-chaka, .. | .. | B. | Sonneratia *acida.* |

## SECTION 2.

### *Tamool, Telinga, Cyngalese, &c.*

## O.

| | | |
|---|---|---|
| Oda, .. .. | T. | Panicum *brizoides.* |
| Odallam, .. .. | M. | Cerbera *Manghas.* |
| Olinda, .. .. | CYNG. | Abrus *precatorius.* |
| Oochinta-kurra, .. | T. | Solanum *trilobatum.* |
| Oochi-useriki, .. | — | Phyllanthus *simplex.* |
| Ooghai, .. .. | TAM. | Salvadora *Persica.* |
| Oolooa, . .. | CYNG. | Trigonella *Fœnum-Græcum.* |
| Oomarie-marum, .. | TAM. | Salsola *elata.* |
| Opie-akoo, .. .. | T. | Monetia *Barleroides.* |
| Ooralay, .. .. | — | Solanum *tuberosum.* |
| Oora-nekra, .. .. | — | Ximenia *Americana.* |
| Oorootora, .. .. | CYNG. | Cassia *Sophora.* |
| Ooru-wee, .. .. | — | Oryza *sativa.* |
| Ootamunnie, . .. | TAM. | Cynanchum *extensum.* |
| Owas, .. .. | CYNG. | Vitis *vinifera.* |

## Section 1.

### *Sanscrit, Bengalee, Hindee, &c.*

# P.

| | | |
|---|---|---|
| Padam, .. .. | H. | Nelumbium *speciosum* or Prunus *cerasus*. |
| Padmachari, .. .. | S. | Nelumbium *speciosum*. |
| Pahari-aiel, .. .. | H. | Mimosa *pennata*. |
| Pakar, .. .. | — | Ficus *venosa*. |
| Pakur, .. .. | B. | Ficus *infectoria*. |
| Palak, .. .. | H. | Spinacea *oleracea*. |
| Palandu, .. .. | S. | Allium *Cepa*. |
| Palanggini, .. .. | — | Manisurus *granalaris*. |
| Pale, .. .. | H. | Ehretia *buxifolia*. |
| Palak, or Palek-joohie, | — | Justicia *nasuta*. |
| Paluk-jooi, .. .. | B. H. | Ixora *undulata*. |
| Palita-mandar; Palta-mandar, .. .. | — | Erythrina *Indica*. |
| Palung; Palunka, .. | — | Beta *Bengalensis*. |
| Palwal, Pulwul, .. | H. | Trichosanthes *dioica*. |
| Pan, .. .. | B. H. | Piper *Betle*. |
| Pana, .. .. | B. | Salvinia *imbricata* or *cucullata*. |
| P—, .. .. | — | Pistia *stratiotes*. |
| Panch-shim, .. .. | — | Dolichos *lignosus (1 var.)* |
| Panee-doorba, .. | — | Agrostis *tenacissima*. |
| P——jamb, .. .. | H. | Eugenia *lanceolaria*. |
| P——kachura, .. | B. | Commelina *Salicifolia*. |
| P——kula, .. .. | — | Damasonium *Indicum*. |
| P——k—, .. .. | B. H. | Mentha *verticillata*. |
| P——lata, .. .. | B. | Gadelupa *uliginosa*. |
| P——mulunga, .. | — | Cyperus *distans*. |
| P——murich, .. | — | Polygonum *flaccidum*. |
| P——phul, .. .. | — | Trapa *bispinosa*. |
| P——syora, .. .. | B. H. | Grewia *sepiaria*. |
| Panie-ke-shumbalie, .. | H. | Vitex *trifolia*. |
| Panialla-jamba, .. | B. | Eugenia *Panialla*. |
| Pani-jaomi, .. .. | H. | Salix *tetrasperma*. |
| Paniyala, .. .. | B. H. | Flacourtia *Cataphracta*. |
| Pan-kakrol, .. .. | B. | Polypodium *unitum*. |

| | | | |
|---|---|---|---|
| **Pan-kooshee,** . | .. | B. | Phyllanthus *multiflorus.* |
| **P——kula,** .. | .. | H. | Limodorum *nutans.* |
| **P——lajuk,** .. | .. | — | Mimosa *natans.* |
| **P——luta,** .. | .. | B. | Hedysarum *gramineum.* |
| **Panshiru,** .. | .. | — | Rottbœllia *compressa.* |
| **Panta,** .. | .. | — | Glycine *debilis.* |
| **Pan-trasee,** .. | .. | — | Phellandrium *stoloniferum.* |
| **Pantub,** .. | .. | — | Jasminum *elongatum.* |
| **Panuar,** .. | .. | H. | Cassia *obtusifolia.* |
| **Papana,** .. | .. | S. | Ixora *Pavetta.* |
| **Papaya; Papya,** | . | B. H. | Carica *Papaya.* |
| **Papura,** .. | .. | H. | Gardenia *latifolia.* |
| **Paral,** .. | .. | — | Bignonia *Chelonoides.* |
| **Pareejat,** .. | .. | B. | Erythrina *fulgens.* |
| **Paribhudra,** .. | .. | S. | E——— *ovalifolia.* |
| **Paris; Paras-pipul,** .. | | H. | Hibiscus *populneus.* |
| **Parnasa,** .. | .. | S. | Ocymum *sanctum.* |
| **Parool,** . | .. | B. | Bignonia *suaveolens.* |
| **Parpata,** .. | .. | S. | Pharnaceum *Cerviana*, or *triflora.* |
| **Parspipul,** .. | .. | H. | Hibiscus *populneus.* |
| **Pashana-bhidee,** | .. | S. | Ocymum *Basilicum.* |
| **Pat,** .. | .. | B. | Corchorus *olitorius*, *(green.)* |
| **Pata,** .. | .. | S. | Sida *lanceolaria.* |
| **P——gruga,** .. | .. | B. | Webera *odorata.* |
| **P——khuree,** .. | .. | B. H. | Saccharum *fuscum.* |
| **Patee,** .. | .. | H. | Cyperus *inundatus.* |
| **P——,** .. | .. | S. | Phrynium *dichotomum.* |
| **P——-neeboo,** . | .. | B. H. | Citrus *acida.* |
| **Patha-umbusta,** | .. | S. | Cissampelos *hexandra.* |
| **Pathur-choor,** | .. | B. | Plectranthus *aromaticus.* |
| **Pat-jooniya,** .. | .. | — | Combretum *acuminatum.* |
| **Patkili,** .. | .. | — | Hibiscus *Rosa-Sinensis.* |
| **Patola,** .. | .. | S. | Trichosanthes *laciniosa.* |
| **Patranga,** .. | .. | — | Swietenia *febrifuga.* |
| **Pat-reem,** .. | .. | B. | Loranthus *bicolor.* |
| **Patee-patee,** .. | .. | — | Phrynium *dichotomum.* |
| **Patuli,** .. | .. | S. B. | Bignonia *suaveolens.* |
| **Patuparni,** .. | .. | S. | Bryonia *grandis.* |
| **Payah-prasadi,** | .. | — | Strychnos *potatorum.* |
| **Paya-tullo,** .. | .. | H. | Bambusa *baccifera.* |
| **Peaj,** .. | .. | B. H. | Allium *Cepa.* |
| **Peela-bhungara,** | .. | H. | Verbesina *calendulacea.* |
| **Peelie-saynd,** . | .. | — | Euphorbia *tortilis.* |
| **Peeplur,** .. | .. | B. | Sophora *robusta.* |

| | | | |
|---|---|---|---|
| Peeraloo, | .. | B. | Gardenia (or Posoqueria) *uliginosa.* |
| Peer-grooj, | .. | H. | Cissampelos *glabra.* |
| Peeta, | .. | S. | Curcuma *longa.* |
| P——kara, | .. | H. | Chrysophyllum *acuminatum.* |
| Peet-shala, | .. | — | Pterocarpus *marsupium.* |
| Peetunga, | .. | B. | Randia *racemosa.* |
| Peeyooksha, | .. | S. | Crotalaria *sericea.* |
| Peeyooli, | .. | B. | C——— *s*———. |
| Pendaloo, | .. | H. | Convolvolus *Batatas.* |
| Peng, | .. | B. | Cynometra *polyandra.* |
| Pengi-nachi, | .. | H. | Panicum *glaucum.* |
| Petaree, | .. | B. | Sida *Asiatica.* |
| Petha, | .. | H. | Curcubita *(sp ?)* |
| Petinar, | .. | B. H. | Panicum *fluitans.* |
| Peyara, | .. | B. | Psidium *pyriferum,* or *pomiferum.* |
| Phenila, | .. | S. | Sapindus *emarginatus.* |
| Phool-shoola, | .. | H. | Hedysarum *lagenaria.* |
| Phoonee-monsa, | .. | — | Cactus *Indicus.* |
| Phul-jamb, | .. | — | Eugenia *terniflora.* |
| Phulsha, | .. | B. H. | Grewia *Asiatica.* |
| Phul-wara, | .. | H. | Bassia *butyracea.* |
| Pia-bausa, | .. | — | Barleria *cristata, (red.)* |
| Pial, | .. | — | Chironjia *sapida.* |
| Piaz, | .. | — | Allium *Cepa.* |
| Pida, | .. | — | Cordia *monoica.* |
| Pilu, | .. | — | Salvadora *Persica,* or Careya *arborea.* |
| Pindalu, | .. | — | Rottlera *Indica.* |
| Pindeetuka, | .. | S. | Vangueria *spinosa.* |
| Pindi, | .. | — | Justicia *Tranquebarensis.* |
| Pinguree, | .. | H. | Echites *acuminata.* |
| Pinnees; Pinnis, | .. | B. | Spinachia *tetrandra.* |
| Pipeera-saree, | .. | — | Salvadora *pentandra.* |
| Pippalyanj, | .. | H. | Croton *sebiferum.* |
| Pippula, | .. | S | Ficus *religiosa.* |
| Pippulee, | .. | S. B. | Piper *longum.* |
| Pippul, | .. | B. H. | P—— *l*———. |
| Pipal, | .. | H. | P—— *l*———. |
| Pipul; Pipal, | .. | — | Ficus *religiosa.* |
| Pipuloo, | .. | — | Piper *longum.* |
| Piraloo, | .. | B. | Gardenia (or Posoqueria) *uliginosa.* |
| Piring, | .. | — | Trigonella *corniculata.* |

| | | |
|---|---|---|
| Pistu, .. .. | H. | Pistacia *officinarum*. |
| Pita-bhringi, . .. | S. | Verbesina *calendulacea*. |
| Pitalee-jamai-pooli-shim, .. .. | B. | Dolichos *lignosus*, *(3 var.)* |
| Pitoli, .. .. | B. H. | Trewia *nudiflora*. |
| Pit-papra, .. .. | H. | Fumaria *officinalis*. |
| Pit-ras, .. .. | — | Curcuma *longa*. |
| Pittuli-pata, .. .. | B. | Phrynium *imbricatum*. |
| Piyalee, .. .. | S. B. | Buchanania *latifolia*. |
| Plucsha, .. .. | S. | Ficus *infectoria*. |
| Poodeena, .. .. | H. | Mentha *sativa*. |
| Poog, .. .. | B. | { Artocarpus *integrifolia*.<br>{ Areca *catechu*. |
| Pooi ; Poi-shak, .. | — | Basella *lucida*. |
| Poonka, .. .. | — | Amaranthus *polygamus*. |
| Poonkhie, .. .. | S. | Galega *purpurea*. |
| Poonk-ka, .. .. | B. | Oldenlandia *crystallina*. |
| Poon-nag ; Poon-naga, | S. B. | Rottlera *tinctoria*. |
| P——— ; P————, | — | Alpinia *nutans*. |
| Poon-nag-chumpa, .. | B. | A——— *n*———. |
| Poonnurnuwa, .. | S. | Boerhavia *procumbens*. |
| Poontureka, .. .. | B. | Nelumbium *speciosum*. |
| Poora-jamb, .. .. | H. | Eugenia *lancæofolia*. |
| P——koi, .. .. | B. | Schleichera *pentapetala*. |
| P——nag-chumpa, .. | B. H. | Alpinia *nutans*. |
| Pootika, .. .. | S. | Basella *rubra*. |
| Pootikarunga, .. | — | Cæsalpinia *Bonducella*. |
| Pootrunjiva, .. .. | — | Nageia *Pootrunjiva*. |
| Post, .. .. | B. H. | Papaver *somniferum*. |
| Potanga, .. .. | S. | Cæsalpinia *Sappan*. |
| Potugula, .. .. | — | Arundo *Karka*. |
| Prabunatha, .. .. | — | Cassia *Tora*. |
| Prakirya, .. .. | — | Guilandina *Bonducella*. |
| Preshoi-purnee, .. | — | (?) |
| Priyungo, .. .. | — | Panicum *Italicum*. |
| Pudma, .. .. | S.B.H. | Nelumbium *speciosum*. |
| P———charinee, .. | S. | Hibiscus *mutabilis*. |
| P———goolunchee, .. | B. | Menispermum *tomentosum*. |
| P———kurubee, .. | B. H. | { Nerium *odorum*, *(red, double.)* |
| Puhari-pippul, .. | H. | Piper *silvaticum*. |
| Pulandoo, .. .. | S. | Allium *Ascalonium*. |
| P———, .. .. | B. | A—— *Cepa*. |
| Pulas, .. .. | B. H. | Butea *frondosa*. |
| Pulasha, .. .. | S. | B——*f*——. |
| Pullee, .. .. | H. | Lindsea *odorata*. |

| | | |
|---|---|---|
| Pulta, .. .. | B. | Trichosanthes *dioica.* |
| Puluku, .. .. | H. | Poa *plumosa.* |
| Pulwul, .. .. | — | Trichosanthes *dioica.* |
| Punarnavi, .. .. | S. | Trianthema *monogynia.* |
| Punarnava, .. .. | — | Boerhavia *diffusa.* |
| Pundaroo, .. .. | H. | Cinchona *excelsa.* |
| Punki, .. .. | B. | Oldenlandia *crystallina.* |
| Punusa, .. .. | S. | Artocarpus *integrifolia.* |
| Purjunee, .. .. | B. | Curcuma *Xanthorhiza.* |
| Purkutta-doomoor, .. | — | Ficus *fruticosa.* |
| Purnasa, .. .. | S. | Ocymum *album*, or *polystachion.* |
| Puroo, .. .. | B. | Allium *Porrum.* |
| Puroosha, .. .. | S. B. | Xylocarpus *Granatum.* |
| Purula, .. .. | H. | Bignonia *suaveolens.* |
| P——, .. .. | — | Luffa *pentandra.* |
| Purush, .. .. | B. H. | Hibiscus *populneus.* |
| P———pipool, .. | — | H——— *populneoides.* |
| Pusoor, .. .. | — | Xylocarpus *Granatum.* |
| Pusuee, .. .. | H. | Oryza *sativa, (wild sort.)* |
| Puthmapoo-todemie, . | S. | Convolvulus *grandiflorus.* |
| Putol, .. .. | B. | Trichosanthes *dioica.* |
| Putolika, .. .. | S. | T—— —— *d——.* |
| Put-puti-chechka, .. | B. H. | Scirpus *articulatus.* |
| Putsun, .. .. | H. | Crotalaria *juncea.* |
| Putta-karie, .. .. | S. | Euphorbia *Nereifolia.* |
| Putteon, .. .. | H. | E- ——— *N-———.* |
| Puttinka-pool, .. | — | Lichen *rotundatus.* |
| Pykassie, .. .. | — | Cassia *fistula.* |

## Section 2.

### *Tamool, Telinga, Cyngalese, &c.*

# P.

| | | |
|---|---|---|
| Paak, | Tam. | Areca *Catechu.* |
| Pacta-valum, | M. | Trichosanthes *Cucumerina.* |
| Padda-nella-kura, | T. | Premna *latifolia.* |
| Padrie, | Tam. | Bignonia *Chelonoides.* |
| Pagada, | T. | Mimusops *Elengi.* |
| Pagara-pula, | Tam. | Phyllanthus *Rhamnoides.* |
| Pail-kura, | T. | Portulacca *meridiana.* |
| Paina-schulli, | M. | Acanthus *Illicifolius.* |
| Pala, | Tam. | Nerium *tinctorium.* |
| Palay, | T. | Asclepias *vomitoria.* |
| Paleroopoo, | — | Doronicum *calcaratum.* |
| Palier-mankeni, | — | Urena *sinuata.* |
| Paloopaghelkodi, | Tam. | Momordica *dioica.* |
| Palseeroo, | T. | Dalbergia *paniculata.* |
| Palta, | — | Mimusops *hexandra.* |
| Paltae, | Tam. | M——— *h*———. |
| Palla-cadija, | T. | Echites *antidysenterica.* |
| P——gurgi, | — | Asclepias *annularia.* |
| P——soucundi, | — | A——— *pseudosarsa.* |
| Palliky, | — | Capparis *acuminata.* |
| Pabudinga, | — | Cucumis *trigonus.* |
| Pampena, | — | Bignonia *Indica.* |
| Panagheri, | — | Cordia *monoica.* |
| Panch-maun, | — | Conocarpus *acuminata.* |
| Pandiki, | — | Kydia *calycina.* |
| Pandipavel, | M. | Momordica *Carantia.* |
| Pania-paniala, | — | Bombax *pentandrum.* |
| Panichikai, | Tam. | Diospyros *glutinosa.* |
| Panitsjika-marum, | M. | D——— *g*———. |
| Pannang-kullo, | Tam. | Borassus *flabelliformis.* |
| Paputta, | T. | Pavetta *Indica.* |
| P———, | Tam. | Ixora *Pavetta.* |
| Parami, | T. | Zizyphus *scandens.* |
| Paratie, | Tam. | Gossypium *herbaceum.* |
| Paringay, | — | Smilax *China.* |
| Passapoo, | T. | Curcuma *longa.* |

| | | |
|---|---|---|
| Passelie-keeray, .. | TAM. | Portulacca *quadrifida*. |
| Pastiki, .. .. | T. | Grewia *salvifolia*. |
| Pata, .. .. | — | Cissampelos *Convolvulacea*. |
| Patalganni, .. . | — | Ophioxylon *serpentinum*. |
| Patanga ; Patangee, .. | CYNG. | Cæsalpinia *Sappan*. |
| Patinga-cottay, .. | TAM. | C——— *S*———. |
| Patpadagam, . .. | CYNG. | Pharnaceum *Cerviana*, or *triflora*. |
| Patrashi, .. .. | TAM. | Mirabilis *Jalapa*. |
| Patsoopoopulataghelin-jerakoo, .. .. | T. | Verbesina *calendulacea*. |
| Patunga, .. .. | — | Briedelia *montana*. |
| Pavala, .. .. | — | Ruellia *Pavala*. |
| P——-poola, . .. | TAM. | Phyllanthus *Rhamnoides*. |
| Pavatti, .. .. | — | Ixora *Pavetti*. |
| Pavel, .. .. | M. | Momordica *muricata*. |
| Pavuttay, .. .. | TAM. | Pavetta *Indica*. |
| Pauncha-tiga, . .. | T. | Cassyata *filiformis*. |
| Pawatti, .. .. | CYNG. | Ixora *Pavetti*. |
| Payana, .. . | M. | Chloroxylon *Dupada*. |
| Paymoostey, . .. | TAM. | Convolvolus *Malabaricus*. |
| Pecheka-boora-gaddi, . | T. | Ambrosinia *unilocularis*. |
| Pedasodi, .. .. | — | Eleusine *stricta*. |
| Pedda-batsalla, .. | — | Basella *lucida*. |
| P——chintu, .. | — | Celastrus *montanus*. |
| P ——doskay, .. | — | Cucumis *Momordica*. |
| P——eita, .. .. | — | (?) |
| P——galli-gheetsa, .. | — | Crotalaria *Laburnifolia*. |
| P——ganti, .. | — | Panicum *spicatum*. |
| P——ghella, . .. | — | Anthistiria *Cymbaria*. |
| P——gillakara, .. | — | Anethum *Panmorium*, or *fœniculum*. |
| P——manieputta, .. | — | Ailanthus *excelsa*. |
| P——patsiroo, .. | — | Mimosa *procera*. |
| P——poil-pail-kura, . | — | Portulacca *quadrifida*. |
| P——shoka-sodi, .. | — | Eleusine *stricta*. |
| P——s———, .. | — | Cyperus *umbellatus*. |
| P——sodi-soloo, .. | — | Eleusine *stricta*. |
| P——waraga-winki, .. | — | Salvadora *Persica*. |
| P——woondoo, .. | — | Panicum *stagninum*. |
| Peddoo-panookoo, .. | — | Rottbœllia *corymbosa*. |
| Peeki-tooma, . .. | — | Mimosa *latronum*. |
| Peelcollie, .. .. | M. | Justicia *nasuta*. |
| Peeliadooghookaila, .. | TAM. | Dolichos, or Carpopogon *pruriens*. |
| Peepul, .. .. | T. | Piper *longum*. |

| | | |
|---|---|---|
| Peerahie, .. .. | TAM. | Trophis *aspera*. |
| Peetandale-cotti, .. | M. | Crotalaria *verrucosa*. |
| Peetoma, .. .. | T. | Mimosa *Farnesiana*. |
| Pemayruttie, . .. | TAM. | Nepeta *Malabarica*. |
| Peneru, .. .. | T. | Physalis *flexuosa*. |
| Penni-vempali, .. | — | Indigofera *hirsuta*. |
| Pepoodel, .. .. | TAM. | Trichosanthes *laciniosa*. |
| Peramootie, .. .. | — | Pavonia *odorata*. |
| Pere-aretei, .. .. | — | Alpinia *Galanga*. |
| Perin-toottie, . .. | — | Sida *Asiatica*. |
| Perinvullie-kelunghu, . | M. | Dioscorea *alata*. |
| Perumarundoo, .. | TAM. | Aristolochia *Indica*. |
| Perumavuttoo, .. | — | Ailanthus *excelsa*. |
| Perundei-codie, .. | — | Cissus *quadrangularis*. |
| Perungyum, .. .. | — | Ferula *Asafœtida*. |
| Perun-siragum, .. | T. | Anethum *Panmorium*, or *fœniculum*. |
| Peti-tora, .. .. | CYNG. | Cassia *Tora*. |
| Petta-mari, .. .. | T. | Ficus *tomentosa*. |
| Peyar, .. .. | — | Grewia *orientalis*. |
| Peycoomutikai, .. | TAM. | Cucumis *Colocynthis*. |
| Phaina-schulli, .. | M. | Acanthus *Ilicifolius*. |
| Phal-modecca, .. | — | Convolvolus *paniculatus*. |
| Pichoola, .. .. | T. | Tamarix *dioica*. |
| Pili-wata-tiga, .. | — | Crotalaria *nummularia*. |
| Pilla-dumpa, . .. | — | Urtica *tuberosa*. |
| Pilli-pessara, . .. | — | Phaseolus *trilobus*. |
| Pindee-koondee, .. | — | Justicia *Tranquebarensis*. |
| Pinnay, .. .. | TAM. | Calophyllum *inophyllum*. |
| Pishanna, .. .. | T. | Ferriola *Buxifolia*. |
| Pissinghie, .. .. | — | Volkameria *inermis*. |
| Pita-wakha, .. .. | CYNG. | Phyllanthus *Niruri*. |
| Pitcha, .. .. | TAM. | Cucurbita *citrullus*. |
| P——ghedie, . .. | CYNG. | C-——— c-———. |
| Piturkurra, .. .. | T. | Chaulmoogra *odorata*. |
| Podœlmaun, .. .. | — | Mimosa *Catechu*. |
| Podootalei, .. .. | TAM. | Verbena *nodiflora*. |
| Poghakoo, .. .. | T. | Nicotiana *Tabacum*. |
| Poghei, .. .. | TAM. | |
| Poi-mooshtie, . .. | — | Cissampelos *Pareira*. |
| Poindi-pooti, . .. | T. | Flagellaria *Indica*. |
| Poka, .. .. | — | Areca *Catechu*. |
| Pokarakai, .. .. | TAM. | Pentaptera *paniculata*. |
| Polaree, .. .. | T. | Antidesma *pubescens*. |
| Ponagunta-kura, .. | — | Achyranthes *triandra*. |
| Ponassa, .. .. | — | Eleusine *Coracana*. |

| | | |
|---|---|---|
| Ponaverie, .. .. | TAM. | Cassia *Sophora.* |
| Ponna-maram, .. | M. | Calophyllum *inophyllum.* |
| Ponnampou-maravara, | — | Limodorum *spatulatum.* |
| Ponnam-taghera, .. | — | Cassia *Sophora.* |
| Pontaletsce, .. .. | — | Lawsonia *spinosa,* or *inermis.* |
| Poo-alla-toomi, .. | T. | Phlomis *Zeylanica.* |
| P—cushalie, . .. | — | Cyperus *Haspan.* |
| Poodalungai, . .. | TAM. | Trichosanthes *anguina.* |
| Poola-gurga, . .. | T. | Rubia *annularia.* |
| P——palla, .. .. | — | Asclepias *microphylla.* |
| Pootas, .. .. | — | Urtica *tenacissima.* |
| Poolavayr, .. .. | TAM. | Phyllanthus *multiflorus.* |
| Pooliaray, .. .. | — | Oxalis *corniculata.* |
| Pooliarileh-kalung, .. | — | Cissus *acida.* |
| Poolie-chinta, .. | T. | Oxalis *corniculata.* |
| Poollium, .. .. | TAM. | Tamarindus *Indica.* |
| Poolugooda, . .. | T. | Phyllanthus *multiflorus.* |
| Poombeh, .. .. | — | Gossypium *herbaceum.* |
| Poonakapoondoo, .. | TAM. | Justicia *Tranquebarensis.* |
| Poona, .. .. | T. T. | Calophyllum *inophyllum.* |
| Poo-natsoo, .. .. | T. | Serpicula *verticillata.* |
| Poonaykallie, .. | TAM. | Dolichos (or Carpopogon) *pruriens.* |
| Poonga-marum, .. | — | Dalbergia *arborea.* |
| Poon-mooshtie, .. | — | Cissampelos *Pareira.* |
| Poorri-gaddi, . .. | T. | Cyperus *Jemenicus.* |
| Poorusharatanum, .. | — | Viola *suffruticosa.* |
| Pootra-juvee, .. .. | — | Ficus *comosa.* |
| Pootsakaia, .. .. | — | Cucumis *Colocynthis.* |
| Pootstrangali, .. | — | Apluda *aristata.* |
| Poottatanim-marum, . | TAM. | Careya *arborea.* |
| Poo-ut, .. .. | M. | Rubia *Munjistha.* |
| Poovandie-cottay, .. | TAM. | Sapindus *emarginatus.* |
| Porasum, .. .. | — | Butea *frondosa.* |
| Poroodonda, .. .. | T. | Ekebergia *Indica.* |
| Portalaykaiantagherie, | TAM. | Verbesina *Calendulacea.* |
| Poti-kakar, .. .. | T. | Momordica *Carantia.* |
| Pot-kuda-pala, .. | CYNG. | Achyranthes *lanata.* |
| Potoo-ederoo, . .. | T. | Arundo *bifaria.* |
| Potri, .. .. | — | Kydia *paterna.* |
| Potu-galli-gheetsa, . | — | Crotalaria *retusa.* |
| Poupadyræ, .. .. | TAM. | Bignonia *Chelonoides.* |
| Poursunghai, . .. | — | Hibiscus *populneus.* |
| Pudda-kanrew, .. | T. | Flacourtia *sapida.* |
| Pukkie, .. .. | — | Trophis *aspera.* |

| | | | |
|---|---|---|---|
| Pulang-kilunggu, | .. | Tam. | Curcuma *Zerumbet.* |
| Pulcollie, .. | .. | M. | Justicia *nasuta.* |
| Pulla-chinta, . | .. | T. | Oxalis *corniculata.* |
| Puloo, .. | .. | — | Bambusa *Balcua.* |
| Punookoo, .. | .. | — | Rottbœllia *compressa.* |
| Punusa, .. | .. | — | Artocarpus *integrifolia.* |
| Puppali, .. | .. | Tam. | Carica *Papaya.* |
| Purpadagum, . | .. | — | { Pharnaceum *Cerviana,* or *triflora.* |
| Purpatakum, . | .. | T. | { P——— *C*———, or *t*———. |
| Putleroo, .. | .. | — | Tribulus *terrestris.* |
| Putoo-toadi, .. | .. | — | Borassus *flabelliformis.* |
| Putri-budinga, | .. | — | Bryonia *scabrella.* |
| Puttamie, .. | .. | Tam. | Pisum *sativum.* |
| Putta-tiga, .. | .. | T. | Capparis *heteroclita.* |
| Puttie, .. | .. | — | Gossypium *herbaceum.* |
| Puwak, .. | .. | Cyng. | Areca *Catechu.* |
| Pydoo-tenghadoo, | .. | T. | Cassia *Sophora.* |

## SECTION 1.

### *Sanscrit, Bengallee, Hindi, &c.*

## Q.

## SECTION 2.

### *Tamool, Telinga, Cyngalese, &c.*

## Q.

| | | | |
|---|---|---|---|
| Quoia-pipalay, | .. | T. | Salicornia *Indica.* |
| Quoiloo, .. | .. | — | S——— *brachiata.* |
| Quoi-tola-kura, | .. | — | Amaranthus *tristis.* |

## Section 1.

### *Sanscrit, Bengalee, Hindee, &c.*

# R.

| | | |
|---|---|---|
| Rachan, .. .. | H. | Ocymum *pilosum.* |
| Racta-bun-pooi, .. | B. | Basella *rubra.* |
| R——suadanshtara, . | S. | Tribulus *terrestris.* |
| Raggee, .. .. | H. | Eleusine *stricta,* or *Coracana.* |
| Rahala, .. .. | — | Cicer *arietinum.* |
| Rahu, .. .. | — | Ocymum *pilosum.* |
| Rai, .. .. | — | Sinapsis *Chinensis.* |
| Rajgagee, .. .. | B. | Vitis *rubifolia.* |
| Rajeeka ; Rajika, .. | S. B. | Sinapsis *ramosa,* or *glauca,* or *Chinensis.* |
| Rajika, .. .. | S. | Eleusine *Coracana.* |
| Rakat-chandan, .. | H. | Pterocarpus *Santalinus.* |
| Rakhal-phul, .. | B. | Ornitrophe *serrata.* |
| Raktotpala, .. .. | S. | Nymphæa *odorata.* |
| Ramanagee-kula, .. | B. | Musa *ornata.* |
| Ram-bagoon, . .. | — | Solanum *hirsutum.* |
| Ramduliya, .. .. | — | Eleocarpus *aristatus.* |
| Ram-katha, .. .. | — | Quercus *semi-serrata.* |
| R—kula, .. .. | B. H. | Musa *sapientium, (wild sort.)* |
| R—til, .. .. | B. | Verbesina *sativa.* |
| R—toolshee, .. | B. H. | Ocymum *gratissimum.* |
| R—turi, .. .. | H. | Hibiscus *longifolius.* |
| Ramutti, .. .. | B. | Cordia *acuminata.* |
| Ranga-makhon-shim, . | — | Dolichos *gladiatus, (red.)* |
| R——moog, . .. | — | Phaseolus *calcaratus.* |
| Rangantheya, .. | — | Amaranthus *atropurpureus.* |
| Ran-goowa, .. .. | — | Areca *triandra.* |
| R—g——sooparee, . | — | A——*gracilis.* |
| Ranjana, .. .. | S. | Pterocarpus *Santalinus.* |
| Ranjun, .. .. | H. | Ixora *Bandhuca.* |
| Rasaut, .. .. | — | Amomum *Anthorrhizum.* |
| Ratlau, .. .. | — | Dioscorea *sativa.* |
| Rawasan, .. .. | — | Dolichos *Sinensis.* |
| Rawkus-gudda, .. | — | Bryonia *epigæa.* |

| | | |
|---|---|---|
| Rawla, .. .. | H. | Panicum *Italicum.* |
| Rechuk, .. .. | B. | Croton *Tiglium.* |
| Reetha, .. .. | — | Sapindus *detergens.* |
| R——, .. .. | — | Mimosa *concina.* |
| Rehan ; Rihan, .. | H. | Ocymum *pilosum.* |
| Rewand-chini, .. | — | Rheum *palmatum.* |
| Rhadonee, .. .. | B. | Apium *involucratum.* |
| Riey, .. .. | H. | Sinapis *Chinensis.* |
| Rishta, .. .. | S. H. | Sapindus *emarginatus.* |
| Ritah, .. .. | H. | { S—— *e*————, or *Saponaria.* |
| Riuasan, .. .. | — | Æschynomene *Sesban.* |
| Roas, .. .. | — | Vicia *Faba.* |
| Rohita-sarushapa, .. | S. | Arabis *Chinensis.* |
| Rohituka, .. .. | — | Andersonia *Rohitoka.* |
| Rohun, .. .. | B. H. | Swietenia *febrifuga.* |
| Rohuna, .. .. | S. | S—— *f*——. |
| Roodrakhya, . .. | B. | Eleocarpus *Ganitrus.* |
| Roodraksha, .. .. | S. | E—— *G*——. |
| Roodrakshya, . .. | B. | E—— *G*——. |
| Rooi, .. .. | H. | Gossypium *herbaceum.* |
| Rosea, .. .. | S. | Salvinia *coccinea.* |
| Roshuniya, .. .. | B. | Spilanthus *oleracea.* |
| Ructa-chundana, .. | — | Adenanthera *pavonina.* |
| R——kumbula, .. | — | Nymphæa *rubra.* |
| R——pudma, .. | — | { Nelumbium *speciosum,* *(red.)* |
| Rujuni-gundha, .. | — | Polyanthes *tuberosa.* |
| Rujunta, .. .. | — | Elsholtzia *villosa.* |
| Rukta-alloo, .. .. | S. | Convolvulus *Batatas.* |
| R—— -baryala, .. | B. | Sida *rhombifolia.* |
| R——canchun, .. | — | Bauhinia *variegata.* |
| R——chitraka, .. | S. | Plumbago *rosea.* |
| R——chunduna, .. | B. H. | Pterocarpus *Santalinus.* |
| Ruktamra, .. .. | S. | Mangifera *sylvatica.* |
| Rukta-pita, .. .. | B. | Ventilago *Maderaspatanum.* |
| R——shaka, . .. | H. | Amaranthus *Gangeticus.* |
| R——shimool, .. | B. | Bombax *heptaphyllum.* |
| R——sirinchee, .. | — | Achyranthes *ferruginea.* |
| R——vindu-chada, .. | S. | Euphorbia *thymifolia.* |
| Ruktuka, .. .. | — | Ixora *Bandhuca.* |
| R——, .. .. | — | Pentapetes *phœnicea.* |
| Rungun, .. .. | B. | Ixora *Bandhuca.* |
| Rusala, .. .. | S. | Saccharum *officinarum.* |
| Rushoon ; Rushoona, | B. H. | Allium *sativum.* |

| | | | |
|---|---|---|---|
| Rusna-jaji, .. | .. | B. H. | Valisneria *alternifolia*. |
| Rut-aloo, .. | .. | H. | Dioscorea *sativa*. |
| Ruthni, .. | .. | — | Mimosa *natans*. |
| Ruttun-puruss, | .. | — | Viola *suffruticosa*. |
| Ruviya, .. | .. | S. B. | Dillenia *speciosa*. |

## Section 2.

### *Tamool, Telinga, Cyngalese, &c.*

## R.

| | | |
|---|---|---|
| Raghi, .. .. | T. | Ficus *religiosa.* |
| Raiy, .. .. | Tam. | Sinapis *Chinensis.* |
| Rajuma, .. .. | T. | Celosia *corymbosa.* |
| Rakisha, .. .. | — | Cyperus *elatus.* |
| Ranawara, .. .. | Cyng. | Cassia *auriculata.* |
| Rassa-usereki, .. | T. | Phyllanthus *longifolius.* |
| Rata-attika, .. .. | Cyng. | Ficus *Carica.* |
| R——endaru, . .. | — | Jatropha *Curcas.* |
| R——innala, .. .. | — | Solanum *tuberosum.* |
| R——kækuna, . .. | — | Canarium *commune.* |
| Rathnetul, .. .. | — | Plumbago *rosea.* |
| Ratipanchie, . .. | T. | Lichen *rotundatus.* |
| Ratu-eka-wæriya, .. | Cyng. | Ophioxylon *serpentinum.* |
| Ratukimbul-wenna, .. | — | Polygonum *barbatum.* |
| Rawa-kada, .. .. | T. | Salsola *nudiflora.* |
| R——salaburta-kanda, | — | Phyllanthus *bacciformis.* |
| Ray, .. .. | — | Ficus *religiosa.* |
| Rayla-kaia, .. .. | — | Cassia *fistula.* |
| Rela, .. .. | — | C—— *f*——. |
| Relloo-gaddi, . .. | — | Saccharum *spontaneum.* |
| Renga ; Rengha, .. | — | Zizyphus *Jujuba.* |
| Rewa, .. .. | — | Poa *procera.* |
| Rewoona, .. .. | — | P— *p*——. |
| Reygha, .. . | — | Zizyphus *Jujuba.* |
| Rhetsa-maun, . .. | — | Fagara *Rhetsa.* |
| Rie, .. .. | Mah. | Sinapis *Chinensis.* |
| Rigrak-tiga, .. .. | T. | Hirea *Indica.* |
| Roodra-joowee, .. | — | Nageia *Putranjiva.* |
| Rosa-kenda, .. .. | Cyng. | Dioscorea *alata.* |
| Ruct-handoon, .. | — | Pterocarpus *Santalinus.* |
| Russa-ghedi, . .. | T. | Solanum *pubescens.* |

## Section 1.

### *Sanscrit, Bengalee, Hindee, &c.*

## S.

| | | |
|---|---|---|
| Saclasuhagan, .. | H. | Hibiscus *phœniceus.* |
| Sada-boree, .. .. | — | Asclepias *pseudosarsa, (narrow leaves.)* |
| S——dhootura, .. | B. H. | Datura *Metel.* |
| S—— hazar-muni, .. | B. | Phyllanthus *Niruri.* |
| S——jamai-pooli, .. | — | Dolichos *lignosus, (var. 3.)* |
| S——j——shim, .. | — | D—— *l*——. |
| S ——jatee, .. .. | — | Barleria *dichotoma.* |
| S——juba, .. .. | H. | Hibiscus *Syriacus.* |
| S——kanoor, .. | B. | Pancratium *triflorum.* |
| Sadbarg, .. .. | H. | Rosa *glandulifera.* |
| Sadul-kuwa, .. .. | — | Melodinus *monogynus.* |
| Saee-kanta, .. .. | — | Mimosa *Suma.* |
| Safriam, .. .. | — | Psidium *pyriferum.* |
| Sagoon, .. .. | B. H. | Tectona *grandis.* |
| Sagwannee, .. .. | H. | Asclepias *echinata.* |
| Sahadevi, .. .. | S. | Conyza *Cinerea.* |
| Sahajna ; Sahunjna, .. | H. | Hyperanthera *Moringa.* |
| Sakchara, .. .. | S. | Lawsonia *spinosa*, or *inermis.* |
| Sakotuka, .. .. | — | Trophis *aspera.* |
| Sal ; Sala, .. .. | S. H. | Shorea *robusta.* |
| Salaee ; Salai, .. | H. | Boswellia *serrata*, or *thurifera.* |
| Salbia, .. .. | — | Salvia *officinalis.* |
| Salsa, .. .. | B. | Ichnocarpus *frutescens.* |
| Samalu, .. .. | H. | Vitex *trifolia.* |
| Samangga, .. .. | S. | Mimosa *pudica.* |
| Samandr-sokh, .. <br> Samoodr-sokh, .. | H. | Convolvulus *argenteus.* |
| Sam-dullum, . .. | — | Elephantophus *scaber.* |
| Sam, .. .. | — | Cupressus *(sp?)* |
| Sami, .. .. | — | Mimosa *albida.* |
| Samoo-druka, . .. | S. | Leea *macrophylla.* |
| Samudra-patra, .. | — | Convolvulus *speciosus.* |
| San, .. .. | H. | Crotalaria *juncea.* |

| | | | |
|---|---|---|---|
| Sanchi-beta, . . | . . | B. | Calamus *Rotang.* |
| Sandhyaraga, . | . . | S. | Polyanthes *tuberosa.* |
| Sangkhi, . . | . . | — | Vinca *parviflora.* |
| Sanwa, . . | . . | H. | Panicum *frumentaceum.* |
| Saom, . . | . . | B. | Fagræa *obovata.* |
| Sarang, . . | . . | H. | Nymphæa *Lotus.* |
| Sapha-nitaha, . | . . | N. | Primula *rotundifolia.* |
| Sar, . . | . . | H. | Saccharum *Sara.* |
| Saral, . . | . . | — | Pinus *longifolia.* |
| Sarass, . . | . . | — | Cupressus *sempervirens.* |
| Sarkara, . . | . . | — | Saccharum *procerum.* |
| Sar-kuchoo, . . | . . | B. | Arum *Nymphœafolia.* |
| Sarmac, . . | . . | H. | Atriplex *(sp ?)* |
| Sarput, . . | . . | — | Saccharum *procerum.* |
| Sarsori, . . | . . | — | Sinapis *dichotoma.* |
| Satapatra, . . | . . | S. | Nelumbium *speciosum.* |
| Satar, . . | . . | H. | Origanum *(sp ?)* |
| Saturi, . . | . . | — | Ruta *graveolens.* |
| Sawan, . . | . . | — | Panicum *(sp ?).* |
| Saynd, . . | . . | — | Euphorbium *antiquorum.* |
| Scamunia, . . | . . | — | Convolvolus *Scammonia.* |
| Seb, . | . . | — | Pyrus *Malus.* |
| Seduari, . . | . . | — | Vitex *trifolia.* |
| Seej, . . | . . | S. | Euphorbia *nereifolia.* |
| Seekekai, . . | . . | — | Mimosa *abstergens.* |
| Seetula-putrika, | . . | — | Phrynium *dichotomum.* |
| Seetul-patee, . | . . | B. H. | P——— *d————.* |
| Sehind, . . | . . | H. | Euphorbia *(sp ?)* |
| Sehooan, . . | . | — | Sinapis *(sp ?)* |
| Sem or Same, . | . . | — | Dolichos *(sp ?)* |
| Semal ; Sembal, | . . | — | Bombax *heptaphyllum.* |
| Send, . . | . . | — | Curcuma *Maderaspatensis.* |
| Sendhi, . . | . . | — | Phœnix *Sylvestris.* |
| Senthi, . . | . . | — | Saccharum *Sara.* |
| Seo, . | . . | — | Pyrus *Malus.* |
| Seora, . . | . . | — | Trophis *aspera.* |
| Seoti, . . | . . | — | Rosa *glandulifera.* |
| Seva, . . | . . | S. | Pyrus *malus.* |
| Sevuti, . . | . . | — | Rosa *glandulifera.* |
| Shado-nuteeya, | . . | B. | Amaranthus *oleraceus.* |
| Shaee, . . | . . | — | Mimosa *Suma.* |
| Shaftalu, . . | . . | H. | Amygdalus *Persica.* |
| Shah-alu, . . | . . | — | Prunus *Cerasus.* |
| S——pusund, | . . | — | Centaurea *moschata.* |
| S——tara, . . | . . | — | Oldenlandia *biflora.* |
| Shaitul, . . | . . | — | Morus *(sp ?)* |

| | | |
|---|---|---|
| Shakul, .. .. | H. | Cytisus *Cajan*. |
| Shal, .. .. | B. H. | Shorea *robusta*. |
| Shala, .. .. | B. | Nauclea *ovalifolia*. |
| Shala-purnee, . .. | S. | Hibiscus *alatum*. |
| Shaleya, .. .. | — | Asparagus *racemosus*. |
| Shalgam ; Shalgram ; Shalgum, .. .. | B. H. | Brassica *rapa*. |
| Shalanchi ; Shalincha, | S. B. | Achyranthes *triandra*. |
| Shalmuli, .. .. | — | Bombax *heptaphyllum*. |
| Shalook, .. .. | B. | Nymphæa *Lotus*. |
| Shaloocha, .. .. | — | Achyranthes *triandra*. |
| Shalpani, .. .. | B. H. | Hedysarum *Gangeticum*. |
| Shalshaeei-babula, .. | B. | Mimosa *tomentosa*. |
| Shama ; Shama-gas, .. | B.H. | Panicum *frumentaceum*. |
| Shamaka, .. .. | S. | P——— *colonum*, *(red.)* |
| Shum-dulun, . .. | B. | Elephantophus *scaber*. |
| Shanchi, .. .. | — | Achyranthes *triandra*. |
| S———sursha, .. | — | Synapis *dichotoma*. |
| Shara, .. .. | — | Trophis *aspera*. |
| Shariva, .. .. | S. | Periploca *Indica*. |
| Shatra, .. .. | H. | Fumaria *officinalis*. |
| Sheel-koil, .. .. | B. | Celastrus *robustus*. |
| Sheem, .. .. | — | Dolichos *gladiatus* or *Lablab*. |
| Sheetahar, .. .. | — | Lycopodium *phlegmaria*. |
| Shelenga, .. .. | — | Achyranthes *triandra*. |
| Sheloo, .. .. | S. | Cordia *latifolia*. |
| Sheora, .. .. | B. | Trophis *aspera*. |
| Shephalika, .. .. | S. B. | Nyctanthes *arbor-tristis*. |
| Shewuti, .. .. | B. H. | Rosa *glandulifera*. |
| Sheyala, .. .. | B. | Valisneria *octandra*. |
| Shial-kanta, .. .. | — | Argemone *Mexicana*. |
| Shibjhool, .. . | — | Cardiospermum *Halicacabum*. |
| Shij, .. .. | B. H. | Euphorbia *nereifolia*. |
| Shimbee, .. .. | S. | Dolichos *gladiatus*, or *Lablab*. |
| Shimeeya-batrajee, .. | B. | Hedysarum *tuberosum*. |
| Shimi-batrajee, .. | H. | Dolichos *glutinosus*. |
| Shimool, .. .. | B. | Bombax *heptaphyllum*. |
| Shingra, .. .. | — | Quercus *lanceofolia*. |
| Shingshupa, .. .. | S. | Dalbergia *Sissoo*. |
| Shiooli, . .. | B. | Nyctanthes *arbor-tristis*. |
| Shireesh, .. .. | S.H.B. | Mimosa *Sirissa*. |
| Shirkisht, .. .. | H. | Ormus *rotundifolia*. |
| Shisham, .. .. | — | Dalbergia *Sissoo*. |
| Shiwanimba, .. .. | S. | Aspalathus *Indica*. |
| Shojina, .. .. | B. | Hyperanthera *Moringa*. |

| | | |
|---|---|---|
| Shola ; Sola, . .. | B. | Æschynomene *paludosa.* |
| Sholee, .. .. | S. | Curcuma *Zedoaria.* |
| Sholista, .. .. | — | C——— Z———. |
| Sholoopha, .. .. | B. | Fumaria *parviflora.* |
| Shona, .. .. | B. H. | Bignonia *Indica.* |
| Shoochi-mookhee, .. | B. | Sanseveria *Zeylanica.* |
| Shook-cheena, .. | — | Smilax *China.* |
| Shookhasa, .. .. | S. | Cucumis *sativus.* |
| Shoola, .. .. | H. | Æschynomene *arborea.* |
| Shoora-aloo, .. .. | B. H. | Dioscorea *nummularia.* |
| Shooshuna, .. .. | B. | Eleagnus *dulcis.* |
| Shoothee, .. .. | — | Curcuma *Zerumbet.* |
| Shoothugnee ; Sho-thugnee, .. | S. B. | Boerhavia *diffusa*, or *procumbens.* |
| Shree-hustinee, .. | S. | Heliotropium *Indicum.* |
| Shudi-mudi, .. .. | B. | Cacalia *sonchifolia.* |
| Shullakee, .. .. | S. | Boswellia *thurifera.* |
| Shumbalie, .. .. | H. | Vitex *Negundo.* |
| Shumee, .. .. | S. | Mimosa *Suma.* |
| S———, .. .. | — | Prosopis *spicigera.* |
| Shuna, .. .. | — | Crotalaria *juncea.* |
| Shunacabarbara, .. | — | Cleome *viscosa.* |
| Shunkinee, .. .. | — | Andropogon *aciculatum.* |
| Shunkur-juta, .. | B. | Hedysarum *pictum.* |
| Shurakasthika, .. | S. | Phrynium *dichotomum.* |
| Shurkura-kunda, .. | — | Convolvulus *Batatas.* |
| Shutuvedhee, . .. | — | Rumex *vesicarius.* |
| Shuta-moolee, .. | — | Asparagus *racemosus.* |
| Shwet (or sada) akund, | B. | Asclepias *gigantea*, (*white.*) |
| S———baryala, .. | — | Sida *rhomboidea.* |
| S———buruna, .. | H. | Randia *stricta.* |
| S———busunta, .. | B. | Acalypha *Indica.* |
| S———b———, .. | H. | Phlomis *biflora.* |
| S———chamni, . | — | Gratiola *Monniera.* |
| S———gothoobi, .. | B. | Kyllingia *monocephala.* |
| S———gurjun, . .. | — | Dipterocarpus *turbinatus.* |
| S———holee, .. .. | B. H. | Pterygodium *sulcatum.* |
| S———kamaluta, .. | B. | Ipomœa *Quamoclit*, (*white.*) |
| S———kherooee, .. | — | Euphorbia *thymifolia.* |
| S———kudum, . .. | — | Nauclea *tetrandra.* |
| S———kurubee, .. | B. H. | Nerium *odorum*, (*white.*) |
| S———moorga, .. | B. | Celosia *argentea.* |
| S———pai, .. .. | — | Eleocarpus *lanceofolia.* |
| S———panee-murich, .. | — | Polygonum *lanatum.* |
| S———pudma, . .. | — | Nelumbium *speciosum.* |
| S———raee, .. .. | — | Sinapis *racemosa.* |

| | | |
|---|---|---|
| Shwet (or sada) sabuni, | H. | Trianthema *obcordata.* |
| S——shimool, .. | B. H. | Bombax *pentandrum.* |
| S——shursha, .. | B. | Brassica *erucoides.* |
| S——turooluta, .. | H. | Ipomœa *Quamoclit,* (*white.*) |
| S——upurajita, . | B. | Clitoria *ternata,* (*white.*) |
| S——vrihutee, .. | S. | Solanum *Indicum,* (*white.*) |
| Shya-kool, .. .. | B. | Zizyphus *scandens,* or Napeia *scabra.* |
| Shyal-kanta, .. .. | — | Z——— *s*———. |
| Shyamaka, .. .. | S. | Bignonia *Indica.* |
| Shymaka, .. .. | — | Panicum *frumentaceum.* |
| Shyama-luta, . .. | B. H. | Echites *frutescens.* |
| Siah-mooslie, . .. | H. | Curculigo *Orchioides.* |
| Siddartha, .. .. | S. | Brassica *erucoides.* |
| Sigroo, .. .. | — | Hyperanthera *Moringa.* |
| Sihoonda, .. .. | — | Euphorbia *antiquorum.* |
| Sij, .. .. | H. | E——— *Nereifolia.* |
| Silapooma, .. .. | — | Juglans *pterococca.* |
| Simar, .. .. | — | Valisneria *octandra.* |
| Sinadika, .. .. | S. | Boerhavia *diffusa.* |
| Sinbalu, .. .. | H. | Vitex *trifolia.* |
| Sindhooka, .. .. | S. | V—— *Negundo.* |
| Sindica, .. .. | — | Diospyros *glutinosa.* |
| Sinduvara, .. .. | — | Vitex *trifolia.* |
| Sinduya, .. .. | — | V—— *Negundo.* |
| Singara, .. .. | H. | Trapa *bispinosa,* or *natans.* |
| Singarhar, .. .. | — | Nyctanthes *arbor-tristis.* |
| Singginjanascha, .. | — | Corchorus *olitorius.* |
| Singhara, .. .. | B. | (?) |
| Singhee, .. .. | S. | Justicia *Adhahota.* |
| Siphal, .. .. | H. | Ægle *marmelos.* |
| Siriari, .. .. | — | Heliotropium *Indicum.* |
| Siris, .. .. | — | Mimosa *Siris.* |
| Sirki, .. .. | — | Saccharum *procerum.* |
| Sissoo, .. .. | B. H. | Dalbergia *Sissoo.* |
| Sitafal, .. .. | H. | Annona *squamosa.* |
| Sitaka-pungerie, .. | — | Lavendula *carnosa.* |
| Sitasiva, .. .. | S. | Anethum *Sowa,* or *graveolens.* |
| Sitalchini, .. .. | H. | Pimenta *vulgaris.* |
| Sitalpatee, .. .. | — | Phrynium *dichotomum.* |
| Sivali, .. .. | — | Valisneria *octandra.* |
| Siwar, .. . | H. | V——— *spiralis.* |
| Sobhanjunya, . .. | S. B. | Hyperanthera *Moringa.* |
| Socha, .. .. | N. | Lonicera *Japonica.* |
| Sod, .. .. | H. | Anethum *Sowa.* |

| | | | |
|---|---|---|---|
| **Soie; Soia,** .. | .. | H. | Anethum *Sowa* or *graveolens.* |
| **Sola,** .. | .. | B. H. | Æschynomene *paludosa.* |
| **Soma-luta,** .. | .. | S. B. | Asclepias *acida.* |
| **Somraj,** .. | .. | H. | Serratula *anthelmintica.* |
| **Somuna,** .. | .. | S. | Triticum *æstivum.* |
| **Sona,** .. | .. | H. | Bauhinia *purpurea.* |
| **Sonali,** .. | .. | B. | Cassia *fistula.* |
| **Sona-moog,** .. | .. | — | Phaseolus *aureus.* |
| **S——mookhee,** | .. | H. | Cassia *Senna.* |
| **S——pat,** .. | .. | B. | C—— *S*——. |
| **Sonballi,** .. | .. | H. | Croton *plicatum.* |
| **Sonf,** .. | .. | — | Anethum *Panmorium* or *fœniculum.* |
| **Sonth,** .. | .. | — | Zinziber *officinalis.* |
| **Soobja,** .. | .. | B. | Sabia *lanceolata.* |
| **Soodali,** .. | .. | — | Cassia *fistula.* |
| **Soodumstra,** .. | .. | S. | Tribulus *terrestris.* |
| **Soodurshun,** . | .. | B. | Crinum *defixum.* |
| **Soodurshuna,** . | .. | S. | C——— *amœnum.* |
| **Soogundha,** .. | .. | — | Alpinia *Galanga.* |
| **Sook-durshun,** | .. | H. | Crinum *Asiaticum* or *Zeylanicum.* |
| **Sookshmuphula,** | .. | S. | Zizyphus *Napeia.* |
| **Sookur-thooti,** | .. | B. | Cnestis *monadelpha.* |
| **Soom,** .. | .. | — | Sarcostema *viminialis.* |
| **Soona,** .. | .. | — | Panax *digitatum.* |
| **Soondhi,** .. | .. | — | Nymphæa *cyanea.* |
| **Soonduree,** .. | .. | S. B. | Heritiera *minor.* |
| **Soonishunnuka,** | .. | S. | Marsilea *quadrifolia.* |
| **Sooparee,** .. | .. | B. H. | Areca *Catechu.* |
| **S———,** .. | .. | B. | Rondeletia *longifolia.* |
| **Sooparshavaka,** | .. | S. | Hibiscus *populneus.* |
| **Soora-yamuni,** | .. | — | H——— *phœniceus.* |
| **Soorea,** .. | .. | B. | Tetranthera *quadrifolia.* |
| **Soorjya-mookhee,** | .. | — | Helianthus *annuus.* |
| **S———muni,** | .. | — | Hibiscus *phœniceus.* |
| **Sooshuni-shak,** | .. | — | Marsilea *quadrifolia.* |
| **Soosni-aloo,** .. | .. | B. H. | Dioscorea *fasciculata.* |
| **Soosuve,** .. | .. | S. | Momordica *muricata.* |
| **Soovurnuka,** | .. | S. B. | Cassia *fistula.* |
| **Sosan,** .. | .. | H. | Lilium *(sp?)* |
| **Sothali,** .. | .. | — | Æschynomene *aspera.* |
| **Sottraj,** .. | .. | — | Tradescantia *axillaris.* |
| **Sowa,** .. | .. | — | Anethum *Sowa* or *graveolens.* |

| | | |
|---|---|---|
| Sowarree, .. .. | B. | Tetranthera *quadrifolia*. |
| Sphootee, .. .. | — | Cucumis *Momordica*. |
| Sprukka, .. .. | S. | Trophis *aspera*. |
| Sringata, .. .. | — | Trapa *bispinosa*. |
| Subjuya, .. .. | H. | Canna *Indica*. |
| Subkyar-sun, . .. | — | (?) |
| Subze, .. .. | — | Ocymum *basilicum*. |
| Suffaid-muhammad, .. | — | Fluggea *leucopyrus*. |
| S——mooslie, .. | — | Asparagus *sarmentosus*. |
| S——-toolsie, .. | — | Ocymum *album*. |
| Suffet-shukurkund-aloo, | B. H. | Convolvulus *Batatas*. |
| S——-turoo-luta, .. | — | Ipomæa *Quamoclit*, (*white*.) |
| S——-gool-mukhmul, | H. | Gomphrena *globosa*,(*white*.) |
| S——-pooi, .. | — | Basella *alba*. |
| Suffri-am, .. .. | — | Psidium *pyriferum*. |
| Sugandha-marichu, .. | S. | Piper *Cubeb*. |
| Sug-ungoor, .. | H. | Atropa *Belladonna*. |
| Suhoora, .. .. | — | Trophis *aspera*. |
| Sujna, .. .. | — | Hyperanthera *Moringa*. |
| Sukandaka, .. .. | S. | Allium *Cepa*. |
| Sukkapat, .. .. | H. | Monetia *Barleroides*. |
| Sukkur-kunda-aloo, .. | B. | Convolvulus *Batatas*. |
| Suloopha; Sulpha, .. | — | Anethum *Sowa*. |
| Sultan-champa, .. | H. | Calophyllum *inophyllum*. |
| Sumac, .. .. | — | Rhus *coriara*. |
| Sumunga, .. .. | S. | Rubia *Munjistha*. |
| Sun, .. .. | B. H. | Crotalaria *juncea*. |
| Sunbul, .. .. | H. | Valeriana *Jatamansi*. |
| Sundel, .. .. | — | Santalum *album*. |
| Sundhi-gool, . .. | B. | Laurus *lanceolaria*. |
| Sun-goolla, .. .. | H. | Calamus *erectus*. |
| Sungkoopie, .. .. | — | Volkameria *inermis*. |
| Suparee, .. .. | — | Areca *Catechu*. |
| Suphee, .. .. | B. | Myrica *integrifolia*. |
| Suphuree-koomra, .. | B. H. | Cucurbita *Melopepo*. |
| Supta-puma, . .. | S. | Echites *scholaris*. |
| Suptula, .. .. | — | Jasminum *Zambac* or *arborescens*. |
| Surajmucki, .. .. | H. | Helianthus *annuus*. |
| Suran, .. .. | — | Arum *campanulatum*. |
| Suranjan, .. .. | — | Colchicum *(sp ?)* |
| Surasarum, .. .. | — | Phyllanthus *rhamnoides*. |
| Surba-juya, .. .. | S. B. | Canna *Indica*. |
| Surshupa, .. | S. | Sinapis *dichotoma*. |
| Suris, .. .. | B. | Mimosa *Smithiana*. |
| Surisha, .. .. | — | Sinapis *dichotoma*. |

| | | | |
|---|---|---|---|
| **Surj,** | .. .. | B. | Shorea *robusta*. |
| **Surpunka,** | .. .. | H. | Calophyllum *inophyllum*. |
| **Surpunkha,** | .. .. | B. | Galega *purpurea*. |
| **Surputnoo,** | .. .. | S. | Solanum *diffusum*. |
| **Sursou,** | .. .. | H. | Phyllanthus *rhamnoides*. |
| **Surul,** | .. .. | B. | Pinus *longifolia*. |
| **Surus,** | .. .. | — | Cupressus *sempervirens*. |
| **Suryavarti,** | .. .. | S. | Croton *plicatum*. |
| **Susha,** | .. .. | B. | Cucumis *sativus*. |
| **Suthri,** | .. .. | H. | Dioscorea *fasciculata*. |
| **Svana-barbara,** | .. | S. | Cleome *viscosa*. |
| **Swadoo-kuntuka,** | .. | — | Flacourtia *sapida*. |
| **Swali,** | .. .. | — | Valisneria *octandra*. |
| **Swarnakshira,** | .. | — | Cleome *felina*. |
| **Swarna-mayahari,** | .. | — | Cassia *Sophora*. |
| **S—— pushpa,** | .. | — | Limodorum *spatulatum*. |
| **Swot,** | .. .. | B. | Sonnerilla *maculata*. |
| **Swati,** | .. .. | — | Panicum *Holcoides*. |
| **Sweta-koonch,** | .. | — | Abrus *precatorius*. |
| **S——mas,** | .. .. | N. | |
| **S——punarnavi,** | .. | S. | Trianthema *monogynia*, (*white*.) |
| **S——shala,** | .. .. | B. | Dalbergia *latifolia*. |
| **Swurunjoothee,** | .. | — | Jasminum *chrysanthemum*. |

## Section 2.

### *Tamool, Telinga, Cyngalese, &c.*

## S.

| | | |
|---|---|---|
| Sadanapa-vedroo, .. | T. | Bambusa *stricta*. |
| Sadda-cooppei, .. | Tam. | Anethum *Sowa* or *graveolens*. |
| Saddika, .. .. | Cyng. | Myristica *moschata*. |
| Sakilla-kampa, .. | T. | Arachis *fruticosa*. |
| Salla-burta, .. .. | — | Hibiscus *rigidus*. |
| S——woondoo, .. | — | Panicum *hirsutum*. |
| Salli-tunga, .. .. | — | Cyperus *compressus*. |
| Samatrapoo-tainkaya, . | — | Cocos *Maldivica*, or Lodoicea *Sechellarum*. |
| Sambrani-chittoo, .. | — | Gratiola *Monniera*. |
| Samutra-cheddie, .. | Tam. | Convolvolus *speciosus*. |
| S———patsa, .. | T. | C——— *s*———. |
| Sanalinga, .. .. | — | Laurus *Cinnamomum*. |
| Sana-yellaci, . .. | — | Alpinia *Cardamomum*. |
| Sandoon, .. .. | Cyng. | Santalum *album*. |
| Sanigheloo, .. .. | — | Cicer *arietinum*. |
| Sangkhaphuli, .. | Tam. | Vinca *parviflora*. |
| Saoohal, .. .. | Cyng. | Salvia *Bengalensis*. |
| Sapatoo-cheddie, .. | Tam. | Hibiscus *Rosa-sinensis*. |
| Sarakonnekai, .. | — | Cassia *fistula*. |
| Sat-sanda, .. .. | Cyng. | Aristolochia *Indica*. |
| Satta-coopa, .. .. | — | Anethum *Sowa* or *graveolens*. |
| Sawil-codie, .. .. | Tam. | Rubia *Munjistha*. |
| Sayawer, .. .. | — | Oldenlandia *umbellata*. |
| Sayselley, . .. | — | Salvia *Bengalensis*. |
| Schædaveli-kelungu, .. | M. | Asparagus *sarmentosus*. |
| Scheratalli-badoo, .. | T. | Dalbergia *scandens*. |
| Scheru-pariti, .. | M. | Hibiscus *Rosa-sinensis*. |
| Schetti-codiveli, .. | — | Plumbago *rosea*. |
| Schunambu-valli, .. | — | Cissus *latifolia*. |
| Seema-avisee, . .. | T. | Cassia *alata*. |
| Seemie-aghatie, .. | Tam. | C—— *a*——. |
| Seera-shengalaneer, .. | — | Conyza *cinerea*. |
| Segapoo-shandanum, . | T. | Pterocarpus *Santalinum*. |

| | | |
|---|---|---|
| Selago-boro-gaddi, .. | T. | Fuirena *ciliaris.* |
| Sema-gherka, .. | — | Agrostis *tenacissima.* |
| Sendoorkum, . .. | TAM. | Carthamus *tinctorius.* |
| Serigada, .. .. | T. | Ehretia *lævis.* |
| Seri-galli-gheetsa, .. | — | Crotalaria *prostrata.* |
| Seringi, .. .. | — | Grislea *tomentosa.* |
| Serroo-samul, . .. | TAM. | Linum *usitatissimum.* |
| Setama-poorgoonooloo, | T. | Cuscuta *reflexa.* |
| Shadamangie, . .. | TAM. | Valeriana *Jatamansi.* |
| Shadray-kullie, .. | — | Euphorbia *antiquorum.* |
| Shaestmantaka, .. | T. | Cordia *Sebestena.* |
| Shakara-koomatei, .. | TAM. | Cucurbita *citrullus.* |
| Shama-kura, . . .. | T. | Arum *colocasia, (var. 2.)* |
| Shanamoo, .. .. | — | Crotalaria *juncea.* |
| Shandana-cottay, .. | TAM. | Santalum *album.* |
| Shangalli-gaddi, .. | T. | Panicum *stagninum.* |
| Shangam-cooppy, .. | TAM. | Volkameria *inermis.* |
| Sharunnay, . . .. | — | Trianthema *monogynia.* |
| Shayng-cottay ; Shay-rang-cottay, .. | — | Semecarpus *Anacardium.* |
| Shayraeet-coochie, .. | — | Gentiana *Chirayta.* |
| Sheeakai, .. .. | — | Mimosa *abstergens.* |
| Sheeikaia, . .. | T. | M—— *a*—— —— |
| Sheelasuttoo-coielloo, . | — | Gentiana *Chirayta.* |
| Sheendie-codie, .. | TAM. | Menispermum *cordifolium.* |
| Shemmarum, . .. | — | Swietenia *febrifuga.* |
| Shemmoolie, . .. | — | Barleria *Prionitis.* |
| Shencodie-vaylie, .. | — | Plumbago *rosea.* |
| Shengalaneer, . .. | — | Nymphæa *odorata.* |
| Sheroo-panookoo, .. | T. | Rottbœllia *compressa.* |
| Sheti-putsa, . . .. | — | Cucumis *Colocynthis.* |
| Shetti-beera, . .. | — | Luffa *amara.* |
| Shevadi, . .. | TAM. | Convolvulus *Turpethum.* |
| Shieri-goomoodoo, .. | T. | Gmelina *parviflora.* |
| Shikroen, .. .. | TAM. | Mimosa *amara.* |
| Shindulja, .. .. | T. | M—— *odoratissima.* |
| Shippur (or Shippuroo) gaddi, .. .. | — | Aristidia *setacea,* or *hystrix.* |
| Sholamini, .. .. | M. | Moræa *Chinensis.* |
| Shumee, .. .. | T. | Prosopis *spicigera.* |
| Shumi, .. .. | — | Adenanthera *aculeata.* |
| Shya-nella-benda, .. | — | Sida *alnifolia.* |
| Simie-attie, .. .. | TAM. | Ficus *Carica.* |
| S——carpoorum, .. | T. | Salvia *Bengalensis.* |
| Siminta, .. .. | — | Æschynomene *Sesban.* |
| Sindrikka, .. .. | CYNG. | Mirabilis *Jalapa.* |

| | | |
|---|---|---|
| Sinnee, .. .. | Tam. | Acalypha *betulina.* |
| Siragum, .. .. | — | Cuminum *Cyminum.* |
| Sirek, .. .. | Mah. | Andropogon *schœnanthus.* |
| Sirimaun, .. .. | T. | Conocarpus *latifolia.* |
| Sirroo-canchoorie, .. | Tam. | Tragia *cannabina.* |
| S——cooringa, .. | — | Periploca *sylvestris.* |
| S——coruttei, .. | — | Trichosanthes *incisa.* |
| S——eetchum, .. | — | Phœnix *farinifera.* |
| S——keeray, . .. | — | Amaranthus *campestris.* |
| Sirrooghoo-kuttalay, . | — | Aloe *littoralis* or *perfoliata.* |
| Sirroo-poolay, . .. | — | Achyranthes *lanata.* |
| Sittamootie, .. .. | Tam. | Pavonia *Zeylanica.* |
| Sittrapaladi, .. .. | — | Euphorbia *thymifolia.* |
| Soda, .. .. | T. | Panicum *paludosum.* |
| Sodi, .. .. | — | Eleusine *Coracana.* |
| Soeloe-marum, .. | Tam. | Mimosa *odoratissima.* |
| Soodooloonoo, .. | Cyng. | Allium *sativum.* |
| Soogundapala, .. | T. | Periploca *Indica.* |
| Sookun-keeray, .. | Tam. | Rumex *vesicatorius.* |
| Sookukada, .. .. | T. | Spermacoce *stricta.* |
| Soondra-woodinika, .. | — | Viscum *verticillatum.* |
| Soora-gada, .. | — | Geronium *fasciculatum.* |
| Soori, .. .. | Cyng. | Rumex *vesicarius.* |
| Sooriya-gaha, . .. | — | Hibiscus *populneus.* |
| Soymido, .. .. | T. | Swietenia *febrifuga.* |
| Sri-gundha, .. .. | Can. | Santalum *album.* |
| Sudab, .. .. | M. | Ruta *graveolens.* |
| Suddapa, .. .. | T. | Anethum *Sowa* or *graveolens.* |
| Suddapo-akoo, .. | — | Ruta *graveolens.* |
| Sukalli, .. .. | — | Trophis *spinosa.* |
| Sukkara-velli, . .. | — | Convolvulus *Batatas.* |
| Sukkaray-vullie, .. | Tam. | C.———— *B————.* |
| Sukkunaroo-pilloo, .. | — | Andropogon *Nardus.* |
| Sulunayi, .. .. | Cyng. | Justicia *repens.* |
| Sunaga, .. .. | T. | Cicer *arietinum.* |
| Sundra, .. .. | — | Mimosa *Sundra.* |
| Sung, .. .. | Tam. | Monetia *Barleroides.* |
| Suroodoo, .. .. | T. | Symphorema *involucrata.* |
| Surootoo, .. .. | — | Carpopogon *capitatum.* |
| Suva, .. .. | Cyng. | Anethum *Sowa* or *graveolens.* |
| Swamy, .. .. | Can. | Swietenia *febrifuga.* |

## Section 1.

### *Sanscrit, Bengalee, Hindee, &c.*

# T.

| | | | |
|---|---|---|---|
| Taba-neeboo, . | .. | B. H. | Citrus *acida.* |
| Tagora, .. | .. | B. | Vitis *barbata.* |
| Taizbul, .. | .. | N. | Piper *Cubeb.* |
| Taj, .. | .. | H. | Laurus *Cassia.* |
| Taj-i-cahrus, . | .. | — | Amaranthus (*sp?*) |
| Tal, .. | .. | B. H. | Borassus *flabelliformis.* |
| Tala-katta, .. | .. | H. | Burmannia *disticha.* |
| T—mool, .. | .. | B. | Ceratostema *variegata.* |
| Talee; Taliera, | .. | S. H. | Corypha *Taliera.* |
| Tali-jooniya, . | .. | B. | Combretum *costatum.* |
| Talisha, .. | .. | S. | Flacourtia *cataphracta.* |
| Talis-putrie, .. | .. | H. | F——— *c*———. |
| Tal-machana, . | .. | — | Barleria *longifolia.* |
| T—moolee, .. | .. | B. | Curculigo *Orchioides.* |
| T—nuroo, .. | .. | — | Scirpus *diphyllus.* |
| Talpota, .. | .. | S. | Cassia *auriculata.* |
| Tamak; Tumak, | .. | B. | Nicotiana *Tabacum.* |
| Tamala-patra, | .. | S. | Laurus *Cassia.* |
| Tamarhindi, .. | .. | H. | Tamarindus *Indicum.* |
| Tambacu, .. | .. | — | Nicotiana *Tabacum.* |

| | | |
|---|---|---|
| Tamboolee, .. .. | S. | Piper *Betle.* |
| Tamra-koota, . .. | H. | Nicotiana *Tabacum.* |
| Tan, .. .. | — | Verbena *nodiflora.* |
| Tapia, .. .. | — | Cratœva *Tapia.* |
| Tapureea, .. .. | B. | Physalis *Peruviana.* |
| Tar, .. .. | H. | Borassus *flabelliformis.* |
| Tar; Taruka, .. | S. B. | Alpinia *Alhugas.* |
| T—- T-——, . .. | — | Curculigo *Orchioides.* |
| Tara-tezac, .. .. | H. | Lepidium *sativum.* |
| Tarbuz, .. . | — | Cucurbita *citrullus.* |
| Tarie, .. .. | — | Borassus *flabelliformis.* |
| Tariyat, .. .. | B. | Corypha *Taliera.* |
| Taruka, .. .. | S. | Alpinia *Alhugas.* |
| Taruni, .. .. | S. B. | Aloe *perfoliata.* |
| Teak-chama, . .. | H. | Prenanthes *asplenifolia.* |
| Tea-parooa, .. .. | B. | Lonicera *Japonica.* |
| Teekor, .. .. | H. | Curcuma *angustifolia.* |
| Teet-conga, .. .. | — | Asclepias *volubilis.* |
| Teetooleeya, . .. | B. | Mimosa *microphylla.* |
| Tej-mool, .. .. | — | Conyza *lanceolaria.* |
| T—pat, .. .. | H. | Laurus *Cassia.* |
| Tejunnuka, .. .. | S. | Saccharum *Sara.* |
| Tekanta-jutee, .. | B. | Monetia *Barleroides.* |
| Tela-koolha, .. .. | — | Momordica *monadelpha.* |
| Telia-gurgun, . .. | — | Dipterocarpus *costatus.* |
| Teling-china, . .. | H. | Lagerstrœmia *Indica.* |
| Telkaiha, .. .. | — | Bryonia *grandis.* |
| Telung-shoora, .. | B. | Limodorum *longifolium.* |
| Tembiri, .. .. | S. | Diospyros *glutinosa.* |
| Tendu, .. .. | H. | D——— *Ebenum.* |
| Teng, .. .. | B. | Saccharum *procerum.* |
| Tenguree, .. .. | — | Stilago *tomentosa.* |
| Tentoolee, .. .. | — | Dalbergia *tamarindifolia.* |
| Teoomeri, .. .. | — | Pæderia *ternata.* |
| Teora, .. .. | — | Lathyrus *sativus.* |
| Teorie, .. .. | — | Convolvolus *Turpethum.* |
| Teparee, .. .. | — | (?) |
| Tepuriya, .. .. | — | Physalis *Peruviana.* |
| Teta, .. .. | H. | Teta *viridiflora.* |
| Thel-koodi, .. .. | — | Oldenlandia *alata.* |
| Thikeree, .. .. | B. | Phaseolus *radiatus.* |
| Thol-pudma, . .. | — | Hibiscus *mutabilis.* |
| Thuhar, .. .. | H. | Euphorbia *Nereifolia.* |
| Tiara, .. .. | B. | Celastrus *monospermus.* |
| Tibiliti, .. .. | N. | C——- *verticillatus.* |
| Ticoray-kullay, .. | B. | Phaseolus *radiatus.* |

| | | |
|---|---|---|
| Tidhara, .. .. | H. | Euphorbia *antiquorum*. |
| Tij, .. .. | B. | Laurus *Cassia*. |
| Tikanta-jutee, .. | — | Monetia *Barleroides*. |
| Tiki-opra, .. .. | — | Melochia *corchorifolia*. |
| Tikrie, .. . | H. | Boerhavia *diffusa*. |
| Tikta-raj, .. .. | B. | Andersonia *Rohitoka*. |
| Tikul, .. . | H. | Garcinia *pedunculata*. |
| Tikur, .. .. | — | Curcuma *angustifolia*. |
| Tikura, .. .. | — | Convolvolus *Turpethum*. |
| Tila, .. .. | S. | Sesamum *Orientale*. |
| Tilaparni, .. .. | — | Pterocarpus *Santalinus*. |
| Till, .. .. | B. H. | Sesamum *Orientale*. |
| Tilla-cheera, .. .. | B. | Casearia *Vareca*. |
| Timmue, .. .. | N. | Piper *Cubeb*. |
| Tinduka, .. .. | S. | Diospyros *glutinosa*. |
| Tinguree, .. .. | B. | Scytalia *rimosa*. |
| Tinisha, .. .. | S. | Dalbergia *Ougeinensis*. |
| Tintili, .. .. | — | Tamarindus *Indica*. |
| Tisi, .. .. | B. H. | Linum *usitatissimum*. |
| Tita-gwaleya, .. .. | B. | Vitis *bracteolata*. |
| T——lao, .. .. | — | Cucurbita?——(*bitter var.*) |
| Tittha-pat, .. .. | — | Corchorus *capsularis*, (*green var.*) |
| Titur-keo, .. .. | — | Dendrobium *clavatum*. |
| Toka-pana, .. .. | H. | Pistia *stratiotes*. |
| Tomri, .. .. | — | Cucurbita *lagenaria*. |
| Tonba, .. .. | — | C——— (*sp ?*)——— |
| Toog, .. .. | — | Connarus *nitidus*. |
| Toogee, .. .. | — | Justicia *lanceolaria*. |
| Toola, .. .. | B. | Sterculia *alata*. |
| T——lodh, .. .. | — | Rondeletia *tinctoria*. |
| Toolati-pari, .. .. | H. | Physalis *minima*. |
| Toolsi; Toolusee, .. | B. H. | Ocymum *villosum*, or *sanctum*. |
| Toom, .. .. | — | Garuga *pinnata*. |
| Toombo, .. .. .. | B. | Cucurbita *lagenaria*. |
| Toon, .. .. | B. H. | Cedrela *Toona*. |
| Toong, .. .. | B. | Rottlera *tinctoria*. |
| Toontoonee-nuteeya, . | — | Amaranthus *fasciatus*. |
| Toot, .. .. | B. H | Morus *Indica*. |
| Tophlu, .. .. | B. | Physalis *Peruviana*. |
| Tori, .. .. | H. | Sinapis —— (?) |
| Toyapippali, .. .. | S. | Croton *sebiferum*. |
| Triangguli, .. .. | H. | Phaseolus *trilobus*. |
| Trikanta-jutee, .. | B. | Monetia *barleroides*. |
| Trinpali, .. .. | H. | Manisuris *granularis*. |

| | | |
|---|---|---|
| **Tripakshi,** .. .. | S. | Coldenia *procumbens.* |
| **Tripungkhi,** .. .. | H. | C—— *p*——— |
| **Triputa,** .. .. | S. | Convolvolus *Turpethum.* |
| **Tryangguli,** .. .. | — | Phaseolus *trilobus.* |
| **Tselkacha,** .. .. | H. | Bryonia *grandis.* |
| **Tuar,** .. .. | — | Cytisus *Cajan.* |
| **Tubee-kura,** .. .. | B. | Unona *dumosa,* or Uvaria *heteroclita.* |
| **Tugura,** .. .. | S.B.H. | Tabernamontana *coronaria, (single.)* |
| **Tula,** .. .. | S. | Morus *Indica.* |
| **T——,** .. .. | B. | Gossypium *herbaceum.* |
| **Tulidun,** .. .. | H. | Solanum *nigrum.* |
| **Tumak,** .. .. | B. | Nicotiana *Tabacum.* |
| **Tumali,** .. .. | — | Diospyros *tomentosa.* |
| **Tumata,** .. .. | S. | Xanthochymus *pictorius.* |
| **Tundooleeya,** .. .. | — | Amaranthus *polygonoides.* |
| **Tunna,** .. .. | S. | Cedrela *Toona.* |
| **Turanj,** .. .. | H. | Citrus *medica.* |
| **Turbooz,** .. .. | B. H. | Cucurbita *citrullus.* |
| **Turbad,** .. .. | H. | Convolvolus *Turpethum.* |
| **Turi,** .. .. | — | Luffa, (or Cucumis) *acutangula.* |
| **Turkolum,** .. .. | S. | Calyptranthes *Jambolana.* |
| **Turmas,** .. .. | H. | Lupinus ?——— |
| **Turoo-luta,** .. .. | B. | Ipomæa *Quamoclit.* |
| **Turulli,** .. .. | H. | Momordica *umbellata.* |
| **Turwur,** .. .. | — | Cassia *auriculata.* |
| **Tushee,** .. .. | B. | Uvaria *dioica.* |
| **Tuverica,** .. .. | S. | Sinapis *(sp ?)* |
| **Twuk-putra,** .. .. | — | Laurus *Cassia.* |

## Section 2.

### *Tamool, Telinga, Cyngalese, &c.*

# T.

| | | |
|---|---|---|
| Taddæ-marum, .. | Tam. | Pterospermum *suberifolia.* |
| Tadda-palla or pullu, . | T. | Ixora *parviflora.* |
| Tagada, .. .. | — | Bignonia *Chelonoides.* |
| T——-tunga, .. | — | Cyperus *dubius.* |
| Tagaray, .. .. | Tam. | Cassia *Tora.* |
| Tagaree ; Tagaroo, .. | T. | Morinda *tinctoria.* |
| Tagarish, .. .. | — | Cassia *Tora.* |
| Tagashay, .. .. | Tam. | C—— *T——.* |
| Takkelam, .. .. | — | Calyptranthes *Jambolana.* |
| Tali-pulli, .. .. | M. | Tradescantia *Malabarica.* |
| Talisha-putrie, .. | T. T. | Flacourtia *cataphracta.* |
| Taloo-dalei, .. .. | Tam. | Clerodendrum *Phlomoides.* |
| Talura, .. .. | — | Shorea *Talura.* |
| Tamalap, .. .. | T. | Piper *Betle.* |
| Tamaray, .. .. | Tam. | Nelumbium *speciosum.* |
| Tamara, .. .. | M. | N——— *s———.* |
| Tambachi, .. .. | Tam. | Ulmus *integrifolia.* |
| Tambatangai, . .. | — | Dolichos *cultratus.* |
| Tambhudda-meerchin-gay, .. .. | Mah. | Capsicum *frutescens.* |
| Tanacoo, .. .. | T. | Gyrocarpus *Jacquini.* |
| Tana-hal, .. .. | Cyng. | Panicum *Italicum.* |
| Tangayree, .. .. | Can. | Cassia *auriculata.* |
| Tangha, .. .. | T. | Cocos *nucifera.* |
| Tanghedoo; Tangheroo, | — | Cassia *auriculata.* |
| Tanidaloo, .. .. | — | Eleusine *Coracana.* |
| Tanikai, .. .. | Tam. | Terminalia *Bellerica.* |
| Tanneer-vittany, .. | — | Asparagus *sarmentosus.* |
| Tantichi, .. .. | T. | Ornitrophe *serrata.* |
| Tatie-kulloo, . .. | — | Borassus *flabelliformis.* |
| Tavatiky, .. .. | — | Ornitrophe *serrata.* |
| Tavashoo-morunghie, . | Tam. | Justicia *Tranquebarensis.* |
| Tayl-kodughoo, .. | — | Heliotropium *Indicum.* |
| T——munnie, . .. | T. | H——— *I———.* |
| Taynga, .. .. | Tam. | Cocus *nucifera.* |
| Taysha, .. .. | — | Piper *dichotomum.* |

| | | |
|---|---|---|
| Teea-dunda, . .. | T. | Momordica *umbellata.* |
| Teek, .. .. | — | Tectona *grandis.* |
| Teerooga, .. .. | — | Caryota *urens.* |
| Tegadu, .. .. | — | Convolvulus *Turpethum.* |
| Tel-domba, .. .. | Cyng. | Calophyllum *inophyllum.* |
| Tel-kohomba, .. | — | Melia *Azadirachta.* |
| Tella-antoo-tiga, .. | T. | Convolvulus *dentatus.* |
| T——barinha, .. | — | Ficus *ampelos.* |
| T——dintona, .. | — | Clitoria *ternata, (white.)* |
| T——gada, .. .. | — | Diospyros *tomentosus.* |
| T——ghelijchroo, .. | — | Trianthema *monogynia, (white.)* |
| T——janoo, . .. | — | Andropogon *Sorghum.* |
| T——jelladoo, .. | — | Asclepias *gigantea*, (*white.*) |
| T——juvi, .. .. | — | Ehretia *aspera.* |
| T——kakisha, .. | — | Gardenia *montana.* |
| T——kalwa, . .. | — | Nymphæa *Lotus.* |
| T——mulaka, .. | — | Solanum *Indicum.* |
| T——poolugooda, .. | — | Fluggea *leucopyrus.* |
| T——tagada, .. | — | Convolvulus *Turpethum.* |
| T——tamara, . .. | — | Nelumbium *speciosum, (white.)* |
| T——tooma, . .. | — | Mimosa *leucophlea*, or *ferruginea.* |
| T——upie, or vuppie, | — | Monetia *Barleroides.* |
| T——userika, .. | — | Phyllanthus *pendulus.* |
| T——woolymera, .. | — | Capparis *trifoliata.* |
| Tel-mee, .. .. | Cyng. | Bassia *longifolia.* |
| Teloki, .. .. | T. | Clerodendrum *phlomoides.* |
| Tenga, .. .. | — | Cocos *nucifera.* |
| Tenkri, .. .. | — | C—— *n-——.* |
| Tenka, .. .. | — | Cordia *Sebestena.* |
| Tenna, .. .. | M. | Panicum *Italicum.* |
| Tenney, .. .. | Tam. | P—— *I-——.* |
| Tettamperel, . .. | M. | Strychnos *potatorum.* |
| Tettan-kottay, .. | Tam. | S-—— *p——.* |
| Tevadarum, .. .. | — | Erythroxylon *areolatum.* |
| Tiga-chemoodoo, .. | T. | Asclepias *acida.* |
| T——jeelooga, .. | — | Hedysarum *Neli-tali.* |
| T——maduga, .. | — | Butea *superba.* |
| T——mushadi, .. | — | Menispermum *polycarpon.* |
| Tilla-kodi, .. .. | — | Carpopogon *atropurpureum.* |
| Tillay-chedday, .. | Tam. | Excoecaria *Cochinchinensis.* |
| Tippa-tiga ; Tippatingay, .. .. | T. | Menispermum *cordifolium.* |

| | | |
|---|---|---|
| Tipilie, .. .. | T. Cy. | Piper *longum*. |
| Tirnoot-patchie, .. | Tam. | Ocymum *basilicum*. |
| Tirucalli, .. .. | — | Euphorbia *Tirucalli*. |
| Tirrooghoo-jemmoodoo, | T. | E——— *tortilis*. |
| T———callie, .. | Tam. | E——- *t*—— |
| Titta-commoodoo, .. | Cyng. | Cucumis *Colocynthis*. |
| Toandi, .. .. | T. | Terminalia *Bellerica*. |
| Todda-vadi, .. .. | M. | Oxalis *sensitiva*. |
| Toema-gherika, .. | T. | Agrostis *tenacissima*. |
| Toldo, .. .. | Can. | Crinum *toxicarum*. |
| Toodavullay, . .. | Tam. | Solanum *trilobatum*. |
| Toolasee, .. .. | — | Ocymum *sanctum*. |
| Toombikai, .. .. | — | Diospyros *glutinosus*. |
| Toomuttikai, . .. | — | Bryonia *callosa*. |
| Toonga-gudda, .. | — | Cyperus *pertenuis*, or *junceafolius*. |
| Toor, .. .. | Mah. | Cytisus *Cajan*. |
| Toora, .. .. | Tam. | Pharnaceum *Mollugo*. |
| Tootra-benda, .. | Cyng. | Sida *Asiatica*. |
| Toottie, .. .. | Tam. | S— *Mauritiana*. |
| T——-akoo, . .. | T. | S— *M*———. |
| Torellega, .. .. | — | Limonia *crenulata*. |
| Tota-kura, .. .. | — | Amaranthus *oleraceus*. |
| Total-vadie, .. .. | Tam. | Mimosa *pudica*. |
| Towaray, .. .. | — | Cytisus *Cajan*. |
| Trasta-walu, . .. | Cyng. | Convolvolus *Turpethum*. |
| Tsaroo-mamadi, .. | T. | Buchanania *latifolia*. |
| Tseeri-koora, . .. | — | Amaranthus *campestris*. |
| Tshama, .. .. | — | Arum *Nymphæafolium*. |
| Tsiapangum, . .. | M. | Cæsalpinia *Sappan*. |
| Tsieru-kirganelli, .. | — | Phyllanthus *urinaria*. |
| T——ponna, .. | — | Calophyllum *Calaba*. |
| Tsietti-mandaru, .. | — | Poinciana *pulcherrima*. |
| Tsillaghenzaloo, .. | T. | Strychnos *potatorum*. |
| Tsilla-cheddie, .. | Tam. | Excoecaria *Cochinchinensis*. |
| Tsinna-avagooda, .. | T. | Trichosanthes *incisa*. |
| T——doolagondie, .. | — | Tragia *cannabina*. |
| T——mootopolaghum, | — | Pavonia *Zeylanica*. |
| Tsinniakoo, .. .. | — | Acalypha *betulina*. |
| Tsjerou-kara, . .. | M. | Webera *tetrandra*. |
| T-——k—, .. | — | Canthium *parviflorum*. |
| T-——mau-maravara, | — | Epidendrum *tenuifolium*. |
| Tsjerroo-uren, .. | — | Melochia *corchorifolia*. |
| Tsjetti-pulli, .. .. | — | Eleusine *Coracana*. |
| Tsjovanna-amelpodi, . | — | Ophioxylon *serpentinum*. |
| Tsulla-ghedaloo, .. | T. | Asparagus *sarmentosus*. |

| | | |
|---|---|---|
| **Tucka-vepa, . . . .** | T. | Media *sempervirens.* |
| **Tumba-codiveli, . .** | M. | Plumbago *Zeylanica.* |
| **Tumbagai, . . . .** | T. | Shorea *Tumbuggaia.* |
| **Tumba-karawilla, . .** | Cyng. | Momordica *dioica.* |
| **Tumbali, . . . .** | Tam. | Diospyros *melanoxylon.* |
| **Tumida, . . . .** | T. | D.——— *m*.——— |
| **Tumika, . . . .** | — | D.——— *glutinosa.* |
| **Tummakaia, . . . .** | — | Dolichos *cultratrus.* |
| **Tunda, . . . .** | Can | Cedrela *Toona.* |
| **Turka-vepa, . . . .** | T. | Olax *Scandens.* |
| **Turkolum, . . . .** | Tam. | Calyptranthes *Jambolana.* |
| **Turulli-amoot-mool, . .** | T. | Momordica *monadelpha.* |

## Section 1.

### *Sanscrit, Bengalee, Hindee, &c.*

## U.

| | | |
|---|---|---|
| Ubdie-narikaylum, .. | S. | Cocos *Maldivica*, or Lodoicea *Sechellarum*. |
| Uch, .. .. | H. | Saccharum *officinarum*. |
| Ulchuleeyaja, . .. | B. | Itea *macrophylla*. |
| Uchyoota, .. .. | S. | Morinda *tinctoria*. |
| Udiram-panum, .. | — | Cacalia *Sonchifolia*. |
| Udambar, .. .. | H. | Ficus *glomerata*. |
| Udumvara, .. .. | S. | F——*Carica*. |
| Ugni-javali, .. .. | — | Grislea *tomentosa*. |
| Ujmood, .. .. | H. | Apium *involucratum*. |
| Ukyo, .. .. | B. | Saccharum *officinarum*. |
| Ulavoo, .. .. | S. | Cucurbita *lagenaria*. |
| Ulsee, .. .. | H. | Linum *usitatissimum*. |
| Ulu, .. .. | — | Saccharum *Cylindricum*. |
| Ulurea, .. .. | S. | Asclepias *gigantea*, (*white*.) |
| Ulut-chandal, .. | H. | Gloriosa *superba*. |
| Umba-vetusa, . .. | S. | Calamus *fasciculatus*. |
| Umbla-bela, .. .. | B. | Arum *bulbiferum*. |
| Umbutee, .. .. | H. | Oxalis *corniculata*. |
| Umla-lonika-chookrika, | S. | O—— *c*—— |
| Umlana, .. .. | — | Gomphrena *globosa*. |
| Umlica, .. .. | — | Tamarindus *Indica*. |
| Umul-koochi, . .. | B. | Cæsalpinia *oleosperma*. |
| Undum, .. .. | H. | Pterocarpus *Santalinus*. |
| Ungoor-shefa, .. | — | Atropa *Belladonna*. |
| Ungootee, .. .. | B. | Hastingia *coccinea*. |
| U———, .. .. | — | Bradleia *nitida*. |
| Unkota, .. .. | S. | Verbena *nodiflora*. |
| Unkotha, .. .. | — | Allangium *hexapetalum*. |
| U———, .. .. | — | Juglans *regia*. |
| Unoo, .. .. | — | Panicum *miliaceum*. |
| Unta-mool, .. .. | H. | Asclepias *asthmatica*. |
| Untarei-tamara, .. | S. | Pistia *stratiotes*. |
| Untcatara, .. .. | H. | Echinops *echinatus*. |
| Untergunga, . .. | — | Pistia *stratiotes*. |
| Ununta, .. .. | S. | Asclepias *pseudosarsa*. |

| | | | |
|---|---|---|---|
| Ununta-mool, | .. | B. H. | Asclepias *asthmatica.* |
| Upamarga, .. | .. | S. | Achyranthes *aspera.* |
| Upanga, .. | .. | B. | A——— *a*—— |
| Uphing, .. | .. | — | Walsura *robusta.* |
| Upurajita, .. | .. | — | Clitoria *ternata, (blue.)* |
| Urimeeda, .. | .. | S. | Mimosa *Farnesiana.* |
| Urishta, .. | .. | — | Xanthium *Indicum.* |
| Urjaka, .. | .. | — | Ocymum *sanctum.* |
| Urjooma, .. | .. | — | Lagerstræmia *Regina.* |
| Urjoon ; Urjoon, | .. | S. B. | Pentaptera *Arjuna.* |
| Urka, .. | .. | — | Asclepias *gigantea, (red.)* |
| U—moola, .. | .. | S. | Aristolochia *Indica.* |
| Urkasi, .. | .. | H. | Tragia *cordata,* or *cordifolia.* |
| Uroona, .. | .. | B. | Rubia *Munjistha.* |
| Urooskura, .. | .. | S. | Semicarpus *Anacarbium.* |
| Urur, .. | .. | B. H. | Cytisus *Cajan.* |
| Urush ; Urusa, | .. | B. | Solanum *pubescens.* |
| Urwee, .. | .. | H. | Arum *Colocasia.* |
| Useer, .. | .. | — | Andropogon *muricatus.* |
| Usory-sowa, .. | .. | N. | Campanula *fulgens.* |
| Usfur, .. | .. | H. | Carthamus *tinctorius.* |
| Usgund, .. | .. | — | Physalis *flexuosa.* |
| Ushlea, .. | .. | B. | Sterculia *lanceofolia.* |
| Ushoka, .. | .. | S. B. | Jonesia *Asoca.* |
| Ushwagundha, | .. | — | Physalis *flexuosa.* |
| Ushwa-shakhota, | .. | S. | Limonia *pentaphylla.* |
| Ushwukurunuka, | .. | — | Shorea *robusta.* |
| Usmadugha, .. | .. | — | Bauhinia *tomentosa.* |
| Usookooli, .. | .. | B. | Cinchona *gratissima.* |
| Usoola, .. | .. | — | Vitex *alata.* |
| Ussu, .. | .. | H. | Jonesia *Asoca.* |
| Ustabunda, .. | .. | — | Premna *spinosa.* |
| Usun, .. | .. | B. H. | Pentaptera *tomentosa.* |
| Usunna, .. | .. | S. | P——— *t*———. |
| Utimookta, .. | .. | — | Gærtnera *racemosa.* |
| Uttimarini, .. | .. | H. | Antirrhinum *cymbalaria.* |
| Uturoosha, .. | .. | S. | Justicia *Adhahota.* |

## SECTION 2.

### *Tamool, Telinga, Cyngalese, &c.*

| | | |
|---|---|---|
| **U.** | | |
| Ubeera, .. .. | T. | Streptium *asperum.* |
| Udivi-gorinta, .. | — | Erythroxylon *monogynum.* |
| U——mulli, .. | — | Jasminum *latifolium.* |
| U——nima, .. | — | Limonia *monophylla.* |
| Uk-gas, .. .. | CYNG. | Saccharum *officinarum.* |
| Ullum, .. .. | T. | Zingiber *officinalis.* |
| Umana, .. .. | M. | Datura *fastuosa.* |
| Undimandari, .. | TAM. | Polyanthes *tuberosa.* |
| Uppoo-punna, .. | T. | Rhizophora *Mangle.* |
| Upu-dali, .. .. | M. | Ruellia *ringens.* |
| Urenka, .. .. | T. | Poa *nutans.* |
| Usereki, .. .. | — | Phyllanthus *Emblica.* |
| Uva, .. .. | — | Dillenia *speciosa.* |

## Section 1.

### *Sanscrit, Bengalee, Hindee, &c.*

## V.

| | | | |
|---|---|---|---|
| Vahisee, .. | .. | S. | Momordica *dioica*. |
| Vaishnava, .. | .. | — | Evolvulus *Alsinioides*. |
| Vajra, .. | .. | — | Euphorbium *antiquorum*. |
| Vajrakantaka, | .. | — | E——— *a* ———. |
| Vajratunda, .. | .. | — | Euphorbia *tortilis*. |
| Vajra-valli, .. | .. | — | Cissus *quadrangularis*. |
| Vakoochie, .. | .. | — | Psoralia *corylifolia*. |
| Vana-raja, .. | .. | — | Bauhinia *parviflora*. |
| V——malli, .. | .. | — | Jasminum *angustifolium*. |
| Vanda, .. | .. | — | Limodorum *spatulatum*. |
| Vandari, .. | .. | — | Tragia *cordata* or *cordifolia*. |
| Vanekili, .. | .. | — | Canna *Indica, (red.)* |
| Varana, .. | .. | — | Cratæva *Tapia*. |
| Vari-purnee, . | .. | — | Pistia *stratiotes*, or Salvinia *imbricata*. |
| Vartta, .. | .. | — | Solanum *melongena*. |
| Varuna, .. | .. | — | Cratæva *Tapia*. |
| Varvar, .. | .. | — | Cleome *pentaphylla*. |
| Vashira, .. | .. | — | Verbena *nodiflora*. |
| Vasiki, .. | .. | — | Justicia *Adhatoda*. |
| Vasooka, .. | .. | S. B. | J——— *A*———. |
| Vastaki, .. | .. | S. | Solanum *melongena*. |
| Vastooka, .. | .. | — | Chenopodium *album*. |
| Vatadalla, .. | .. | — | Zizyphus *trinervius*. |
| Vata-ghni, .. | .. | — | Clerodendrum *Phlomoides*. |
| Veeruna, .. | .. | — | Andropogon *muricatum*. |
| Veeshamoosti, | . | — | Strychnos *Nux-vomica*. |
| Velaitie-capoor, | .. | H. | Salvia *Bengalensis*. |
| Vellajung, .. | .. | S. | Piper *nigrum*. |
| Venee, .. | .. | — | Andropogon *serratum*. |
| Vetra; Vetusa, | .. | — | Calamus *Rotang*. |
| Vidara, .. | .. | — | Flacourtia *cataphracta*. |
| Vidaree, .. | .. | — | Convolvolus *paniculatus*. |
| Vidyumatrie, . | .. | — | Justicia *Adhahota*. |
| Vikusa, .. | .. | — | Rubia *Munjistha*. |
| Vilatie-mindie, | .. | B. | Myrtus *communis*. |

| | | |
|---|---|---|
| Vilva ; Vilwa, .. | S. | Ægle *Marmelos*, or Crateva *religiosa*. |
| Vimba, .. .. | — | Bryonia *grandis*. |
| Vimbika, .. .. | — | Momordica *monadelpha*. |
| Viratara, .. .. | — | Andropogon *muricatum*. |
| Viravriksha, .. .. | — | Mimosa *cinerea*. |
| Vishalee, .. .. | — | Cucumis *Colocynthis*. |
| Vishavriksha, . .. | — | Andrachne *Cadishaw*. |
| Vishulya-krit, . .. | — | Echites *dichotoma*. |
| Viswa-toolsie, . . | — | Ocymum *album*. |
| Vreehibheda, . .. | — | Panicum *miliaceum*. |
| Vributee, .. .. | — | Solanum *Indicum*. |
| Vrikshadunee, .. | — | Loranthus *bicolor*. |
| Vrishchi-putree, .. | — | Tragia *involucrata*. |
| V——roha, .. | — | Cymbidium *tessalloides*. |
| Vucha, .. .. | — | Acorus *Calamus*. |
| Vudura, .. . | — | Zizyphus *scandens*. |
| Vuka, .. .. | — | Æschynomene *grandiflora*. |
| Vula ; Vulahwa, .. | — | Crinum *Asiaticum*. |
| Vuna-ardrukum, .. | — | Zinziber *Cassumuniar*. |
| V——huridra, .. | — | Curcuma *Zedoaria*. |
| V——rista, .. .. | — | C—— Z——. |
| Vunda, .. .. | — | Loranthus *bicolor*. |
| Vungsha, .. .. | — | Bambusa *Arundinacea*. |
| Vurichoora, .. .. | — | Celosia *cristata, (yellow.)* |
| Vuroona, .. .. | — | Capparis *trifoliata*. |
| Vurtulika, .. .. | H. | Mimosa *cinerea*. |

## Section 2.

### *Tamool, Telinga, Cyngalese, &c.*

### V.

| | | | |
|---|---|---|---|
| Vaag-marum, . | . . | Tam. | Bignonia *Indica.* |
| Vada-kodi, . . | . . | M. | Justicia *Gandarussa.* |
| Vadamvittiloo, | . . | T. | Terminalia *Catappa.* |
| Vaesamboo, . . | . . | Cyng. | Acorus *Calamus.* |
| Vaivinta, . . | . . | T. | Cleome *pentaphylla.* |
| Vakil, . . | . . | — | Andropogon *muricatus.* |
| Valei, . . | . . | Tam. | Musa *Paradisiaca.* |
| Val-mellaghoo, | . . | — | Piper *Cubeb.* |
| Valumbirikai, . | . . | — | Helicteres *Isora.* |
| Valumbrikaca, | . . | T. | H——— *I———.* |
| Vankuda, . . | . . | — | Solanum *Jacquini.* |
| Vara-moolie, . . | . . | Tam. | Barleria *Prionitis.* |
| V——poola, . . | . . | — | Fluggea *leucopyrus.* |
| Varie-coomuttei-kai, . . | | — | Cucumis *Colocynthis.* |
| Vassamboo, . . | . . | — | Acorus *Calamus.* |
| Vassunta-gundha, | . . | T. | Rottleria *tinctoria.* |
| Vatana, . . | . . | Cyng. | Pisum *sativum.* |
| Vata-tirupie, . | . . | Tam. | Cissampelos *Pareira.* |
| Vatunghie-cottay, | . . | — | Cæsalpinia *Sappan.* |
| Vaydoobooriki, | . . | — | Ballota *disticha.* |
| Vaymboo, . . | . . | M. | Acorus *Calamus.* |
| Vaylie, . . | . . | Tam. | Cleome *pentaphylla.* |
| V——partie, . | . . | — | Cynanchum *extensum.* |
| Vaympa, . . | . . | T. | Melia *Azadirachta.* |
| Vaympalie, . . | . . | — | Galega *purpurea.* |
| Vaypum, . . | . . | T. Tam. | Melia *Azadirachta.* |
| Vedroo, . . | . . | T. | Bambusa *Arundinacea.* |
| Vedditalung, . | . . | Tam. | Mimosa *cinerea.* |
| Veelivie, . . | . . | — | Stroemia *tetrandra.* |
| Veelvie, . . | . . | — | Cratæva *religiosa.* |
| Veel-velum, . . | . . | — | Mimosa *leucophlea.* |
| Velatie-aghatie, | . . | T. | Cassia *alata.* |
| Vellacoy, . . | . . | M. | Musa *Paradisiaca.* |
| Vellangay, . . | . . | Tam. | Feronia *Elephantum.* |
| Velli-gudda, . . | . . | T. | Allium *sativum.* |
| Vellitooroo, . . | . . | — | Mimosa *cinerea.* |

| | | |
|---|---|---|
| Vendium, .. .. | TAM. | Trigonella *Fœnum-Grecum.* |
| Venegayum, .. .. | — | Allium *Cepa.* |
| Veni-vell-getta, .. | CYNG. | Menispermum *fenestratum.* |
| Vepa ; Vepam, .. | T. T. | Melia *Azadirachta.* |
| Veppalei, .. .. | TAM. | Echites, or Nerium, *anti-dysentericum.* |
| Vepoodipatsa, .. | T. | Ocymum *basilicum.* |
| Veri-nella-vemos, .. | — | Oldenlandia *herbacea.* |
| V——talli-napi, .. | — | Xanthium *Indicum.* |
| Veru-gudu-chawa, .. | — | Dalbergia *latifolia.* |
| Verrugung, .. .. | TAM. | Arum *macrorhizon.* |
| Vesha-mangaloo, .. | T. | Crinum *Asiaticum.* |
| Veshei-moonghie, .. | TAM. | C—— *A*——. |
| Vettilei, .. .. | — | Piper *Betel.* |
| Vidi-marum, . .. | — | Cordia *Myxa.* |
| Vilpalei, .. .. | — | Asclepias *lactifera.* |
| Vistnookrandie, .. | — | Evolvulus *Alsinioides.* |
| V———krandum, .. | T. | E——— *A*———. |
| Vittie-vayr, .. .. | TAM. | Andropogon *muricatum.* |
| Voellarekoo, .. .. | — | Exacum *hysopifolium.* |
| Vudza, .. .. | T. | Acorus *calamus.* |
| Vuelie, .. .. | — | Strœmia *tetrandra.* |
| Vukka, .. .. | — | Areca *Catechu.* |
| Vul-ademboo, . .. | TAM. | Convolvolus *grandiflorus.* |
| Vullam-marum, .. | — | Feronia *elephantum.* |
| Vullarei, .. .. | — | Hydrocotyle *Asiatica.* |
| Vaillay-oomatay, .. | — | Datura *Metel.* |
| V———poondoo, .. | — | Allium *sativum.* |
| V———sharunnay, .. | — | Trianthema *monogynia.* |
| Vum-maray, . .. | — | Swietenia *chloroxylon.* |
| Vulvaylum, .. .. | — | Mimosa *ferruginea.* |
| Vun-paratie, . .. | — | Gossypium *herbaceum.* |
| Vuttei-khilloo-khilloo-pie, .. .. | — | Crotalaria *verrucosa.* |
| V——pemayruttie, .. | — | Ballota *disticha.* |

## Section 1.

### *Sanscrit, Bengalee, Hindee, &c.*

## W.

| | | | |
|---|---|---|---|
| Walooa, | .. .. | B. | Ternstrœmia *serrata*. |
| Waluka, | .. .. | S. | Lavendula *carnosa*. |
| Wampee, | .. .. | H. | Cookia *punctata*. |
| Warahi, | .. .. | S. | Curculigo *Orchioides*. |
| Wari, | .. .. | — | Asparagus *racemosus*. |
| Wully-kola, | .. .. | B. H. | Musa *Sapientum*. |

## Section 2.

### *Tamool, Telinga, Cyngalese, &c.*

| W. | | |
|---|---|---|
| Wadata-toka-guddee, | T. | Eleusine *calycina*. |
| Wadda-kaha, . . . | Cyng. | Acorus *calamus*. |
| Wadimki, . . . . | — | Loranthus *scurrula*. |
| Wæl-boo-renda, . . | Cyng. | Volkameria *inermis*. |
| W—heeræssa, . . | — | Cissus *quadrangularis*. |
| W—kayila, . . . . | — | Phyllanthus *multiflorus*. |
| W—kolundo, . . | — | Artemisia *Maderaspatensis* or *Indica*. |
| W—koopaymenya, . . | — | Acalypha *Indica*. |
| W—kotala, . . . . | — | Torenia *Asiatica*. |
| W—midi, . . . . | — | Vitis *vinifera*. |
| W—nidi-kumba, . . . | — | Mimosa *pudica*. |
| W—tib-batu, . . | — | Solanum *trilobatum*. |
| Wæta-hik, . . . . | — | Amyris *Zeylanica*. |
| Wagattæ, . . . . | Tam. | Gardenia *uliginosa*. |
| Waka, . . . . | T. | Carissa *Carandas, (black.)* |
| Wakloo ; Wakoyloo, . | — | C—— *diffusa*. |
| Walaba, . . . . | Cyng. | Cleome *viscosa*. |
| Wal-eka-wæriya, . . | — | Ophiorhiza *Mungos*. |
| W—gummaris, . | — | Piper *Cubeb*. |
| Walkaha, . . . . | — | Curcuma *Zedoaria*. |
| Wallag-doora, . . | T. | Mimosa *octandra*. |
| Wallaray-kilangoo, . . | — | Solanum *tuberosum*. |
| Wallika-dooda, . . | — | Cæsalpinia *lacerans*. |
| Wallursi, . . . . | — | Walsura *piscidea*. |
| Walsaman-pichcha, . . | Cyng. | Jasminum *angustifolium*. |
| Walsura, . . . . | Tam. | Walsura *piscidea*. |
| Wandukolli, . . . . | T. | Cassia *alata*. |
| Wangari-dookoodoo, . | — | Sesuvium *portulacastrum*. |
| Wangkai, . . . . | — | Solanum *melongena*. |
| Wangkari, . . . . | Tam. | S—— *m*——. |
| Wara-tarae, . . . . | — | Mimosa *cinerea*. |
| Watusæwendara, . . | Cyng. | Andropogon *Nardus*. |
| Wawinti, . . . . | T. | Cleome *pentaphylla*. |
| Wayalakoo, . . . . | — | Vitex *Negundo*. |
| Wellipanna-kelingoo, . | M. | Polypodium *taxifolium*. |

| | | | |
|---|---|---|---|
| Well-madatta, | .. | CYNG. | Rubia *Munjistha*. |
| Werkoodie, .. | .. | TAM. | Strœmia *tetrandra*. |
| Whonnay, .. | .. | CAN. | Pterocarpus *Santalinus*. |
| Widdatilam, . | .. | TAM. | Mentha *sativa*. |
| Wistnu-kranti, | .. | CYNG. | Evolvulus *Alsinioides*. |
| Woada, .. | .. | T. | Panicum *brizoides*. |
| Wodachoe-marum, | .. | TAM. | Cluytia *collina*. |
| Wodoowunghai, | .. | — | Andrachne *Cadishaw*. |
| Woetiwear, .. | .. | T. | Andropogon *muricatus*. |
| Wolam, .. | .. | — | Panicum *interruptum*. |
| Wominta, .. | .. | CYNG. | Sinapis *ramosa*. |
| Woni, .. | .. | T. | Mimosa *ferruginea*. |
| Wooda, .. | .. | — | Panicum *brizoides*. |
| W——talum, | .. | — | Poa *bifaria*. |
| Woodia, .. | .. | — | Odina *Woodier*. |
| Woodiam, .. | .. | TAM. | O—— *W————*. |
| Woodoo-gaddi, | .. | T. | Panicum *brizoides*. |
| Woolawooloo, | .. | — | Dolichos *biflorus*. |
| Wooligudda, . | .. | — | Allium *Cepa*. |
| Woolisi, .. | .. | — | Buchnera *Asiatica*. |
| Woomæ-marum, | .. | TAM. | Melia *sempervirens*. |
| Woondoo, .. | .. | T. | Panicum *colonum, (red.)* |
| W————, .. | . | — | P———— *hirsutum*. |
| Woorsipala, . . | .. | — | Cissus *acida*. |
| Woosherike-poo, | .. | — | Phyllanthus *Emblica*. |
| Worga, .. | .. | — | Panicum *miliaceum*. |

SECTION 1.

*Sanscrit, Bengalee, Hindi, &c.*

## Y.

| | | | |
|---|---|---|---|
| Yasa ; Yavusa, | .. | S. | Hedysarum *Alhagi*. |
| Yastimadhuca, | .. | — | Glycirrhiza *glabra*. |
| Yeb-rooj, .. | .. | B. | Atropa *Mandragoragora*. |
| Yoothika, .. | .. | S. | Jasminum *auriculatum*. |
| Y —— purnee, | .. | — | Justicia *nasuta*. |
| Yugaphala, .. | .. | — | Cynanche *extensum*. |

## Section 2.

### *Tamool, Telinga, Cyngalese, &c.*

## Y.

| | | |
|---|---|---|
| Yælim-buriki, .. | T. | Schleichera *trija*. |
| Yamskalung, . .. | Tam. | Dioscorea *alata*. |
| Yaydersie, .. .. | — | Elettaria *Cardamomum*. |
| Yalakooloo, .. .. | T. | E—— C———. |
| Yeanadari-tiga, .. | — | Thunbergia *fragrans*. |
| Yeati-mallier, . .. | — | Polygonum *tomentosum*. |
| Yecada, .. .. | Can. | Asclepias *gigantea*. |
| Yedda; Yeddi, .. | T. | Andropogon *contortum*. |
| Yellinga-wadinika, .. | — | Loranthus *bicolor*. |
| Yelloo-tungoo-gaddi, . | — | Agrostis *Coromandeliana*. |
| Yennapootoo-nulikeh-jemmoodoo, .. | — | Cacalia *Kleinia*. |
| Yercum, .. .. | Tam. | Asclepias *gigantea*. |
| Yerra-cittramoolum, . | T. | Plumbago *rosea*. |
| Y——chirtli, .. | — | Ventilago *Maderaspatanum* |
| Y——katha, .. | — | Lettsomia *aggregata*. |
| Y——kalwa, .. | — | Papaver *somniferum*, (*red var.*) |
| Y——pulleroo, .. | Tam. | Tribulus *terrestris*, (*sm. var.*) |
| Y——tamaray, .. | T. | Nelumbium *speciosum*. |
| Y——yerra, .. .. | — | Ficus *benjamina*. |
| Yettie, .. .. | — | Strychnos *Nux-vomica*. |
| Yettroo, .. .. | — | Mimosa *cinerea*. |

## Section 1.

### *Sanscrit, Bengalee, Hindi, &c.*

| Z. | | | |
|---|---|---|---|
| Zafran, | .. .. | H. | Crocus *sativus.* |
| Zarawand, | .. .. | — | Aristolochia (*sp ?*) |
| Zard-alu, | .. .. | — | Prunus *Armeniaca.* |
| Z——chob, | .. .. | — | Curcuma *longa.* |
| Zira, | .. .. | — | Cuminum *Cyminum.* |
| Zufa, | .. .. | — | Hyssopus (*sp ?*) |
| Zumeenkund, | .. | — | (?) |

## Section 2.

### *Tamool, Telinga, Cyngalese, &c.*

| | | | |
|---|---|---|---|
| Zootupakoo, | .. | T. | Cynanche *extensum.* |